The Place of the French Revolution in History

PROBLEMS IN EUROPEAN CIVILIZATION SERIES

The Place of the French Revolution in History

Edited with introduction, commentary, and translations by

Marvin R. Cox

University of Connecticut

Houghton Mifflin Company   Boston   New York

Editor-in-Chief: Jean L. Woy
Assistant Editors: Keith Mahoney/Leah Strauss
Associate Project Editor: Gabrielle Stone
Associate Production/Design Coordinator: Deborah Frydman
Manufacturing Coordinator: Michael O'Dea
Marketing Manager: Sandra McGuire

Cover Image: Sarah Melhado
Cover Design: An officer of the National Guard takes an oath. 18th c. Coll.
Chauvac Claretie, France. Giraudon/Art Resource, NY.

Printed in the U.S.A.

Library of Congress Catalog Number: 97-72458

ISBN: 0-395-81531-2

123456789-DH-01 00 99 98 97

Contents

Preface   ix

Chronology of the Revolution   x

Introduction: Change and Continuity in the
Historiography of the French Revolution   1

I   An Aristocratic Overview   15
   Alexis de Tocqueville
     A Bourgeois Revolution   15
       Why Great Revolutions Will Become Rare   16
       The Political and Social Condition of France   20

     The Triumph of the Centralizing State   29
       The Old Regime and the French Revolution   29

II   Positivist Perspectives   41
   Hippolyte Taine
     The Fulfillment of the Enlightenment   41
       The Spirit and Doctrine of the Enlightenment   42
       The Origins of Contemporary France   49

   Alphonse Aulard
     The Genesis of Middle-Class Democracy   54
       A Political History of the French Revolution   54

III   Marxist Interpretations   67

Jean Jaurès

The Overthrow of Feudalism by the Capitalist
Bourgeoisie   67

Socialist History of the French Revolution   68

Albert Mathiez

Capitalist Revolution and Crucible of
Socialism   75

The French Revolution   75

Georges Lefebvre

A Revolution of Peasants and Bourgeois
Buccaneers   90

The French Revolution and the Peasants   91

The French Revolution   102

Albert Soboul

A Revolution of *Sans-Culottes* and
Montagnards   123

The Parisian Sans-Culottes   124

IV   Post-Marxist Interpretations   141

François Furet

The Beginnings of Modern Mass Politics   141

Interpreting the French Revolution   142

Revolutionary France, 1770–1880   153

Mona Ozouf

The Transfer of the Sacred   170

Festivals of the French Revolution   170

Lynn Hunt

A Revolution in Political Culture   182

*Politics, Culture, and Class in the
French Revolution*   183

Robert Darnton

A Conflict Between "Possibilism" and
"The Givenness of Things"   187

*What Was Revolutionary about the
French Revolution?*   187

V Postmodern Perspectives   201

François Crouzet

Industrial Anticlimax and Economic
Watershed   201

*The Economic Consequences of the French
Revolution: Reflections on a Debate*   202

William Hamilton Sewell, Jr.

Revolutionary Artisans and the Formation of the
French Working Class   212

*Artisans, Factory Workers, and the Formation of the
French Working Class*   213

Darlene G. Levy and Harriet Applewhite

Revolutionary Women and the Radicalization of French Politics   230

Women, Radicalization, and the Fall of the French Monarchy   231

Tzvetan Todorov

The Birth of Conflicting Nationalist Traditions   248

On Human Diversity: Nationalism, Racism, and Exoticism   249

Suggestions for Further Reading   265

Preface

From the time the French Revolution broke out, it has been recognized as a climactic event. There is widespread agreement that, in conjunction with the Industrial Revolution which began a few years earlier, the French Revolution put an end to the old order in Europe and set modern history in motion. This book consists of selections from the works of historians who have interpreted the revolution's climactic character. The selections cover a span of roughly a hundred and fifty years, from the middle of the last century to the present. Thus, the book offers a brief survey of the historiography of the French Revolution.

Two features of this historiography stand out: the determination of successive generations of historians to break with their predecessors and provide a definitive verdict on the revolution's significance, and the recurrence among these same historians of different versions of two conflicting, mutually exclusive interpretations.

These interpretations are ultimately traceable to the revolutionary period, and their recurrence testifies to the hold of early readings of events on subsequent historians, but the selections show that tradition alone cannot explain the persistence of conflicting views. Each interpretation is amply supported by documentary evidence. Disagreements about the revolution's place in history thus reflect the complexity of the revolution itself. Though technically a single, relatively brief event, it contained a variety of conflicting strains, each of which had an enduring impact on the future.

Many people helped make this book possible, but I would like to single out the following for special recognition. For contributing ideas and information, my friends John Thompson, James Friguglietti, and Lawrence Langer. For encouraging me to pursue the project, my colleagues Richard Brown, Thomas Paterson, and Edmund Wehrle. For keeping me going, my wife Diane and my daughter Kate. For keeping me in line, my mentors at Houghton Mifflin Keith Mahoney, Gabrielle Stone, and Leah Strauss. I also owe a debt of thanks to two former students: Jared Parker, who did much of the spadework on the selections, and James Coon, who helped me make sense of Marxist historical thinking.

Marvin R. Cox

Chronology of the Revolution

1787	February 22	Meeting of First Assembly of Notables
1788	August 8	Louis XVI's assent to calling of Estates-General
	August 25	Necker reappointed
	September 25	Paris *Parlement* decrees separate meetings of three estates
	December 27	Royal Council decrees doubling the number of Third Estate's representatives
1789	January	Sieyes publishes *Qu'est-ce que la Tiers Etat?*
	May 5	Convocation of Estates-General: Third Estate calls for joint meetings with First and Second Estates; clergy and nobles meet separately
	June 17	Third Estate declares itself "National Assembly"
	June 19	Majority of clergy join National Assembly
	June 20	Exclusion of National Assembly from meeting hall; "Tennis Court" oath to continue deliberations until constitution enacted
	June 23	Louis XVI addresses Estates-General; calls for separate meetings of Estates
	June 27	Louis XVI orders clergy and nobility to join National Assembly
	Late June– early July	Kings summons troops to vicinity of Paris and Versailles; Necker dismissed
	July 14	Storming of Bastille
	Late July– early August	Municipal revolutions, peasant revolts, Great Fear
	August 4	National Assembly decrees abolition of feudalism

	August 26	National Assembly enacts Declaration of Rights of Man and the Citizen
	September	King withholds sanction of August reforms
	September 11	National Assembly grants suspensive, rather than absolute, veto to king
	October 5–6	"October Days": women of Paris march on Versailles; royal family and National Assembly subsequently removed to Paris
	October 29	Decree restricting vote to "active" (propertied) citizens
	November 2	National Assembly appropriates property of church
	December 14–22	Abolition of historic provinces; division of national territory into departments
	December 19	First issue of *assignats* (revolutionary currency)
1790	January 28	Jews given equal rights
	February 13	Suppression of most religious orders and monastic vows
	May 22	National Assembly renounces wars of conquest
	June 19	Noble titles and status abolished
	July 12	Civil Constitution of the Clergy
	July 14	Festival of the Federation (first Bastille Day)
	October 26	King authorizes secret negotiations with foreign courts for intervention to stop revolution
	October 29	Revolt of slaves and black freemen in San Domingo
	November	Publication of Burke's *Reflections on the French Revolution*
	November 27	Decree requiring civic oath for clergy
1791	March 2	Suppression of guilds and monopolies
	March 10	Papal letter condemning Civil Constitution and Declaration of Rights
	April 13	Papal bull condemning Civil Constitution of Clergy
	May 15	Children of black freemen in colonies granted equal rights with whites

	June 14	Le Chapelier Law outlawing worker "combinations"
	June 20	King flees Paris to join *émigrés* and foreign armies
	June 25	King, captured at Varennes, returned to Paris, powers suspended
	July 15	King's powers restored
	July 17	Massacre by National Guards of crowds in *Champs de mars* signing petition against king's reinstatement
	August 17	*Emigrés* summoned to return to France within month
	August 27	Declaration of Pillnitz: King of Prussia, Emperor of Austria proclaim support for joint action of European monarchs to restore powers of Louis XVI
	September 28	Slavery abolished in France, maintained in colonies
	September 30	Dissolution of National Assembly
	October 1	First meeting of Legislative Assembly
	November 9	*Emigrés* placed under suspicion of conspiracy against nation, summoned to return
	November 12	Royal veto of decree against *émigrés*
	November 29	Priests refusing to take oath to constitution suspended from functions
	December 19	Royal veto of decree against "nonjuring" priests
1792	January 2	January 1, 1789 declared beginning of "Age of Liberty"
	February 9	Decree appropriating *émigré* property by nation
	March 10–23	Resignation of moderate ministry under pressure from assembly, appointment of Girondin ministers
	April 20	Declaration of war against Hapsburg monarchy (Austria)
	June 12	King dismisses Girondin ministers, appoints proroyalist cabinet

	June 19	Royal veto of second decree against nonjuring priests and of assembly of revolutionary troops in Paris
	June 20	Invasion of Tuilleries palace by crowds protesting royal veto; threats to royal family
	July 21	Decree declaring nation (*la patrie*) to be in danger
	July 25	Brunswick Manifesto demanding people of Paris submit to king or face punishment by invading armies
		Neighborhood assemblies in Paris (*sections*) authorized to meet in permanent session
	August 3	Majority of Paris *sections* demand deposition of king
	August 10	"Second French Revolution": Tuilleries palace stormed, king suspended from functions, Girondin ministers reinstated
	August 19	Defection of Lafayette to Austrians
	August 23	Fall of Longwy to Prussians
	September 2	Fall of Verdun to Prussians
	September 2–6	"September Massacre" of prisoners in Paris jails
	September 20	French victory over Prussians at Valmy
	September 21	First meeting of convention; monarchy abolished
	September 22	Decree dating all future acts from "Year I" of newly established republic
	October 6	Enactment of revolutionary calendar
	October 21	French armies take Mainz
	November 6	Invasion of Belgium; French victory at Jemappes
	November 19	Official French offer of aid to foreign peoples seeking freedom
	November 27	French annexation of Savoy
1793	January 14–17	King's trial
	January 21	Execution of Louis XVI
	February 1	Declaration of war against Great Britain and Holland

March 7	Declaration of war against Spain
March 9	Members of Convention (*représentants en mission*) sent to departments and to armies to coordinate war effort
March 10	Establishment of Revolutionary Tribunal
March 11	Beginnings of Vendée insurrection
March 21	Surveillance committees set up in all localities (*communes*)
April 6	First Committee of Public Safety; defection of General Dumouriez to Austrians
May 4	First *Maximum* on grain prices
May 31– June 2	Suspension and expulsion of Girondins from Convention under pressure of Paris crowd
June 6	"Federalist" risings in support of Girondins at Bordeaux and Marseilles
June 24	Convention ratifies Constitution of 1793 (never applied)
July 17	Definitive abolition, without compensation, of feudal obligations
July 27	Robespierre joins Committee of Public Safety
August 1	Adoption of metric system
August 23	Universal military service (*levée en masse*) enacted
August 27	Fall of Toulon to British
September 5	Convention declares Terror "order of the day" under pressure of Paris crowd
September 17	Law of Suspects
September 22	Beginning of "Year II" of the republic
September 29	General *maximum* on prices and wages
October 9	Suppression of "federalist" insurrection in Lyons
October 10	Government declared to be "revolutionary" for duration of war
October 16	Execution of Marie Antoinette
October 24–31	Trial and execution of Girondins
December 19	French retake Toulon
December 23	Republicans retake Vendée

1794	January 27	Decree extending French language into non-Francophone provinces
	February 4	Abolition of slavery in French colonies
	February 26–March 3	Vote to sequester property of "suspects" for distribution to poor
	March 24	Execution of *sans-culottes* leaders (Hébertistes)
	April 6	Execution of Danton and his followers in convention
	June 8	Festival of Supreme Being
	June 10	Law of 22 Prairial suspending rights of accused and inaugurating the Great Terror
	June 16	Battle of Fleurus: French retake Belgium
	July 23	Maximum on wages
	July 26	Robespierre's last speech to convention
	July 27	9th *Thermidor*: fall of Robespierre
	July 28–29	Execution of Robespierre and 115 followers
	July 30–December 24	Thermidorean Reaction: reorganization of Revolutionary Tribunal and Committee of Public Safety, closing of Jacobin Club, return of surviving Girondins to Convention, abolition of Maximum
1795	February 21	Decree establishing freedom of worship
	April–May	"White Terror" in southern France
	April 5	Peace with Prussia (Treaty of Basle)
	May 16	Peace with Holland; recognition of "Batavian Republic"
	May 20	1 *Prairial*: *sans-culottes* rising
	May 23	Paris *sections* disarmed
	June 8	Death of Louis XVII; comte de Provence becomes pretender to French throne (Louis XVIII)
	July 22	Peace with Spain
	August 22	Convention ratifies "Constitution of Year III"
	October 1	Annexation of Belgium
	October 5	13 *Vendémiaire*: Parisian insurrection defeated
	October 22	Convention disbands; beginning of Directory

1796	May 10	Battle of Lodi: Bonaparte defeats Austrians; arrest of Babeuf (Conspiracy of Equals)
	November 15–17	Bonaparte's victory at Arcola
1797	January 14	Bonaparte's victory over Austrians at Rivoli
	March–April	Royalist victory in legislative elections
	May 26	Babeuf sentenced to death
	September 4	Coup d'état: royalist legislators purged
1798	May 11	Further purge of Jacobins and royalists from legislature
	May 19	Departure of Bonaparte's expedition to Egypt
	July 21	Bonaparte victory in battle of the Pyramids
	August 1	Battle of the Nile: French fleet defeated
1799	April	Jacobin victory in legislative elections
	October 9	Bonaparte's return to France
	November 9–10	18 *Brumaire*: Bonaparte's *coup d'état*

Introduction: Change and Continuity in the Historiography of the French Revolution

Over the past twenty-five years the study of the French Revolution has undergone what historians of science call a "paradigm shift." In simple terms, this means that the revolution has been reinterpreted. Through much of the twentieth century it was perceived to be a social revolution in which France's traditional ruling class, the feudal aristocracy, was overthrown and replaced by a new ruling class, the bourgeoisie. The most influential version of this interpretation was set forth by Georges Lefebvre in a famous textbook, a selection from which is included in Section III of this book.

By the time of Lefebvre's death in 1959, his concept of a "Bourgeois Revolution" had become virtually an orthodoxy among historians—a belief too universally accepted to be easily challenged. Aspects of this "orthodoxy" were nonetheless called into question by a number of research historians, particularly in Great Britain and the United States. In 1964 the results of their research were synthesized by Alfred Cobban, an English historian hitherto known mainly as an expert on Edmund Burke, in a book called *The Social Interpretation of the French Revolution.* Cobban's book consists of a sustained attack on the "orthodoxy's" basic proposition. Using Lefebvre's own objective criteria, and in some cases Lefebvre's data, Cobban demonstrated that the ruling class that rose to power in the revolution's wake could not plausibly be classified as a bourgeoisie because it was similar to the prerevolutionary ruling class, which Lefebvre called an "aristocracy."

By the early 1970s, Lefebvre's "orthodoxy" had been discredited. Since then, other historians have attempted to replace it with new interpretations. Selections from the works of four of these historians comprise Section IV of this book. Underlying these selections is the assumption that inasmuch as the bourgeoisie did not overthrow the aristocracy, the revolution was primarily political rather than social. This political revolution had to do not so much with changes in laws and institutions as with changes in political consciousness, what Lynn Hunt calls "political

1

culture." To François Furet, the most important of the four, the revolution in political culture consisted primarily of the substitution of a new form of absolutism, popular sovereignty, for the old absolutist doctrine of the Divine Right of Kings. Hunt herself emphasizes the creation of a new system of symbols and a new political idiom by means of which the sovereign people were activated. Mona Ozouf focuses on the festivals of the revolution—celebrations of a putatively secular regime that actually were religious rituals designed to endow the new sovereign state with something of the sacred character of the fallen monarchy. To Robert Darnton these changes in language, symbol, and ceremonial eventuate in a reconstruction of what the revolutionaries took to be reality.

On a more complex level, the "paradigm shift" also has involved a change in historians' perceptions of the revolution's place in history. To Lefebvre and other proponents of the "orthodoxy," the bourgeoisie of the Bourgeois Revolution was a capitalist class. The main significance of its rise to power was that, in the phrase of another historian in Section III, Albert Soboul, it "paved the way for capitalism." The Bourgeois Revolution specifically marked the point at which conditions were created for the passage of industrial capitalism from Great Britain to France and thence to the rest of the European continent and the world.

This idea derives from Karl Marx's philosophy of history, dialectical materialism, according to which humankind progresses by stages from conditions of scarcity to conditions of abundance. The passage from feudalism, the last stage of the agrarian era, to industrial capitalism is a major climacteric in this progression. The French Revolution, transmitting industry to the larger world, caps the climax.

This proposition also was called into question by Alfred Cobban. His basic case against the "orthodoxy" is that the postrevolutionary ruling class consisted primarily of landowners rather than capitalists. Such a class was hardly likely to have "paved the way" for industry, and Cobban went on to demonstrate that it did not: After the revolution, as before, the French economy was agrarian.

Cobban's ultimate message seemed to be that the French Revolution had little impact on the modern world. Post-Marxist historians do not go so far. Ozouf and Furet suggest that the political culture of the French Revolution was a major influence on the totalitarian regimes of the twentieth century. (Furet, conversely, links the rejection of the Marxist interpretation to the decline of communism in eastern Europe and in France itself.) But the post-Marxists accept Cobban's contention that the revolution could not have been a world-historical socioeconomic climacteric.

To Furet, this claim is the latest manifestation of a delusion dating back to the revolution, "the myth of the founding event." Furet says that for nearly two hundred years Frenchmen suffering from this delusion have refought the revolution's battles. But the delusion's impact on historiography has been even more decisive than its influence on French politics. Virtually all historians of the revolution have subscribed to some version of the myth.

The salient feature of Furet's historical vision is the absence of this delusion. He is able to recognize, as previous historians could not, that the revolution was something of an anticlimax or a climax only in the sense that, against all objective evidence, it convinced the French that they had entered a new era. Furet's hope is that his postdelusional perspective will allow other historians to free themselves of the myth. Once they recognize that the revolution is over, they will regard it with the same detachment that historians of early Middle Ages bring to their study of the Merovingians. They will stop reliving and commemorating the revolution and begin to "take it apart."

Furet clearly believes that the terms in which he and his followers have reinterpreted the revolution mark as sharp a break in historiography as the revolutionary period was once thought to have made in the historical process itself. In some ways he is right to think this. The post-Marxists' focus on political culture has disclosed little-known aspects of revolutionary consciousness. This focus in turn reflects the influence of new disciplines. Robert Darnton approaches the revolution from the perspective of cultural anthropology, Lynn Hunt from a background in historicist literary criticism. Ozouf and Furet himself belong to the *Annales* school, named for a journal that fosters the study of historically distinctive forms of collective consciousness called *mentalités*.

In suggesting that the revision of the Marxist interpretation is the first genuine watershed in the historiography of the revolution, however, Furet gives a misleading impression of the post-Marxists' place within this historiography and oversimplifies the historiographical tradition itself. "Paradigm shifts," in which historians have tried to discredit earlier interpretations and transcend previous partisan quarrels, have been a recurrent feature of the historiography of the French Revolution.

This book begins with selections from Alexis de Tocqueville, who initiated a "paradigm shift" around the middle of the last century. Tocqueville is one of the rare historians whom Furet recognizes as a precursor, and he stands in something of the same relation to an earlier historiographical generation, the liberals of the Restoration, as Furet does to the Marxists. Tocqueville's particular quarrel was with François Guizot, the leading liberal historian (later chief minister to Louis Philippe, the king who came to power after the Bourbons were overthrown in 1830). To Guizot, the revolution was a political watershed that ended centuries of arbitrary absolutist rule and created conditions for the emergence of a constitutional monarchy in which the rights of the individual would be guaranteed. Tocqueville takes issue with every aspect of this interpretation. He disputes Guizot's assumption that the revolution had transformed the country by demonstrating that many changes attributed to it had occurred before it erupted. He argues that the revolution did not inaugurate an age of liberal constitutional development but rather accelerated a process of administrative centralization, begun by the absolute monarchy, that led to the despotism of Napoleon I and, in Tocqueville's own time, to the dictatorship of his nephew, Louis Bonaparte.

Tocqueville's sober writing style represents a reaction against romanticism — the dominant mode of expression among the liberal historians of the Restoration. In the years following Tocqueville's death in 1859, this reaction gathered force among French thinkers and culminated in a widespread conversion to a new philosophy, positivism. This philosophy laid down the principle that all branches of knowledge are destined to transcend metaphysics (of which romanticism was one expression) and reach the same level of precision and positive social usefulness as the physical sciences.

The selections in Section II are from the writings of two men who attempted to apply positivism to the study of the French Revolution during the early years of the Third Republic, the regime that succeeded Louis Bonaparte's Second Empire in 1870. Both writers claim to have based their histories on a scientific examination of relevant documents, but the selections demonstrate that neither was able to write a definitive objective interpretation. Hippolyte Taine, whose writings come first in this section, wrote a highly partisan indictment of the revolution — and indirectly of the Third Republic, which he believed had emanated from it. The second selection, from the writings of another positivist, Alphonse Aulard, makes an equally partisan case against Taine and for the revolution.

The publication of Jean Jaurès' *Histoire socialiste* at the turn of the twentieth century marks another "paradigm shift" — away from the variegated perspectives of previous histories to Marxism. Jaurès' interpretation was the first to define the revolution as a decisive juncture in the history of industrial capitalism and the first, by extension, to link the stages of human development to changes in the means of production. This assumption subsequently influenced Marxist and non-Marxist historians alike. Mathiez assumes that the revolution's place in the process of industrialization makes it a world-historical event. Furet assumes that because it had no impact on this process, it could not have been a socioeconomic revolution.

The selection from *L'Histoire socialiste* in Section III indicates that Jaurès himself had a different perception of the historiographical significance of his work. His intention was to shift the focus of research away from political history, which had been Aulard's concern, to social and economic history—particularly the history of the poor. The excerpts from Lefebvre's essay on the peasantry and Soboul's study of the Parisian *sans-culottes* show that this aspect of Jaurès' work was to have lasting influence as well.

These selections also demonstrate that continuity is as much a feature of revolutionary historiography as "paradigm shifts." This continuity, however, does not consist primarily, as Furet maintains, of an ongoing commemoration of the "founding event." It consists rather of a complex pattern of recurrence: interpretations that periodically reappear but which at each appearance reflect the intellectual and political changes that underlie the "paradigm shifts."

The Bourgeois Revolution is one of these recurrent interpretations. Its basic features were prefigured in a celebrated pamphlet entitled *Qu'est-ce que le tiers état?* that the abbé Sieyès wrote at the beginning of the revolution. A later version of the interpretation appears in the writings of Tocqueville. In the selection from his *Democracy in America*, the revolutionary rise to power of the middle classes in both the United States and France is interpreted as a major stage in the transition from aristocratic to democratic social conditions—and as the last major social revolution in Western Civilization.

In the other selections Tocqueville's ideas about the Bourgeois Revolution figure prominently in the case he makes against the historical arguments of Guizot. To Guizot, the overthrow of the feudal aristocracy by the bourgeoisie is the climax of a process lasting several centuries during which middle-class merchants and bureaucrats assist the kings in building the nation and opening the road to freedom. Tocqueville interprets it as the final triumph of mediocre men of property and un-scrupulous functionaries who laid the foundations for absolutism and later served as willing agents of Bonapartist despotism.

Where Tocqueville saw the Bourgeois Revolution as a precondi-tion of the Second Empire, Aulard, writing some fifteen years after the Second Empire had fallen, perceived it as the genesis of a tradition that culminated in a liberal democratic republic. In this interpretation the bourgeoisie is once again an historical hero. But to Aulard the heroic bourgeoisie is more complex than it had been to Guizot. Aulard be-rates the class because it initially attempted to create a constitutional monarchy to be run for its own benefit. Only later, under pressure from the counterrevolution, would the middle class make common cause with the people and commit itself to the republic.

The same ambiguous relationship between bourgeoisie and com-mon people reappears in Jaurès' *Histoire socialiste* and in subsequent Marxist histories, but in other respects the Marxist interpretation is dif-ferent from previous versions of the Bourgeois Revolution. The bour-geoisie itself is transformed from a modest middle class of merchants, *rentiers*, and propertied professionals into a capitalist class of large-scale entrepreneurs. A more important change has to do with Marxist percep-tions of the revolution's impact on the future. Like Tocqueville, most previous historians had seen the events of the late eighteenth century as France's last major social upheaval. In the selection from *L'Histoire socialiste*, the Bourgeois Revolution brings forth not only an industrial economy but also a new working class, the industrial proletariat, and thus sets in motion a scenario of social conflict between workers and bourgeois that will lead to another revolution and the beginnings of what Jaurès calls "communist humanity."

Albert Mathiez, the next historian in Section III, saw in the final months of the Terror the "blood red crucible" of this future class struggle, as well as of the socialist economy that Bolshevik revolutionaries were at-tempting to establish in Russia. Other selections in this section reveal how subsequent developments, and more detailed research by Marxist historians, called Mathiez' conclusions into question. Soboul argues that the Parisian *sans-culottes* had little in common with a proletariat and that the seemingly socialist Montagnard program of 1794 was in reality an im-practical bourgeois experiment in poor relief. In an earlier essay Lefebvre identifies the peasantry as an autonomous and largely anticapitalist force and criticizes Jaurès and Mathiez for forcing the rural revolution into the framework of a bourgeois capitalist offensive. In the selection from his text, Lefebvre demonstrates that the postrevolutionary ruling class was not the bourgeoisie that initiated and led the revolution and that in all its incarnations the bourgeoisie was more an eclectic propertied class than the purely capitalist class that Jaurès had imagined.

Another recurrent interpretation is the idea that the revolution was the fulfillment of the Enlightenment. Like the Bourgeois Revolution, this concept dates to the revolutionary period itself—specifically to an essay entitled *Reflections on the French Revolution* that Edmund Burke published in 1790. In the early nineteenth century Burke's essay had considerable influence on conservative critics of the revolution, but his ideas did not figure in a full-dress history until the appearance of Taine's *Origins of Contemporary France.*

Taine's positivism put him at a far remove from Burke, who was a spiritual father of romanticism. As the selection shows, much of Taine's work represents an attempt to subject the leaders and crowds of the revolution to sociologic analysis, an unknown discipline in the eighteenth century. In other respects, however, *The Origins of Contemporary France* echoes and amplifies major themes in *Reflections on the French Revolution.*

In the first part of the selection Taine elaborates on Burke's major theme by explaining how a superficial rationalism and a classical taste for elegantly expressed ideas predisposed eighteenth-century Frenchmen to accept the utopian ideal of an egalitarian society. Subsequent passages show how this abstract vision seized the minds of revolutionaries who stampeded the nation into a hopeless attempt to realize this vision.

This interpretation contrasts at every major point with the idea of a Bourgeois Revolution. It is most obviously different in its account of the revolution's causes. Tocqueville, Aulard, and the Marxist historians explain the onset of the revolution primarily in terms of concrete developments in the material world—the expansion of the monarchy, the rise of the people, the emergence of the capitalist economy. Taine, following Burke, explains it primarily in terms of visions and ideas—forces that operate in people's minds. The social character of the revolutionaries is also different in the two interpretations. In every version of the Bourgeois Revolution the bourgeoisie is part and parcel of French society. To Aulard and the Marxists this is true of the revolutionary crowds as well. To Taine the revolutionary leaders are rootless, ill-paid ideologues and men of letters, the mobs they lead the pathological flotsam and jetsam of the lower classes. On a deeper level the two interpretations offer conflicting views of the revolution's place in history. In every version the Bourgeois Revolution is the culmination of a long historical process—its origins traceable to the beginnings of the monarchy for Tocqueville and to the birth of trade for Lefebvre. To Taine, as again to Burke before him, the revolution is unhistorical, even antihistorical, a violation of the historical process. In the selection he attempts to demonstrate how recently minted Enlightenment ideas deflect the French from a program of reforms appropriate to their distinctive historical experience and set them off on a disastrous experimental tangent that leads inexorably to the Terror. The ultimate message of Taine's work is that the deflection of French history from its natural course reached its climax in the Paris Commune, a radical rising against the monarchists who ruled the early Third Republic, which Taine saw as the ultimate expression of Enlightenment egalitarianism.

In the early twentieth century Taine's ideas were developed by a royalist historian, Augustin Cochin, who explained the workings of all modern democracies, including American machine politics, in terms of the influence of dedicated minorities. After Cochin's death, the historiographical tradition emanating from Taine and Burke went into relative decline. Many of Taine's ideas reappear, however, in the writings of post-Marxist historians.

The disciplines that have most conspicuously influenced the post-Marxists—cultural anthropology and the *Annales* school—did not, of course, exist in Taine's time. Their accounts of revolutionary political culture make very little of aspects of Enlightenment thinking such as classicism and rationalism that were important to Taine. Nor is there any indication that their misgivings about the egalitarian aspects of this culture extend to other forms of political democracy, as was the case with Taine.

The selections in Section IV, however, also show that the post-Marxist historians have at least as much in common with Taine as the Marxists themselves had with earlier historians of the Bourgeois Revolution. There are conspicuous similarities between their respective social visions. The "Grub Street" writers and blood-thirsty mobs in Darnton's essay bear more than a passing resemblance to the rootless ideologues and poverty-stricken sociopaths of *Les Origines de France contemporaine*.

More important in terms of basic continuity is the reappearance of the thesis that the revolution was the fulfillment of the Enlightenment. The post-Marxists make little of Montesquieu and Voltaire, but Rousseau looms as large in their writings as in Taine's. His ideas are recurrent themes in their interpretation of revolutionary culture. The *Social Contract*, according to Lynn Hunt, is the source of the notion of reconstructing society. Furet maintains that the principle of "popular sovereignty" derives from the concept of the "general will." To Ozouf, Rousseau provides a blueprint for the revolutionaries' civic religion. The post-Marxists also associate Rousseau with less easily definable aspects of the revolutionary *mentalité*: the exaltation of the poor at the expense of the rich, of feeling over reason. It is to the change in sensibility inspired by Rousseau's writings that Robert Darnton attributes the vague but compelling conviction of infinite possibility that lay behind the revolutionary obsession with human regeneration.

The post-Marxists also share Taine's ideas about the revolution's place in history. This is implicit in Hunt's emphasis on the revolutionaries' determination to reconstruct society and all but explicit in Ozouf's argument that the creators of the revolutionary festivals repudiated 800 years of shared historical experience. Corollary to the sense of infinite possibility in Darnton's essay is a self-conscious break with the past. But the most important connections between post-Marxist interpretations and Taine's vision of the revolution's place in history appear in the selection from Furet's *Revolutionary France*. For him as for Burke and Taine, the revolution sets the country on an aberrant historical course. As early as 1789, Furet says, revolutionary idealism deflects France from the path of moderate reform onto a radical trajectory that eventuates in the Reign of Terror. Much of the rest of Furet's work chronicles the baleful consequences of violating the historical process. The message of the final passage in the selection is that the cycle of revolution and reaction that began in 1789 ended only in the later nineteenth century when moderate positivist republicans like Jules Ferry managed to exorcize the revolutionary *mentalité* and establish a conservative republic.

The reappearance of Taine's ideas in Furet's writings indicates that Furet has been no more successful than Taine in his quest for detachment. Like Taine, he sides with the revolution's critics in an old historiographical quarrel. The selections in Section V suggest that the quarrel between proponents and critics of the revolution may not be over. The writers in this section subscribe to aspects of the idea of a Bourgeois Revolution. Like previous advocates of this idea, they believe that the revolution made substantive contributions to progress. But these selections also illustrate a more complex feature of the intellectual climate that has taken shape since the most recent "paradigm shift."

Prior to the revision of the Marxist interpretation, "orthodoxies" prevailed in other areas of social science—Freudianism in psychology, structural linguistics in philology. There are few examples of such intellectual hegemony today. In any given field different scholars take different approaches to their subjects and incorporate insights from conflicting interpretations. In most fields a variety of "paradigms" have had to learn to coexist. The traditional term for this situation would be "eclectic." The prevailing term is "postmodern."

The selections in this section illustrate postmodern diversity. These scholars, as indicated, accept aspects of the concept of a Bourgeois Revolution. Yet none is a Marxist historian. None in fact is an historian of the revolution. But all four have insights into its history that point to new interpretations and perspectives.

The first selection in the final section is from an article by a French economic historian, François Crouzet. The article summarizes evidence that argues against the Marxist thesis that the revolution paved the way for industrialization. But it also raises serious questions about Furet's assumption that pre- and postrevolutionary conditions were fundamentally similar. Crouzet argues that the revolution changed, and even improved, the economic condition of France's peasant majority. He also suggests that the revolution brought a new class to power—men who had little in common with capitalists but who bore a significant resemblance to what Tocqueville and Guizot would have called a "bourgeoisie."

The second selection is from an article by an American labor historian, William Sewell. It focuses on France's artisan class in the eighteenth and early nineteenth centuries. Like Furet and his followers, Sewell distances himself from Marxist concepts and categories, which have been pervasive in labor history. He is especially critical of Albert Soboul. Where Soboul treats the artisans as archaic social remnants that will give way to a genuine proletariat once postrevolutionary industrialization is underway, Sewell argues that they were the only significant working class in this still preindustrial country until after the middle of the nineteenth century. Sewell's approach, like Robert Darnton's, derives from cultural anthropology, and like Ozouf and Hunt, he is concerned with the idiom and symbols of revolutionary political culture. Yet, like Soboul, and Marx before him, Sewell perceives France's nineteenth-century working class, however defined, as the original constituency of socialism. Under the impact of the revolution it develops its own distinctive socialist ideology by reworking in universalist terms the collectivist ideas of the guilds. But the new ideology also results, Sewell says, from changes that the revolution made in the economic conditions under which the working class lived — the suppression of the guilds, the inauguration of a new system which, though not industrial, was clearly capitalist by eighteenth-century standards. Related changes in working conditions resulted from the rise to power of what he persists in calling a "bourgeoisie."

The topic of the selection by Darlene Levy and Harriet Applewhite is the role of women during the revolution's radical period between 1792 and 1794. This is a time of triumph to Marxist and republican historians alike — the high point of the offensive against feudalism, the first appearance of popular democracy. To Levy and Applewhite it is a tragic story. Women, they show, made a major contribution to this process of radicalization and to the success of the revolution as a whole. Their male counterparts, however, failed not only to acknowledge this contribution but also actually repudiated the revolutionary women. At the point where the revolution became most democratic, by including large numbers of *sans-culotte* men, women were excluded from the political process. In assessing the ultimate historical significance of the revolution, however, Levy and Applewhite are closer to Aulard than to Ozouf and Hunt. It remains a significant event in the emergence of liberal democracy and even in the history of women. Despite their ultimate failure, the feminist radicals of the revolution forced women's rights onto the agenda of Western Civilization.

The perceptions of the last writer in the section, Tzvetan Todorov, are influenced by his original academic discipline, structural linguistics, and by his experience growing up in communist Bulgaria. His concern in this selection is with the catalytic impact of the Enlightenment and the revolution on the emergence of nationalism. He is critical of the exclusivist, aggressive, expansionist nationalism of the revolution's radical period and, by extension, like the post-Marxist historians, of the political culture that inspired it — a culture in which, again like them, he sees precedents for totalitarianism in eastern Europe. The selection also shows, however, that to him this was not the only significant form of nationalism to emerge in France during the Enlightenment and the revolution. Alongside it, particularly during the revolution's early period, was another strain, tolerant and peaceable, inward-looking but cosmopolitan, that focused primarily on integrating the French into a liberal national community. This nationalism was in turn the expression of a very different political culture which, though ultimately defeated, has an honorable place in the history of the revolution and was to have important sequels in the future. Todorov finds the origins of this liberal political culture in the rational, classical Enlightenment of Montesquieu and Voltaire, which has receded from view in post-Marxist interpretations. His own interpretation of the revolution's significance harks back to Guizot and the Restoration liberals who also saw in revolutionary political culture the expression of an eclectic Bourgeois Revolution — aberrant and fraught with peril in its final phases but full of promise for the future in its heroic beginnings.

France Under the Old Regime. From *France In Modern Times, Fifth Edition,* by Cordon Wright. Copyright © 1995, 1987, 1981, by W. W. Norton & Company, Inc. Copyright © 1974, 1960 by Rand McNally College Publishing Company. Reprinted by permission of W. W. Norton & Company, Inc.

France in the Nineteenth Century. From *France In Modern Times, Fifth Edition*, by Gordon Wright. Copyright © 1995, 1987, 1981, by W. W. Norton & Company, Inc. Copyright © 1974, 1960 by Rand McNally College Publishing Company. Reprinted by permission of W. W. Norton & Company, Inc.

I An Aristocratic Overview

Alexis de Tocqueville

A Bourgeois Revolution

Since the publication of *L'Ancien Régime et la Révolution* in 1856, historians of all persuasions have admired Alexis de Tocqueville (1805–1859). This widespread appeal has given him a reputation for standing above the partisan quarrels that have influenced revolutionary historiography. In his own time Tocqueville lived in the thick of the political fray. His career as a public figure began with the appearance in 1835 of *De la Démocratie en Amérique*—a book that is as much a commentary on conditions in France as an account of society in the United States. Later, during the July Monarchy, he served as an opposition deputy in the lower house of parliament. He again served as a

From "Why Great Revolutions Will Become Rare" from *Democracy In America* by Alexis de Tocqueville. Edited by J. P. Meyer and Max Lerner. Translated by George Lawrence. English translation copyright © 1965 by Harper & Row, Publishers, Inc. Copyright renewed. Reprinted by permission of HarperCollins Publishers, Inc.

deputy, and briefly as foreign minister, under the short-lived Second Republic. He was also a prominent figure in the political *salons* of the early Second Empire. Throughout his public life he criticized the inability of the French to govern themselves—a failing that he attributed to their unfortunate history. His negative assessment of the revolution's place in history on view in these selections from Tocqueville's writings reflects this conviction. Tocqueville also was an aristocrat. His class background gave him a long-range historical perspective unique among major nineteenth-century French thinkers but was a source of prejudice. Directly or indirectly, in all three selections, he compares the bourgeoisie unfavorably with the nobility.

Why Great Revolutions Will Become Rare

When a people has lived for centuries under a system of castes and classes, it can only reach a democratic state of society through a long series of more or less painful transformations. These must involve violent efforts and many vicissitudes, in the course of which property, opinions, and power are all subject to swift changes.

Even when this great revolution has come to an end, the revolutionary habits created thereby and by the profound disturbances thereon ensuing will long endure.

As all this takes place just at the time when social conditions are being leveled, the conclusion has been drawn that there must be a hidden connection and secret link between equality itself and revolutions, so that neither can occur without the other.

On this point reason and experience seem agreed.

Among a people where ranks are more or less equal, there is no apparent connection between men to hold them firmly in place. None of them have any permanent right or power to give commands, and none is bound by his social condition to obey. Each man, having some education and some resources, can choose his own road and go along separately from all the rest.

The same causes which make the citizens independent of each other daily prompt new and restless longings and constantly goad them on.

It therefore seems natural to suppose that in a democratic society ideas, things, and men must eternally be changing shape and position and that ages of democracy must be times of swift and constant transformation.

But is this in fact so? Does equality of social conditions habitually and permanently drive men toward revolutions? Does it contain some disturbing principle which prevents society from settling down and inclines the citizens constantly to change their laws, principles, and mores? I do not think so.

Almost every revolution which has changed the shape of nations has been made to consolidate or destroy inequality. Disregarding the secondary causes which have had some effect on the great convulsions in the world, you will almost always find that equality was at the heart of the matter. Either the poor were bent on snatching the property of the rich, or the rich were trying to hold the poor down. So, then, if you could establish a state of society in which each man had something to keep and little to snatch, you would have done much for the peace of the world.

I realize that among a great people there will always be some very poor and some very rich citizens. But the poor, instead of forming the vast majority of the population as is always the case in aristocratic societies, are but few, and the law has not drawn them together by the link of an irremediable and hereditary state of wretchedness.

The rich, on their side, are scattered and powerless. They have no conspicuous privileges, and even their wealth, being no longer incorporated and bound up with the soil, is impalpable and, as it were, invisible. As there is no longer a race of poor men, so there is not a race of rich men; the rich daily rise out of the crowd and constantly return thither. Hence they do not form a distinct class, easily identified and plundered; moreover, there are a thousand hidden threads connecting them with the mass of citizens, so that the people would hardly know how to attack them without harming itself. In democratic societies between these two extremes there is an innumerable crowd who are much alike, who, though not exactly rich nor yet quite poor, have enough property to want order and not enough to excite envy.

Such men are the natural enemies of violent commotion; their immobility keeps all above and below them quiet, and assures the stability of the body social.

I am not suggesting that they are themselves satisfied with their actual position or that they would feel any natural abhorrence toward a revolution if they could share the plunder without suffering the calamities; on the contrary, their eagerness to get rich is unparalleled, but their trouble is to know whom to despoil. The same social condition which prompts their longings restrains them within necessary limits. It gives men both greater freedom to change and less interest in doing so.

Not only do men in democracies feel no natural inclination for revolutions, but they are afraid of them.

Any revolution is more or less a threat to property. Most inhabitants of a democracy have property. And not only have they got property, but they live in the conditions in which men attach most value to property.

If one studies each class of which society is composed closely, it is easy to see that passions due to ownership are keenest among the middle classes.

The poor often do not trouble much about their possessions, for their suffering from what they lack is much greater than their enjoyment of what they have. The rich have many other passions to gratify besides those connected with wealth, and moreover, the long and troublesome management of a great fortune sometimes makes them in the end insensible to its charms.

But men whose comfortable existence is equally far from wealth and poverty set immense value on their possessions. As they are still very close to poverty, they see its privations in detail and are afraid of them; nothing but a scanty fortune, the cynosure of all their hopes and fears, keeps them therefrom. The constant care which it occasions daily attaches them to their property; their continual exertions to increase it make it even more precious to them. The idea of giving up the smallest part of it is insufferable to them, and the thought of losing it completely strikes them as the worst of all evils. Now, it is just the number of the eager and restless small property owners which equality of conditions constantly increases.

Hence the majority of citizens in a democracy do not see clearly what they could gain by a revolution, but they constantly see a thousand ways in which they could lose by one.

I have shown elsewhere in this work how equality naturally leads men to go in for industry and trade and that it tends to increase and distribute real property. I pointed out that it inspires every man with a constant and eager desire to increase his well-being. Nothing is more opposed to revolutionary passions than all this.

The final result of a revolution might serve the interests of industry and trade, but its first effect will almost always be the ruin of industrialists and traders.

In revolution the owners of personal property have more to fear than all others, for their property is often both easy to seize and capable of disappearing completely at any moment.

Therefore the more widely personal property is distributed and increased and the greater the number of those enjoying it, the less is a nation inclined to revolution.

Moreover, whatever a man's calling and whatever type of property he owns, one characteristic is common to all.

No one is fully satisfied with his present fortune, and all are constantly trying a thousand various ways to improve it. Consider any individual at any period in his life, and you will always find him preoccupied with fresh plans to increase his comfort. Do not talk to him about the interests and rights of the human race; that little private business of his for the moment absorbs all his thoughts, and he hopes that public disturbances can be put off to some other time.

This not only prevents them from causing revolutions, but also deters them from wanting them. Violent political passions have little hold on men whose whole thoughts are bent on the pursuit of well-being. Their excitement about small matters makes them calm about great ones.

It is therefore a mistake to suppose that once equality has become something long established and undisputed, molding manners to its taste, men will easily allow themselves to be thrown into danger by some rash leader or bold innovator.

I am not making out that the inhabitants of democracies are by nature stationary; on the contrary, I think that such a society is always on the move and that none of its members knows what rest is; but I think that all bestir themselves within certain limits which they hardly ever pass. Daily they change, alter, and renew things of secondary importance, but they are very careful not to touch fundamentals. They love change, but they are afraid of revolutions.

I have no hesitation in saying that most of the maxims which are generally called democratic in France would be outlawed by the American democracy. That is easily understood. In America there exist democratic ideas and passions; in Europe we still have revolutionary ones.

The Political and Social Condition of France

. . . For half a century almost every nation of Europe has been more or less acted upon by French revolutionary influences, but generally without any distinct perception of the fact. They have obeyed a common impulse, without being conscious of the force which gave it.

If we study the countries in the immediate neighbourhood of France, we discover many events, customs, and ideas which are easily traceable, either directly or indirectly, to the French Revolution. At the same time we cannot fail to perceive, that in the very same countries there exists great ignorance of the causes which produced and of the effects which followed that revolution, even in France itself. . . .

The ideas and feelings of every age are connected with those of the age that preceded it, by invisible but almost omnipotent ties. One generation may anathematize the preceding generations, but it is far easier to combat than to avoid resembling them. It is impossible, therefore, to describe a nation at any given epoch, without stating what it was half a century before. This is especially necessary when the question relates to a people who, for the last fifty years, have been in an almost continual state of revolution. . . .

It is proposed [here] . . . to give some explanation of the state of France previously to the great revolution of 1789, for want of which her present condition would be difficult to comprehend. . . .

It will perhaps be not without some difficulty that we shall convey to the English reader of the present day a clear conception of the noblesse of France. English has no word which expresses exactly the old French idea of a noblesse. The word "nobility" expresses more, the word "gentry" less. Neither is the word "aristocracy" one which can be applied to the case without explanation. By aristocracy . . . is commonly understood the aggregate of the higher classes. The French noblesse was an aristocratic body, but we should be wrong in saying that it alone formed the aristocracy of the country, for by its side were to be found classes as enlightened, as wealthy, and almost as influential as itself. The French noblesse,

"The Political and Social State of France," *The London and Westminister Review* (III, April–July, 1836), translated by John Stuart Mill.

therefore, was to aristocracy as is understood in England, what the species is to the genus; it formed a caste, and not the entire aristocracy. . . . Not that a man could not be made noble in France by the purchase of certain offices, . . . but the fact of being ennobled, . . . did not, properly speaking, introduce him into those of the noblesse. The noble of recent date halted, as it were, on the confines of the two orders; somewhat above the one, but below the other. He perceived afar the promised land which his posterity alone could enter. Birth, therefore, was in reality the only source whence the noblesse sprung. Men were born noble—they did not become so. . . .

Noble families recognized among themselves a species of theoretic equality, founded on their common privilege of birth. . . . There existed, nevertheless, great differences of condition among the nobles. Some still possessed large landed estates, others had scarcely the means of subsistence in their paternal manor-house. Some passed the greater part of their time at court, others proudly cherished, at the extremity of their province, a hereditary obscurity. To some, custom opened the road to the highest dignities of the state, whilst others, after having attained the utmost limit of their hopes, a moderate rank in the army, returned peaceably to their homes, to quit them no more.

A certain community of spirit nevertheless existed among all the members of this great body. . . .

The French noblesse, having originated, like all the other feudal aristocracies, in conquest, had, like them, . . . enjoyed enormous privileges. It had monopolized almost all the intelligence and wealth of society. It had possessed all the land, and been master of the inhabitants.

But at the close of the eighteenth century the French noblesse presented but a shadow of its former self. It had lost its influence over both the prince and the people. The king still chose from its ranks the principal officers of government. Upon the people the influence of the noblesse was still less. Between a king and a body of nobles there is a natural affinity, . . . but a union of the aristocracy and the people is not in the ordinary course of events; only by sustained efforts can it be brought about and maintained.

In truth there are but two modes by which an aristocracy can maintain its influence over the people; by governing them, or by uniting with them for the purpose of checking the Government. The nobles must either remain the people's masters, or must become their leaders. . . . The French noblesse was far from placing itself at the head of the other classes in resistance to the abuses of the royal power; on the contrary, it was the kings who formerly united themselves, first with the people to struggle against the tyranny of the nobles, and afterwards with the nobles to maintain the people in obedience.

On the other hand, the noblesse had long ceased to take an active part in the details of government. The general government of the state was usually in the hands of nobles; they commanded the armies, and filled the chief offices in the ministry and about the courts; but they took no share . . . in that part of the public business which comes into immediate contact with the people. . . . The king's officers, who administered justice, levied taxes, maintained guidance of the people. . . .The lesser nobles, confined to the provinces by narrow circumstances, led an idle, useless and restless existence.

In thus abandoning to others the details of the public administration, and aspiring only to the more important offices of the state, the French noblesse had shown that they were more attached to the semblance of power than to power itself. . . . It is in governing the village that an aristocracy lays the foundation of the power which afterwards serves it to control the state.

The French nobles had preserved a certain number of exclusive rights, which distinguished them from, and raised them above, the rest of the citizens; but it was easy to discover that among the privileges of their fathers, the French noblesse had only retained those which make aristocracies hated, and not those which cause them to be respected or beloved. . . . The nobles were exempt from some of the taxes, and they levied from the inhabitants of their domains . . . a great number of annual contributions. These rights did not increase to any great extent the wealth of the nobles, but they erected the order of nobility into an object of general hatred and envy.

The most dangerous of all privileges . . . are pecuniary privileges. Every one can appreciate them at a glance, and sees clearly how much he is injured by them. The privileges, therefore, which confer pecuniary profit, are at once less valuable and more dangerous to the possessor than those which confer power. The French nobles, by preserving the former in preference to the latter, had maintained that feature of inequality of condition which is offensive and renounced that which is serviceable. They oppressed and impoverished the people, but did not rule over them. . . .

Independently of these lucrative privileges, the French noblesse had retained a vast number of purely honorary distinctions, such as titles, order of precedence in public, and the privilege of adopting a certain costume, and wearing certain arms. [All] . . . were alike incapable of being of the slightest service, and might be productive of danger. When once the reality of power has been abandoned, to wish to retain its semblance is to play a dangerous game. Those who possess the appearance of power, without its substance, . . . are no longer capable of protecting themselves against the hatred they excite.

All that we have said of laws and customs may be extended to opinions. . . . The modern nobles had abandoned most of the ideas of their ancestors, but there were still several of a very hurtful character in which they were obstinately attached. At the head of these must be placed the prejudice which interdicted to persons of noble birth the pursuits of commercial industry. . . .

The consequence of this was, that the families of the noblesse, while they were liable in common with others to the chances of ruin, were precluded from the ordinary means of increasing their fortunes. The noblesse, therefore . . . was gradually becoming impoverished; and thus, after having abandoned the direct road to power, they remained equally strangers to the by-roads which might possibly conduct to it.

A nobleman would have deemed himself degraded by an alliance with the daughter of a rich *roturier*. Nevertheless such unions were not uncommon among them; for their fortunes decreased more rapidly than their desires. These plebeian alliances, while they enriched [some noblemen], put the finishing stroke to the ruin of that influence over opinion, which was the only power the [noblesse] . . . retained.

In the eighteenth century the feudal laws relative to entails were still in vigour, but these laws had little effect in keeping together the fortunes of the nobles. . . . When the nobles are not tormented by the desire of enriching themselves, and when the other classes of the nation are tolerably content with the lot which Providence has assigned to them, the law of entail being then in complete accordance with the tendency of opinions and habits, the result of the whole is a universal slumber and immobility. . . . Each generation of nobles maintains without difficulty the rank which the preceding generation occupied.

But in a nation where all except the nobles are seeking to enrich themselves, the territorial possessions of the noblesse become a sort of prize which all the other classes endeavour to catch at. The ignorance of the nobles, their passions . . . [and] foibles . . . are put in requisition to draw into the general current of circulation the mass of landed property which they possess; and in a short time the noblesse themselves seldom fail to assist in the work.

The commons having only the privilege of wealth to oppose to the privileges of all kinds which their rivals enjoy, do not fail to display their opulence with every kind of ostentation. This excites the emulation of the nobles. . . . Embarrassment soon manifests itself in the fortunes of the nobles; their incomes become inadequate to their wants; and they themselves, ultimately feeling inconvenienced by the very laws which are made to keep them rich and powerful, seek by every means in their power to elude those laws. . . . There is something more powerful than the constant operation of laws in one direction, . . . the constant operation of human passions in the contrary direction.

At the breaking out of the French revolution, the laws of France still assigned to the eldest son of a noble almost all the family estates. He was, in his turn, compelled to transmit them to his descendants unimpaired. . . . Nevertheless, many domains of feudal origin had already passed from the hands of the noblesse, and many others had been divided.

Not only did the noblesse comprise in its ranks very rich and very poor men—a circumstance which by no means conflicts with the notion of a . . . noblesse—but it included very many persons who were neither rich nor poor, but possessed moderate fortunes. This state of things already savoured more of democracy than of aristocracy; and if the composition of the French noblesse had been closely examined, it would have been found to be in reality a sort of democratic body, clothed in relation to all other classes with the privileges of an aristocracy.

But the danger which menaced the nobles arose much more from what was passing around them, than from what occurred within their own circle. . . . At the same time that the wealth of the French noblesse was dwindling, and their political and social influence fading away, another class of the nation was rapidly acquiring monied wealth, and even coming into contact with the government. The noblesse was thus . . . becoming both positively and relatively weaker. The new, encroaching class, which seemed to elevat[e] . . . itself on the ruins of the other, had received the name of *tiers-état*.

At the first glance it might be thought that in France the *tiers-état* was composed of the middle class, and stood between the aristocracy and the people. But this was not the case. The *tiers-état* . . . also comprised elements which were naturally foreign to these classes: the richest merchant, the most opulent banker, the most skillful manufacturer, the man of letters, the man of science, . . . as well as the small farmer, the shopkeeper, and the peasant. . . . The tiers-état . . . included rich and poor, the ignorant and the instructed. The tiers état had thus within itself an aristocracy of its own. . . . It formed of itself a complete people, which co-existed with the privileged order, but which was perfectly capable of existing by itself, apart from them. It had opinions, prejudices, and a national spirit of its own.

Thus the tiers-état and the noblesse were intermixed on the same soil, but they formed . . . two distinct nations, which, though living under the same laws, remained strangers to each other. But of these two nations the one was incessantly recruiting its strength, the other was losing something every day, and never regaining anything.

The creation of this new people in the midst of the French nation threatened the very existence of the noblesse. The state of isolation in which the nobles lived was a still greater source of danger to them. . . . This complete division between the tiers-état and the nobles not only accelerated the fall of the noblesse, but threatened to leave in France no aristocracy whatever. . . .

In the middle ages, . . . birth was the principal source of all social advantages; but in the middle ages the nobles were also rich, and had called into alliance with them the priests, who were the instructed. Society yielded . . . to these two classes of men a complete obedience. . . . But in the eighteenth century many of the wealthy . . . were not noble, and many . . . nobles were no longer rich. The same . . . [was true] in respect to intelligence. The tiers-état . . . one member of . . . the natural aristocracy, but separated from the main body . . . was sure to destroy it by declaring war against it.

The division which existed in France between the different aristocratic elements, established in the aristocracy itself a sort of intestine war, by which democracy alone was destined to profit. Rejected by the noblesse, the principal members of the tiers-état were obliged, in combating those adversaries, to arm themselves with principles, convenient for their immediate purpose, but ultimately dangerous to themselves. . . . The tiers-état was one portion of the aristocracy which [used] . . . the principle of equality . . . as a means of overthrowing the particular barrier which was opposed to themselves. . . .

The idea spread . . . by degrees through the nation, that equality alone was conformable to the natural order of things, and was the foundation on which all well-regulated society should be built. . . .

Custom, in general, follows much more closely than law, the changes of opinion. The aristocratic principle still triumphed in political institutions, but manners had already become democratic. . . .

A circumstance which favoured singularly this mixture of classes in society, was the position gradually acquired by the literary class. The French noblesse had at all times held out their hands to literary men, and liked to associate with them; but this was especially the case in the eighteenth century. . . .

They occupied . . . a brilliant position, but one which was ill-defined and perpetually contested. They shared in the pleasures of the great, and remained strangers to their rights. The nobles were sufficiently near to them to exhibit to them in detail all the advantages reserved for superiority of birth, but at the same time kept themselves sufficiently distant to prevent them from participating in . . . those advantages. Equality was thus placed before their eyes as a phantom. . . . Accordingly the class of literary men thus favoured by the noblesse formed the most discontented portion of the tiers-état, and might be heard railing at privileges even in the palaces of the privileged.

Whilst the upper classes were gradually lowering themselves, the middle classes were gradually raising themselves, and an insensible movement was bringing them daily nearer to each other. Changes were going on in the distribution of property which . . . facilitated the growth . . . of democracy.

Almost all foreigners imagine that, in France, the division of landed property first commenced from the [revolutionary] epoch. . . . This is an error. At the moment when the revolution broke out, the lands, in a great number of provinces, were already considerably divided. The revolution did but extend to the territory what had previously been peculiar to some of its parts.

We have seen that, long before the French revolution, landed property had come to be no longer the principal source of consideration of power. During the same period industry and commerce had not made a very rapid progress; and the people, already sufficiently enlightened to conceive and desire a better condition than their own, had not yet acquired intelligence to disclose to them the most ready means of attaining it. The land, whilst it ceased to be an object of luxury to the rich, became . . . the only object of industry to the poor. The former disposed of it, to facilitate and increase his pleasures; the other purchased it, to improve his circumstances. In this manner landed property was silently passing out of the hands of the nobles, and becoming divided among the people.

While the ancient proprietors of the soil were thus losing their estates, a multitude of commoners came gradually to acquire considerable propeily. But they only did so by great efforts, and . . . most imperfect processes. Thus the large territorial fortunes daily diminished, without much contemporaneous amassing of large capital; and in the place of a few vast domains, were created many small ones, the slow and painful fruit of labour and economy.

These changes in the distribution of landed property facilitated in a singular manner the great political revolution which was on the eve of taking place. . . . There is nothing . . . more favourable to the reign of democracy than the division of the land into small independent properties. . . .

In France, at the close of the eighteenth century, the principle of the inequality of rights still ruled despotically in political society. . . . Of all the systems of government of which inequality is the basis, they had preserved the most exclusive and . . . the most intractable. A man must be noble before he could serve the state. . . .

The details of the French institutions were in accordance with this principle. Entails, the right of primogeniture, . . . seignorial rights . . . all the remains of the ancient feudal society still existed. . . . In France, nevertheless, everything had for a long time been in progress towards democracy. He who . . . had pictured to himself the state of moral impotence into which the clergy had fallen—the impoverishment and degradation of the noblesse—the wealth and intelligence of the tiers-état—the remarkable division of landed property which already existed—the great number of middling, and the small number of large fortunes; who had recollected the theories professed at this epoch, the principles tacitly but almost universally admitted—he . . . who had embraced in one view all these different objects, could not have failed to conclude that the France of that day, with her noblesse, her state religion, her aristocratic laws and customs, was already, taken altogether, the most really democratic nation of Europe; and that the French at the close of the eighteenth century, by their social state, their civil constitution, their ideas and their manners, had already outstripped greatly even those among the nations of the present day who tend most conspicuously towards democracy.

It is not only in the progress she was making towards equality of conditions, that France of the eighteenth century approximated to the France of our day. Many other features of the national physiognomy, which are usually looked upon as new, had already made their appearance.

In a society where there exists great equality of conditions, the citizens, being so nearly equal among themselves, are naturally led to place the details of administration in the hands of the only power which stands forth conspicuously in an elevated situation above them all; namely, the central government of the state.

A democratic people tends towards centralization, as it were, by instinct. In France it was not only the central government, but the king in particular, who was exclusively vested with this power. . . .

In France, the extension of the royal power to embrace every part of the public administration regularly kept pace with the rise and progressive development of the democratic classes. In proportion as conditions became more equalized, the king penetrated more deeply and more habitually into the management of the local affairs. . . .

The kings of France had been singularly assisted in this tendency, by the support which, during so many ages, had been afforded to them by the lawyers. In a country like France, where there existed . . . a noblesse and a clergy, who had within themselves a large portion of the intelligence and almost all the riches of the country, the natural chiefs of the democracy were the lawyers. French lawyers themselves aspired to govern in the name of the people, they laboured assiduously to ruin the noblesse for the aggrandizement of the throne [and] lent themselves to the despotic purposes of the kings, with singular readiness and with infinite art.

. . . Kings seize upon absolute power by force; lawyers give it the sanction of legality. When the two are united, the result is a despotism which scarcely allows a breathing-place to human nature. . . .

Independently of the general causes of which we have spoken, there existed in France many of an accidental and secondary nature, which hastened the concentration of all power in the hands of the king. . . .

France had formerly been made up of provinces, acquired by treaties or conquered by arms, and which long remained in the position of foreigners towards one another. In proportion as the central power was enabled to subject these different portions of territory to a uniform system of administration, the differences which previously existed among them vanished; and, in proportion as these differences subsided, the central power found greater facilities in extending its sphere of action over all parts of the country. Thus the unity of the people facilitated the unity of the government, and the unity of government aided in blending the people into one nation. . . .

If we now close the page of history, and, after having allowed half a century to elapse, come to consider what the intervening time has produced—we observe immense changes; but, in the midst of new and unheard-of things, we easily recognise the same characteristic features which struck us half a century earlier. The effects, therefore, said to be produced by the French revolution, are usually exaggerated.

Without doubt, there never was a revolution more powerful, more rapid, more destructive, and more creative than the French revolution. It would, however, be deceiving ourselves strangely, to believe that there arose out of it a French people entirely new, and that an edifice had been erected whose foundation had not existed before. The French revolution has created a multitude of accessory and secondary things; but, of all the things of principal importance, it has only developed the germs previously existing. It has regulated, arranged, and legalized the effects of a great cause, but has not been itself that cause. . . .

All that the revolution has done, would have been done, sooner or later, without it. It was but a violent and rapid process, by the aid of which the changes already effected in society were extended to the government; laws were made to conform themselves to manners; and the direction already taken by opinions, was communicated to the outward world.

The Triumph of the Centralizing State

The Old Regime and the French Revolution

Though the Old Regime is not far removed from us . . . , it seems already to have disappeared into the mists of time. The radical revolution which stands between that era and ours has obscured everything that it did not destroy, making changes that normally take centuries. Thus few today can answer the simple question: How was the countryside administered

From Alexis de Tocqueville, *L'Ancien Régime et la Révolution*, Book II in *Oeuvres complètes*, J. P. Mayer, ed., 18 vols. (Paris, 1951–1986), editor's translation, pp. 100–105, 119–120, 130–132, 141–142, 168–177, 219–225, 232–243.

before 1789? And indeed that question cannot be answered accurately and in detail without a thorough study of the archives. . . .

Many times I have heard it said of the nobility that it had ceased to play a role in the nation's government, but had held on to the administration of the countryside right to the end, the seigneur ruled over his peasants. This appears to be an error. . . .

In the eighteenth century all parish affairs were managed by a certain number of functionaries who were neither agents nor appointees of the seigneur. . . . Not only did the seigneur have no active role in the management of local affairs, he did not even oversee it. All parish officials were under the supervision of the central authority. . . . The seigneur rarely acted even as an intermediary . . . between the king and the people of the parish. . . . The seigneur was just another inhabitant, separated and isolated from the others by his immunities and privileges. He was superior by virtue of his status, not his power. . . .

Beyond the parish at the level of the canton, the same situation prevailed. The nobles were no longer in charge of the administration. . . . This situation was unique to France. Everywhere else the basic characteristic of the old feudal society survived in some form: land ownership still entailed the right to rule the local population. . . .

French noblemen had long since ceased to play a role in public administration—with one single exception, justice. The most important among them retained the right of naming judges who acted in their name and from time to time issued police regulations within the boundaries of their domains; but over time the central government had limited and subordinated the seigneur's judicial powers. . . . [Of] all the nobility's specific rights, the political aspect had disappeared; only the pecuniary prerogative remained, and was greatly augmented. . . .

I am speaking of those privileges which above all others bore the name of feudal rights; for it was these which touched the people. . . . Today it is difficult to determine what these rights consisted of in 1789. Their number had once been immense . . . and many had disappeared or been transformed. . . . Nonetheless . . . all the surviving rights may be classified under a few main headings. To one degree or another they were all bound up with the soil or its produce. Each weighed upon those who farmed it. . . .

What I wish to emphasize at this point is that throughout Europe . . . precisely the same feudal rights were to be found, and that in most countries they weighed much more heavily upon the population than in

France. . . . Moreover, several of the feudal rights which most offended our forebears . . . were to be found . . . among the English. A small number still exist there today. Yet they did not prevent English agriculture from being the richest and most highly developed in the world. The English people are hardly aware of their existence.

When I began my research in the provincial archives on the parishes of the Old Regime, I was surprised to discover in these impoverished and downtrodden communities several features which had once impressed me in the rural townships of America . . . that I had then wrongly taken to be a distinctive characteristic of the New World. In neither one was there a permanent assembly, or an official municipal government. Both were administered by selectmen who worked in isolation with each other under the authority of the community as a whole. Both from time to time had town meetings where the inhabitants, joining together, elected their judges and managed their affairs. The French and American Systems were in a word alike — inasmuch as a corpse can resemble a living body.

However different their destinies, these two bodies had a common origin. . . . Transported from feudal Europe and left wholly on its own, the rural parish of the Middle Ages became the *township* of New England. In France, cut off from the seigneur but under constant pressure from the State, it took the distinctive form which I shall now describe.

In the eighteenth century the number of parish officers, . . . varied from province to province. . . . In most parishes only two remained: the Collector and the Syndic. These town officials were usually elected . . . but in every case they became agents of the State rather than representatives of the community. . . . The seigneur, as noted, stood aloof from matters of municipal administration. He was no longer involved even in a supervisory capacity. . . . As his power declined, those functions which had once sustained his power now appeared to be beneath his consideration. His pride would have been wounded had he been asked to become involved. He no longer governed, but his privileges and his very presence in the parish made it impossible to replace the old system with a good parish government. The very presence of such a peculiar and privileged individual undermined or weakened the rule of law. . . .

The correspondence of Old Regime officials shows that similarities between their institutions and ours makes for similarities between the administrations of the two periods. They seem to join hands across the chasm that the Revolution made. . . . So that everything could be controlled from Paris a thousand regulatory mechanisms had to be invented. The quantity of documents was already huge, and the delays resulting from these administrative procedures were so long that, by my reckoning, it took at least a year for a parish to receive authorization to repair a church steeple. . . .

I used to think that the administrators of our own day were the first to be obsessed with statistics, but I was wrong. Toward the end of the eighteenth century little printed forms were frequently circulated. . . . The information obtained by these means was as detailed, and as unreliable, as that which is provided today. . . .

The functionaries of the administration, bourgeois almost to a man, already constituted a class with its own traditions and virtues, its own sense of pride and honor, its own distinctive spirit. It was the aristocracy of the new society, fully formed and full of life, which was waiting for the revolution to clear a space for it in the top ranks of society. . . .

While beyond its boundaries Paris was becoming all-powerful, another change which deserves mention was occurring within it. . . . [It] was becoming a city of factories and manufacturing establishments. . . . By the eve of the Revolution the number of factories had so vastly increased in Paris that the government finally became alarmed—for largely imaginary reasons, however. The true danger that such a concentration might produce was not recognized. . . .

Paris had mastered France and the army which would master Paris had already assembled. . . . Few would deny that administrative centralization and the omnipotence of Paris are largely responsible for the overthrow of all the governments that have succeeded one another over the past fifty years. Without undue effort I shall demonstrate that the same phenomenon played a large role in the sudden and violent fall of the monarchy and that it should be ranked among the primary causes of this first revolution from which all the others followed.

The reader who closes my book at this point will have a very incomplete picture of government under the Old Regime and will have trouble understanding the society which made the Revolution. . . . He might conclude that, divided and shut in upon themselves, under the rule of a vast and powerful monarch, the French were virtually servile. But this was not the case. Though the government managed the nation's common interests according to its whim, it did not yet control the lives of individuals.

In the midst of the many institutions which laid the groundwork for absolute rule, freedom had managed to survive. It was a peculiar kind of freedom which is hard to imagine today. Understanding it requires close scrutiny. . . . While the government was taking over local government and expanding throughout the political sphere, certain institutions which it had allowed to survive or had itself created . . . impeded its action, and maintained in many souls a spirit of resistance.

The centralizing state had the same penchants, the same goals, the same procedures which we see today; but it did not yet have the same power. In its eagerness to make money by any and all means, the government had put most public posts up for sale and had thus deprived itself of the prerogative of hiring and dismissing functionaries at will. Its love of money counterbalanced its will to power. In order to function it was therefore repeatedly forced to rely on agents whom it had not trained for its purposes and whom it could not subordinate. Edicts which were meant to be fiats became half-measures in execution. This strange and unsound state of affairs served as a kind of check on the omnipotence of the central power. . . .

The government did not yet have at its disposal that immense store of favors, subsidies, honors, and cash which it can pass around today. Its capacity for bribery was as limited as its powers of coercion. . . . Its sphere of action was immense, but it moved slowly and hesitantly, as if it were fumbling in the dark. By concealing the limits of the state's jurisdiction this fearsome darkness both worked against the rights of the king's subjects, by favoring the subversion of liberties, and for the subjects' defense.

Acutely aware of how recently it had come into existence, and of how humble the origins of its agents were, the administration was always hesitant about taking decisive action and drew back when it encountered resistance. . . .

A number of the privileges, prejudices, and false notions which are most inimical to the establishment of a sound and beneficent administration inspired among many of the king's subjects a spirit of independence and a willingness to stand up to abuses of authority.

Noblemen looked down on the regular administration. . . . Right up to the point where they lost the last of their powers they clung to something of that ancestral pride which set them in opposition both to servitude and the rule of law. They cared little about the freedom of their fellow citizens and willingly acquiesced in the royal power's oppression of those around them. But they would not put up with royal oppression themselves. . . . At the moment the Revolution broke out, this nobility, which was to fall with the throne, still maintained a much haughtier attitude in its relations with the king and its agents, and spoke in a much less guarded language, than did the Third Estate, which would soon overthrow the monarchy. The nobles demanded virtually every guarantee against the abuse of power that we enjoyed during our thirty-seven years of representative government. . . . It is to be regretted that . . . the French nobility was struck down and uprooted. The nation was thus deprived of an indispensable portion of its substance, and our liberties suffered a wound which time will never heal. A class which for centuries has marched ahead of all the others takes on . . . a certain natural confidence, . . . which makes of it the main point of resistance in the body social. It imbues other classes with the manly virtues which animate it. Once such a class is extirpated even its enemies are drained of energy. Nothing can ever fully replace it. The class may recover its titles and its property, but never the soul of its forebears.

The bourgeoisie of the Old Regime was also more inclined to show an independent spirit than its contemporary counterpart. Several of its conformist vices actually contributed to this result. . . . [T]he bureaucratic positions which this class occupied were even more numerous then than now, and the middle class was equally avid to fill them. But what a difference between the two eras! Since most of these positions were neither given by, nor wrested from, the government, they enhanced the status of the office-holder without putting him at the mercy of the government. The very situation . . . which nowadays keeps many people in an abject state of subservience served before the Revolution to maintain the bourgeoisie's self-respect. . . .

Modern methods of curbing dissent had not yet been perfected. France was not yet the soundless desert in which we live today. The nation resounded with noise. Though political liberty was not yet in evidence, a voice once raised reverberated. . . . It was primarily the judicial system which in those days provided the oppressed with a means of expression. . . . Our judges had tenured positions and did not seek to rise to higher ranks—two essential preconditions of judicial independence. The monarchical state had managed to deprive the regular tribunals of any competence regarding cases in which public authority had a stake, but it feared these courts even as it undermined them. If it prevented them from ruling in these cases, it dared not stop them from hearing grievances and stating opinions. . . . The irregular intervention of the courts in political affairs, though often contrary to the interests of sound administration, thus served on occasion to protect human rights.

These judicial practices had a considerable influence on the behavior of the nation as a whole. A number of ideas which are inimical to servitude had spread from the courts: the belief that all issues may be debated, that every verdict is subject to appeal, that debates should be publicized, the taste for legal procedures. This was the only aspect of a free people's education that the Old Regime bequeathed to us. The administration itself had absorbed much of the language and many of the practices of the courts. The king felt obliged to justify his edicts before he implemented them. . . . The decrees of his councils were introduced with lengthy preambles. The business of all the ancient administrative bodies was conducted in public. All these ways of doing things set limits on the monarch's arbitrariness.

Only the common people, especially the people of the countryside, lacked the means of resisting oppression—other than by violence. Most of the defensive measures which I have just described were beyond their grasp. Only those who had a social status which allowed them to be seen and heard had recourse to these means. But above the level of the common people there was not a man in France who, if he had sufficient courage, could not temper his obedience and resist while appearing to obey. The king spoke to the nation as a leader rather than a master. At the beginning of his reign Louis XVI said "We glory in the fact that we rule over a free and generous nation." . . .

Frenchmen of the eighteenth century had little knowledge of that passion for material well-being which leads so easily to servitude. This deep-rooted, ineradicable passion of the indolent is fully compatible with private virtues—love of family, regular habits, respect for religion, even a tepid and perfunctory religious faith. It allows for personal honesty but not for heroism. Those over whom it has a hold do well enough in the routines of daily life but in their civic lives are cowards. . . .

Old Regime Frenchmen were both better and worse than ourselves—reveling in the joys and pleasures of life, more irregular in their behavior, more extravagant in their passions than we. . . . The upper classes were concerned with making their lives beautiful rather than comfortable, in building an illustrious reputation rather than getting rich. Even the middle classes were not wholly absorbed in the quest for material well-being. Refinement was often more important to them than the pursuit of wealth.

We use the wrong criterion when we assume that submission to royal authority was a sign of moral baseness. . . . Though subservient to the king, Frenchmen of the Old Regime never abased themselves before an illegitimate or questionable authority which, though little honored . . . has the power to help or do harm. . . . The king inspired in his subjects feelings which not even the most dictatorial of the rulers who have since appeared could arouse. The Revolution has so thoroughly eradicated these feelings that we find them hard to understand. Under the Old Regime the king's subjects loved him as they loved their fathers and respected him as they respected God. Their obedience to even the most arbitrary of his commands had more to do with affection than with compulsion. . . . Let us not disdain our ancestors. We have no right to. Would to God we might regain a little of their greatness of soul. . . .

Far from being a time of dependence and servility . . . the Old Regime allowed for greater freedom than our own day. But it was an ill-defined and intermittent kind of freedom, hemmed in by class distinctions, bound up with immunities and privileges. It made possible both defiance of the law and arbitrary rule and provided not even the most minimal necessary guarantees for the generality of citizens. And yet, though narrow and misshapen, it was a fertile kind of freedom. . . .

At this point the French were no longer satisfied with improvements in the management of their affairs. They wanted to manage things for themselves. It thus became apparent that a vast upheaval loomed ahead which would be carried out not simply in the people's name but by the people's hand. . . . I think that from this moment forward the radical revolution which would destroy all that was best and worst in the Old Regime became inevitable. A people so ill-prepared to take matters into its own hands was bound to wreck everything in its path. . . . An absolute monarch would have been a less dangerous innovator. . . . [If] the Revolution . . . had been undertaken by an enlightened despot, rather than a people acting in the name of popular sovereignty, we would have had a better chance of developing into a free nation. . . .

When the love of liberty was rekindled in the bosom of the French, they had already absorbed a number of ideas about running a government which are not simply hard to reconcile with free institutions, but are virtually antithetical to their establishment. In their view the ideal society was one in which functionaries constitute the only aristocracy and a centralized, all-powerful administration puts private citizens in tutelage. However much they might aspire to freedom, they had no intention of renouncing this fundamental notion, and tried to make it compatible with the concept of liberty. They set about doing this by combining an all-powerful centralized administration and a preponderant legislative body, bureaucratic administration and elected government. The collectivity of the nation was made sovereign; the individual citizen reduced to a condition of utter dependence. . . .

About thirty years before the Revolution . . . there was a perceptible stirring at every level of society such as had never previously been witnessed . . Every year this life force spread and gained momentum. The whole country appeared to be revitalized. . . . [Yet] the French found their lot less bearable as it improved, a phenomenon that recurs repeatedly in history. . . . Revolutions do not always happen when conditions become worse. It often happens that a people which had submitted without complaint to the most oppressive laws violently rejects them when the burden is lightened. In almost every case the regime which a revolution destroys is superior to the one which came immediately before it, and the most dangerous moment for a bad government comes at the moment when it begins to reform itself. . . .

For a long time the government itself had been insinuating into the minds of the people . . . revolutionary ideas which were inimical to individual rights and conducive to violence. . . . The king set the example by showing contempt for the oldest and seemingly the most stable institutions. Louis XV undermined the monarchy and hastened the coming of the revolution as much by experimentation as by depravity, as much by his actions as by his inertia. When the people beheld the fall and disappearance of a high court that was nearly as old, and apparently as well-established, as the monarchy itself, there spread among them a vague feeling that violent and uncertain times were at hand when nothing old would be respected and nothing new could not be tried. Throughout his brief reign Louis XVI constantly talked of reform and held out the prospect of destroying many institutions which the Revolution finished off. After doing away with some of the worst features of our traditional legislation, he promptly put the same laws back into place and in so doing gave the impression of wanting to weaken the foundations and leave the final work of destruction to others. . . . Among the reforms he himself undertook, some made sudden unexpecte changes in long-standing and deep-rooted practices and concomitantly violated well-established rights. These acts set the stage for the Revolution not so much by clearing the way for it as by showing the people how to carry it out. What made things worse was the high-mindedness that lay behind the actions of the king and his ministers. No precedent is more dangerous than the example of violence undertaken with good intentions by men of substance.

By means of his edicts Louis XIV had long before planted the idea that every landed estate in the kingdom had been granted to its occupant conditionally and that the real proprietor was the state. All other landowners had only dubious title to their property. This doctrine derived from feudal legislation, but it was professed in France only when feudalism had entered its death throes. . . . It is the fundamental concept of socialism [which] first took root, ironically, under an absolute monarchy. . . .

Thus it was that a well-meaning and firmly established government gave the people daily lessons in criminal behavior appropriate to times of revolution and tyranny. . . . The Old Regime taught these dangerous lessons to the lower classes right to the end. . . . Yet we should remember that despite their arbitrary, and even violent, acts the authorities were kind at heart.

After a careful survey of these well-documented facts I have no hesitation in saying that much of the behavior which we associate with the Revolution stems from methods which the government used against the common people during the final two centuries of the monarchy. The Old Regime set a number of precedents for the revolutionaries. They merely added their peculiar genius for brutality. . . .

Several other revolutions have occurred in France since 1789, revolutions which virtually transformed the country's system of government. Most of these revolutions erupted suddenly and succeeded by means of force in violation of prevailing laws. Yet the disorder which resulted from them was never far-reaching or longstanding. Most people hardly felt their effects and sometimes hardly noticed them.

The reason for this is that since 1789, amid the ruins of successive political constitutions, the state administration has remained in place. Dynasties and regimes have come and gone, but our daily routines have neither been interrupted nor disturbed. In ordinary business each of us has remained subject to familiar rules and regulations, to the same jurisdictions, often indeed to the same petty officials. For, though each revolution has cut off the head of the government, the body of the administration has remained intact and fully functional. The same functionaries have carried out the same functions in the name of the king, the republic, and thereafter the emperor; then, in our century, as fortunes changed, and the cycle began again, the same men once more judged and administered, first for the king, then for the republic, then as before for the emperor. What did the master's name matter to them? They were less concerned with being good citizens than with being good judges or administrators. . . . Once the initial shock had passed, it always seemed as if the country had not budged. . . .

Siege of the Bastille, 14 July 1789. Anonymous, 18th Century. Giraudon/Art Resource, N.Y. Musée de la Ville de Paris, Musée Carnavalet, Paris, France.

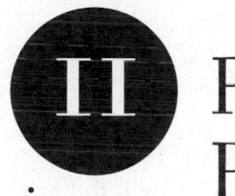
Positivist
Perspectives

Hippolyte Taine

The Fulfillment of
the Enlightenment

Hippolyte Taine (1828–1893) was one of the major thinkers of the Second Empire. He made his mark initially by applying positivist methods to the study of literature. He also made a name for himself as a critic of the Bonapartist regime—a stance that gave him high standing among radical republicans. The appearance early in the Third Republic of *Les Origines de la France contemporaine*, from which these selections are taken, represented Taine's attempt to extend his positivist methodology from literary criticism to history. It also identified him—to the considerable surprise of republicans— as a deeply conservative monarchist. A constant feature of Taine's thought at each stage of his career was his admiration for England, which he held up to his countrymen as an example of sound empirical thinking and healthy historical development.

The Spirit and Doctrine
of the Enlightenment

Preface

I regret the dissatisfaction which I foresee this work will cause to many
of my countrymen. My excuse is, that almost all of them, more fortunate
than myself, have political principles which serve them in forming their
judgments of the past. I had none; if, indeed, I had any motive in undertaking this work, it was to seek for political principles. Thus far I have
attained to scarcely more than one; and this is so simple that it will seem
puerile, and that I hardly dare enunciate it. Nevertheless I have adhered
to it, and in what the reader is about to peruse my judgments are all
derived from that; its truth is the measure of theirs. It consists wholly in
this observation: that *human society, especially a modern society, is a vast
and complicated thing.* Hence the difficulty in knowing and comprehending it. For the same reason it is not easy to handle the subject well.
It follows that a cultivated mind is much better able to do this than an
uncultivated mind, and a man specially qualified than one who is not.
From these two last truths flow many other consequences, which, if the
reader deigns to reflect on them, he will have no trouble in defining. . . .

Another volume would be required to criticize authorities. For this
I have no room, and I merely state the rule that I have observed. The
most trustworthy testimony is that of the eyewitness, especially when this
witness is an honourable, attentive, and intelligent man, writing on the
spot, at the moment, and under the dictation of the facts themselves—if
it is manifest that his sole object is to preserve or furnish information,
if his work is not a piece of polemics planned for the needs of a cause, or
a passage of eloquence arranged for popular effect, but a legal deposi-
tion, a secret report, a confidential dispatch, a private letter, or a personal
memento. The nearer a document approaches this type, the more it
merits confidence, and supplies superior materials—I have found many
of this character in the national archives. . . .

Hippolyte Taine, The Fulfillment of the Enlightenment, selections from "The Spirit and
Doctrine of the Enlightenment" in *The Influence of the Enlightenment on the French
Revolution*, William F. Church, ed., D.C. Heath & Co., 1964, 25–38.

I. The Composition of the Revolutionary Spirit: Science, The First Element

The philosophy of the eighteenth century contained poison, and of a kind as potent as it was peculiar; for, not only is it a long historic elaboration, the final and condensed essence of the tendency of the thought of the century, but again, its two principal ingredients have this peculiarity that, separate, they are salutary and in combination they form a venomous compound.

The first scientific discovery, admirable on all sides, and beneficent in its nature . . . is made up of masses of facts slowly accumulated and then summarily presented or in rapid succession. For the first time in history the sciences expand and affirm each other to the extent of providing . . . a definite and demonstrated system of the universe, that of Newton.

Such is the course to be pursued with all the sciences and especially with the moral and political sciences. To consider in turn each distinct province of human activity, to decompose the leading notions out of which we form our conceptions, those of religion, society and government, those of utility, wealth and exchange, those of justice, right and duty; to revert to palpable facts, to first experiences . . . ; to recompose our ideas with this, to fix its meaning and determine its value; to substitute for the vague and vulgar notion with which we started, the precise scientific definition we arrive at . . . constituted the prevalent method taught by the philosophers under the name of analysis, and which sums up the whole progress of the century. Up to this point, and no farther, they are right· truth, every truth, is found in observable objects and only from thence can it be derived. . . . The operation . . . is productive only when the vein is rich and we possess the means of extracting the ore. To obtain a just notion of government, . . . a man must be a historian . . . and economist, and have gathered up myriads of facts; and, . . . he must possess a vast erudition and practiced and special acuteness. . . . [I]f none of these conditions are complied with, the same operation in the hands of . . . drawing-room amateurs, and oratorical charlatans in public places, will undoubtedly end only in mischievous compounds and in destructive explosions. Nevertheless a good law remains good even when the ignorant and the impetuous make a bad use of it, and if we of today resume the abortive effort of the eighteenth century it is within the liens it transmitted to us.

II. The Classic Spirit, The Second Element

This grand and magnificent edifice of new truths resembles a tower of which the first story, quickly finished, at once becomes accessible to the public. The public ascends the structure and is requested by its constructors to look about, . . . right before it and on the ground, so as to know the country on which it dwells. The point of view is certainly favourable and the recommendation is judicious. To conclude, however, that the public will see accurately would not be warranted, for the state of its eyes must be examined, to ascertain whether it is near- or far-sighted. . . . In like manner the French of the eighteenth century must be considered, the structure of their inward vision . . . [its] fixed form. . . .

This fixed form consists of the classic spirit, and this, applied to the scientific acquisitions of the period, produces the philosophy of the century and the doctrines of the Revolution. . . . [L]et us study its formation.

Its establishment is coeval with that of the regular monarchy and polished intercourse, and it accompanies these, not accidentally but in the natural order of things. For it is the work of the new public which the new regime and new habits then formed, consisting of an aristocracy rendered listless by the encroaching monarchy, of people well born and well educated who, withdrawn from activity, . . . devote their leisure to enjoying the calm or refined pleasures of the intellect. . . . [T]hey find no other occupation. . . . [T]o talk, to listen, to entertain themselves agreeably and with ease, on all subjects, . . . of any interest to the men, and especially to the women, of society is their great affair.

In the eighteenth century they constitute the sovereign authority. In the great crowd of "imbeciles," sprinkled with vulgar pedants, there is, says Voltaire, "a small group apart called good society, which . . . forms the flower of humanity; for it the greatest men have labored; it is that which creates fame." . . . Under a strong pressure of this kind the mind necessarily accommodates itself to the tastes, and the degree of attention and of instruction of its public. Hence the classic mould—formed out of the habit of speaking, writing and thinking for a drawing-room audience. . . .

There is accordingly, a radical defect in the classic spirit, . . . at first, kept within proper bounds, contributes toward the production . . . which, in accordance with the universal law, goes on increasing and turns into a vice through the natural effect of age, use, and success. . . . In the eighteenth century the portrayal of living realities, an actual individual, just as he is in nature and in history . . . is improper. The capacity to receive and contain all these is wanting. Whatever can be discarded is cast aside, and to such an extent that nothing is left at last but . . . a hollow abstraction. . . .

To pursue in every research, . . . without either reserve or precaution, the mathematical method, to derive, limit and isolate a few of the simplest generalized notions; and then, setting experience aside, comparing them, combining them, and, from the artificial compound thus obtained, deducing all the consequences they involve by pure reasoning, is the natural process of the classic spirit. It is so deeply implanted as to be equally encountered among the partisans of innate ideas as with the partisans of sensation . . . Rousseau . . . Condorcet and Sieyès. . . . [T]hey leave experience behind them. . . . Through intellectual incapacity and literary pride they omit the characteristic detail . . . the significant, convincing and complete example. . . . [W]e are always in the air, in the empty space of pure generalities.

Sieyès holds history in profound contempt, and believes that he had "perfected the science of politics" at one stroke. . . . Rousseau, by means of a contract, founds political association, and, with this given idea, he deduces the constitution, government and laws of every system of social equity. . . .

III. Combination of the Two Elements

Out of the scientific acquisitions thus set forth, elaborated by the spirit we have just described, is born a doctrine seemingly a revelation and which, under this title, assumes to regulate the government of human affairs. On the approach of 1789 it is generally admitted that man is living in "a century of light," in "the age of reason"; that, previously, the human species was in its infancy and that now it has attained to its "majority." Truth, finally, is made manifest and, for the first time, its reign on earth is apparent. Everybody must be ruled by it, for, in its nature, it is universal. The philosophy of the eighteenth century, in these two articles of faith, resembles a religion, the puritanism of the seventeenth century. . . . We see the same outburst of faith, hope and enthusiasm, . . . the same rigidity and intolerance, the same ambition to recast man and to remodel human life according to a preconceived type. . . . It differs, however, from the preceding religions in this respect, that instead of imposing itself in the name of God, it imposes itself in the name of reason.

The authority, indeed, was a new one. Up to this time, in the control of human actions and opinions, reason had played but a small and subordinate part. Both the motive and its direction, were obtained elsewhere; faith and obedience were an inheritance; a man was a Christian and a subject because he was born Christian and subject. Surrounding his budding philosophy . . . is a system of recognized laws, . . . a reigning religion; all the stones of this structure hold together. . . . But what does the common cement consist of and what is its first foundation? Who authorizes all these civil regulations which control marriages, testaments, inheritances, contracts, property and persons . . . ? In the first place immemorial custom, varying . . . according to . . . the quality and condition of the person; and next, the will of the king. . . . Who authorizes . . . this sovereignty of the prince? . . . [In the first place], eight centuries of possession, a hereditary right similar to that by which each one enjoys his own field and domain, a property established in a family and transmitted from . . . the first founder of the state to his last living successor; and . . . a religion directing men to submit to the constituted powers. . . . [W]ho . . . authorizes this religion? . . . [F]irst, eighteen centuries of tradition, . . . the steady belief of sixty preceding generations; and . . . at the beginning of it, the presence and teachings of Christ; . . . further back, the creation of the world, the command and the voice of God. Thus, throughout the moral and social order of things the past justifies the present. . . . Reason . . . is only a subaltern, . . . forced by religion and the monarchy to labor in their behalf. . . . So long as reason is limited to this function its work is that of a councillor of state. . . . Far from proving destructive it consolidates. . . .

But here the parts become inverted; tradition descends from the upper to the lower rank while reason ascends from the latter to the former. On the one hand religion and the monarchy . . . under Louis XIV . . . and . . . Louis XV . . . demolish piece by piece the basis of hereditary reverence and filial obedience so long serving them as a foundation . . . ; hence the authority of tradition insensibly declines and disappears. On the other hand science . . . erects piece by piece a basis of universal trust and deference, raising itself up from an interesting subject of curiosity to the rank of a public power; hence the authority of reason augments and occupies its place. . . . Investigation penetrates into the forbidden sanctuary. Instead of deference there is verification, and religion, the state, the law, custom, all the organs, in short, of moral practical life, become subject to analysis, to be preserved, restored or replaced, according to the prescriptions of the new doctrine.

. . . Hereditary prejudice is a sort of reason [which operates] unconsciously. . . . [L]ike science, it issues from a long accumulation of experiences. . . . [I]n its leading features, it is indispensable. . . . If the leading prejudices of the community should suddenly disappear, man . . . would at once fall back into a savage condition and . . . become . . . a restless, famished, wandering, hunted brute. There was a time when this heritage was lacking; there are populations today with which it is still utterly lacking. To abstain from eating human flesh, . . . to be one husband of but one woman, to hold in horror incest and unnatural practices, to be the sole and absolute owner of a distinct field, . . . all these observances, formerly unknown and slowly established, compose the civilization of human beings. . . . In general the older and more universal a custom, the more it is based on profound motives. . . .

If there are valid reasons for legitimating custom there are reasons of higher import for the consecration of religion. . . .

This is no barren formula. A sentiment of such grandeur resembles an illumination. . . . Religion in its nature is a metaphysical poem accompanied by faith. Under this title it is popular and efficacious; for, apart from an invisible select few, a pure abstract idea is only an empty term, and truth, to be apparent, must be clothed with a body. It requires a form of worship, a legend and ceremonies in order to address the people, women, children, the credulous. . . . [T]hroughout society, religion [is] at once a natural and precious instrumentality. On the one hand men require it for the contemplation of infinity and to live properly, if it were suddenly to be taken away from them, . . . they would do greater injury to their neighbors.

. . . When . . . after religion and habit, we regard the state, that . . . armed power possessing both physical force and moral authority, we find for it an almost equally noble origin. In Europe at least . . . it is, in its origin and essence, a military foundation in which heroism constitutes itself the champion of right. . . . [I]n the chaos of mixed races and . . . crumbling societies, some man has arisen who, through his ascendancy, rallies around him a loyal band . . . re-establishing order, reviving agriculture, founding a patrimony and transmitting as property to his descendants his office of hereditary justiciary. . . . [A] great public office is . . . fixed in one family; thenceforth the nation possess a vital centre and each right obtains a visible protector. . . .

Such are the valid claims of hereditary prejudice; like instinct, we see in it a blind form of reason. . . . [R]eason herself is obliged to borrow its forms. The inspiration of a doctrine is due to its blind activity. . . . [T]o convert itself into a spring of action, it must lodge itself in minds in the shape of an accepted belief; then only does it . . . become a social force. But, through the same process, it ceases to be critical and clairvoyant; it no longer tolerates doubt or contradiction. We, of the present day, believe in infinite progress about the same as people once believed in original sin; we still accept ready-made opinions from above, the Academy of Sciences taking the place of the ancient councils. . . . [R]eason would greatly err in resenting the leadership of prejudices in human affairs, since, to take this lead, she must herself become prejudice.

Unfortunately, in the eighteenth century, reason was classic. . . . [T]here was no knowledge of history; there was a repugnance to erudition. . . .

Unable to comprehend the past, they were unable to comprehend the present. They had no accurate conception of the mechanic, of the provincial bourgeois; these were . . . wholly transformed through philosophic theories and sentimental mistiness.

The structure of the still primitive mind of the people was never imagined, the narrowness of their mechanical, routine existence, devoted to manual labor, absorbed with anxieties for daily bread, . . . their deep-seated rancor, their inveterate distrust, . . . their lack of capacity for conceiving abstract right and of comprehending public events, . . . their blind fury like that of bulls, and all those traits of character the Revolution was about to bring to light. . . . The classic reason declined to go so far as to laboriously study the ancient man and the actual man. . . .

Ancient institutions lose their divine prestige; they are simply human works. . . . Scepticism enters through all the breaches. With regard to Christianity it at once changes into open hostility. . . .

A return to nature, meaning by this the abolition of society, is the war-cry . . . coming from the Rousseau battalion and that of the socialists who, in their turn, march up to the assault of the established regime. . . . [T]he distinctive machinery it employs consists likewise of a new conception of human nature. Rousseau derived this conception wholly from the spectacle he contemplated in his own breast: a strange, original and superior man, who, from his infancy, harbored within him a germ of insanity and who finally became wholly insane. . . . Rousseau generalizes; occupied with himself, even to infatuation, and regarding no one in the world but himself he imagines man accordingly. . . . [H]is vices and his baseness must be attributed to circumstances.

The wrong is thus all on the side of society. In like manner [Rousseau says] "Nature made man to be happy and good, while society has made him depraved and miserable."

Civilization, which boasts of its splendor, is simply the restlessness of over-excited, servile monkeys each . . . corrupting the other to attain to super-refinement, discomfort and ennui. Human culture . . . is in itself bad, while the fruit it produces is merely . . . poison. . .

If civilization is bad, society is worse. For this could not have been established except by destroying primitive equality, while its two principal institutions, property and government, are usurpations. . . .

The first property right was a robbery by which an individual abstracted from the community a portion of the public domain. Nothing could justify the outrage. . . .

The Origins of Contemporary France

In every important insurrection there are similar evil-doers and vagabonds, enemies to the law, savage, prowling desperadoes, who, like wolves, roam about wherever they scent a prey. It is they who serve as the directors and executioners of public or private malice. . . . They are known by their acts, by their love of destruction for the sake of destruction, by their foreign accent, by their savage faces and their rags. . . . Henceforth these constitute the new leaders. . . . The example is contagious; the beginning was the craving for bread, the end is murder and incendiarism; the savagery which is unchained adding its unlimited violence to the limited revolt of necessity.

Bad as it is, this savagery might, perhaps, have been overcome, in spite of the dearth and of the brigands; but what renders it irresistible is the belief of its being authorised, and that by those whose duty it is to repress it. Here and there words and actions of a brutal frankness break forth, and reveal beyond the sombre present a more threatening future. . . . The publicans insinuate to them . . . that . . . the King, in favour of the re-assembling of the three orders, has granted three days'

The Origins of Contemporary France, selections from *The Ancient* (Chicago, University of Chicago Press, 1974). John Durand, translator, I, 1–2, 14–15, 23–25, 53, 83, 88–91; II, 214–215; III, 218–219.

freedom from all duties. . . . Upon this the crowd, rushing off to the barriers, . . . burn or demolish the bureaux, destroy the registers, . . . carry off the money and pillage the wine on hand in the depot. . . .

. . . It is in the centre that the convulsive shocks are strongest. Nothing is lacking to aggravate the insurrection—neither the most lively provocations to stimulate it, nor the most numerous bands to carry it out. The environs of Paris all furnish recruits for it; nowhere are there so many miserable wretches. . . . Robberies of grain take place everywhere. . . . Along with the abuse of property they are led, by a natural impulse, to attack property itself. . . .

For those who are most compromised Paris is the nearest refuge. . . . Bands rise up around the capital, just as in countries where human society has not yet been formed, or has ceased to exist. . . . All hover around Paris and are there engulfed as in a sewer, the unfortunate along with criminals. . . . During the first days of May a change in the appearance of the crowd is remarked; there mingle in it "a number of foreigners, from all countries, most of them in rags, armed with big sticks, and whose very aspect announces what is to be feared from them." Already, before this final influx, the public sink is full to overflowing. Think of the extraordinary and rapid increase of population in Paris, the multitude of artisans brought there by recent demolitions and constructions, all the craftsmen whom the stagnation of manufactures, . . . the rigour of winter and the dearness of bread have reduced to extreme distress. . . .

Clearly a new leaven has been infused among the ignorant and brutal masses, and the new ideas are producing their effect. They have been insensibly filtering for a long time from layer to layer, and after having gained over the aristocracy, the whole of the lettered portion of the Third-Estate, the lawyers, the schools, all the young, they have insinuated themselves drop by drop and by a thousand fissures into the class which supports itself by the labour of its own hands. . . .

. . . [M]an returns to his original feeble state, while power is vested in passing aggregates which spring up like whirling vortices amongst the human dust. . . . Each band in its own canton lays its rude hands on the wheels within its reach, wrenching or breaking them haphazard. . . . Thus do unchained negroes, each pulling and hauling his own way, undertake to manage a ship of which they have just obtained the mastery. . . . In such a state of things white men are hardly worth more than black ones; for, not only is the band, whose aim is violence, composed of those who are most destitute, most wildly enthusiastic, and most inclined to destructiveness and to license, but also, as this band tumultuously carries out its violent action, each individual the most brutal, the most irrational, and most corrupt, descends lower than himself, even to the darkness, the madness, and the savagery of the dregs of society. . . . All . . . restraints . . . are wanting to the man who plunges into insurrection. . . . His anger is exasperated by peril and resistance. . . . Add to this the clamours, the drunkenness, the spectacle of destruction, the nervous tremor of the body strained beyond its powers of endurance, and we can comprehend how, from the peasant, the labourer, and the bourgeois, pacified and tamed by an old civilisation, we see all of a sudden spring forth the barbarian, and, still worse, the primitive animal, the grinning, sanguinary, wanton baboon, who chuckles while he slays. . . . Such is the actual government to which France is given up. . . . [T]he best qualified most judicious and profoundest observer of the Revolution will find nothing to compare to it but the invasion of the Roman Empire in the fourth century. . . .

. . . [T]he real sovereign, who is the mob, is very soon apparent. On the 15th of July it undertakes the demolition of the Bastille of its own accord, and this popular act is sanctioned; for it is necessary that appearances should be kept up; even to give orders after the blow is dealt, and to follow when it is impossible to lead. . . . It is under this constant pressure that the Government is carried on; and the elect of the people, the most esteemed magistrates, those who are in best repute, are at the mercy of the throng who clamour at their doors. . . .

Administrators and members of district assemblies, agitators of barracks, coffee-houses, clubs and public thoroughfares, writers of pamphlets, penny-a-liners are multiplying as fast as buzzing insects are hatched on a sultry night. After the 14th of July thousands of places have presented themselves to unrestrained ambitions; "attorneys, notaries' clerks, artists, merchants, shopmen, comedians, and especially advocates; each wants to be either an officer, a director, a councillor, or a minister." . . . Philosophy, fallen into such hands, seems to parody itself, and nothing equals its emptiness, unless it be its mischievousness and success. Lawyers . . . roll out the high-sounding dogmas of the revolutionary catechism. . . . The journals and pamphlets are written in the same style. Every brain is filled with the fumes of conceit and of big words; the leader of the crowd is he who raves the most, and he guides the wild enthusiasm which he increases.

Let us consider the most popular of these chiefs; they are the green or the dry fruit of literature, and of the bar. . . . Their empty, unpractised minds are wholly void of political conceptions; they have no capacity or practical experience. . . .

Let us picture to ourselves these directors of public opinion as we find them three months before this. . . . Danton, . . . second-rate lawyer, coming out of a hovel in Champagne, . . . Brissot, a strolling Bohemian, formerly employé of literary pirates, . . . and, finally, Marat—a writer that has been hissed, an abortive scholar and philosopher. . . . Is it to be supposed that, borne so high by such a sudden jerk of fortune, they wish to put on the drag and again descend? . . . [I]s it not clear that they will aid with all their might the revolt which hoists them towards the loftiest summits? . . . With the full weight of their inexperience, incapacity, and improvidence, of their fears, credulity, and dogmatic obstinacy, they urge on popular attacks. . . .

Such is the work of the Constituent Assembly. In several of its laws, especially those which relate to private interests, in the institution of civil regulations, in the penal and rural codes, in the first attempts at, and the promise of, a uniform civil code, in the enunciation of a few simple regulations regarding taxation, procedure, and administration, it planted good seed. But in all that relates to political institutions and social organization its proceedings are those of an academy of Utopians, and not those of practical legislators. . . . On the sick body intrusted to it, it performed amputations which were as useless as they were excessive, and applied bandages as inadequate as they were injurious. With the exception of two or three restrictions admitted inadvertently, . . . it carried out its principle to the end, the principle of Rousseau. It deliberately refused to consider man as he really was under its own eyes, and persisted in seeing nothing in him but the abstract being created in books. Consequently, . . . the Assembly destroyed on the one hand the time-honoured, spontaneous, and lasting societies formed by geographical position, history, common occupations and interests, and on the other, those natural chiefs whose name, repute, education, independence, and earnestness designated them as the best qualified to occupy high positions. In one direction it despoils and permits the ruin and proscription of the superior class, the nobles, . . . and the upper middle class. In another it dispossesses and breaks up all historic or natural corporations, religious congregations, clerical bodies, provinces, parliaments, societies of art and of all other professions and pursuits. This done, every tie or bond which holds men together is found to be severed; all subordination and every graduated scale of rank have disappeared. There is no longer rank and file, or commander-in-chief. Nothing remains but individual particles, twenty-six millions of equal and disconnected atoms . . . The new Constitution . . . reduces the King to the position of an honorary president, suspected and called in question by a disorganized State. Between him and the legislative body it interposes nothing but sources of conflict, and suppresses all means of concord. The monarch has no hold whatever on the administrative departments which he must direct; and the mutual independence of the powers, from the centre to the extremities of the State, everywhere produces indifference, negligence, and disobedience between the injunctions issued and their execution. France is a federation of forty thousand municipal sovereignties, in which the authority of legal magistrates varies according to the caprice of active citizens. . . .

. . . The sudden and surprising concord of all volitions and all intelligences is to revive the golden age on earth. It is proper, accordingly, to regard the social contract as a festival, an affecting, sublime idyl, in which, from one end of France to the other, all, hand in hand, should assemble and swear to the new compact, with song, with dance, with tears of joy, with shouts of gladness, the worthy beginning of public felicity. With unanimous assent, indeed, the idyl is performed as if according to a written programme.

. . . [T]he excitement spreads from month to month and from province to province. . . . But local unions are not sufficient to complete the organization of France; a general union of all Frenchmen must take place. Many of the various National Guards have already written to Paris for the purpose of affiliating themselves with the National Guard there; and . . . the Parisian municipal body having proposed it, the Assembly decrees the universal federation. It is to take place on the 14th of July, . . . everywhere on the same day, both at the centre and at the extremities of the kingdom. There is to be one in the principal town of each district and of each department, and one at the capital. . . . Fourteen thousand representatives of the National Guard of the provinces appear on the Champ de Mars, the theatre of the festival. . . . All rise to their feet and swear fidelity to the nation, to the law, to the King and to the new Constitution. When the report of the cannon is heard which announces the taking of the oath, those of the Parisians who have remained at home, men, women, and children, raise their hands in the direction of the Champ de Mars and likewise make their affirmation. In every principal town of every district, department, and commune in France there is the same oath on the same day. Never was there a more perfect social compact heard of. Here, for the first time in the world, everybody beholds a veritable legitimate society, for it is founded on free pledges, on solemn stipulations, and on actual consent. They possess the authentic act and the dated official report of it.

There is still something more—the time and the occasion betoken a union of all hearts. The barriers which have hitherto separated men from each other are all removed and without effort. . . .

Alphonse Aulard

The Genesis of Middle-Class Democracy

Like Taine, Alphonse Aulard (1849–1928) began his career as a professor of literature (Italian literature, specifically). After changing fields, he became a thorough-going positivist professional—one of the first historians in France to apply German techniques to documentary research and the very first to be named professor of the history of the French Revolution at the Sorbonne. Positivism's hold on Aulard is apparent not only in his methodology but also in his narrative. He presents the radicalization of the revolution as an empirical process in which the French are gradually won over to republicanism by the lessons of experience. The selection included here also reflects Aulard's sympathies for radical socialism, a major republican movement of the late nineteenth and early twentieth centuries that officially advocated measures such as the income tax that contemporaries considered anticapitalist but which in practice was mainly anticlerical.

A *Political History of the French Revolution*

No one on the eve of the Revolution had ever dreamed of the establishment of a republic in France: it was a form of government that seemed impossible in a great State in course of unification. It was through the

F. V. A. Aulard, The Genesis of Middle-Class Democracy, selections from *A Political History of the French Revolution*, 4 vols., (London, Unwin, Chapman & Hall, 1910). I, 125–126, 145–146, 155–160, 179–180, 195–196, 209–211, 265; II, 39, 277–278, 293–295; III, 132–133, 137–138, 142, 157–158, 163, 181–183, 191; IV, 277–278, 281–282.

King that men sought to establish a free government. Men wished to organise the monarchy, not to destroy it. No one dreamed of calling the ignorant mass of the people to political life; the necessary revolution was to be brought about by the better class of the nation, the educated, property-owning class. It was believed that the people . . . could only prove an instrument of reaction in the hands of the privileged. However, the future date of democracy was announced in the proclamation of the principle of the sovereignty of the people; and the republic, the logical form of democracy, was prepared by the diffusion of republican ideas— for example, from America; by the sight of an impotent monarchy. . . . The ruling classes of society were steeped in republicanism. Such a state of mind was so prevalent that if the King, in whom men saw the historically indispensable guide to a new France, were to fail in his mission, or discard, for example, his authority as hereditary defender of French independence, a republic would be accepted without dislike and without enthusiasm, first by the better class, and then by the mass of the nation. . . .

The principal events at the outset of the Revolution, caused the supreme power to slip from the hands of the King into those of the nation; and through the municipal revolution, . . . thirty thousand communes, united to form a nation under the actual sovereignty of the French people: in other words, a kind of united republic in process of formation, in which the King would no longer have more than a nominal authority.

The Constituent Assembly had partially ratified this state of things . . . by the Declaration of Rights; then modified it, in a conservative, or rather reactionary, manner, by organising the monarchy and by establishing the *bourgeoisie* as a politically privileged class.

We will first examine the Declaration of Rights, which is the most remarkable fact in the history of the growth of democratic and republican ideas. . . .

Here we may usefully recall the fact that every one was unanimously agreed that the way must be cleared by a "declaration of rights of man and citizen." This was a matter of proclaiming, in the French tongue, the same principles that the Anglo-Americans had proclaimed.

No one, or scarcely a soul, contested the truth of these principles, in favour of which there was a wide and profound current of opinion.

. . . To proclaim them at this moment was to settle the principles from which the Constitution should issue. It was to strike the supreme blow at absolute power. It was to consecrate, to ratify the Revolution . . . except for the fact that it does not proclaim liberty of conscience, the Declaration of Rights is definitely republican and democratic. . . .

The Declaration may be considered from two points of view: as destroying the past, or as constructing the future.

Today, in retrospection, we consider it especially from the second point of view—that is to say, as the political and social programme of France from the year 1789. The men of the Revolution considered it especially from the first point of view, as the notification of the decease of the old style of government; and, as the preamble infers, as a safeguard against the possible resurrection of the old style. . . .

As to the other point of view, from which the Declaration is regarded as the programme of a reorganisation of society, the members of the Assembly left it purposely in semi-obscurity, because it was to some extent inconsistent with the middle-class government they were about to establish.

The principle of the equality of rights is democracy; it is universal suffrage, to speak of the political effects of the principle alone, and the Assembly was about to establish a property-owners' suffrage.

The principle of the sovereignty of the nation is republicanism, and the Assembly intended to maintain the monarchy.

These consequences were foreseen, not by the masses, but by the members of the Assembly and by educated folk. And it was precisely on this account that the middle class hesitated to issue a Declaration of Rights. . . .

There was at first no organised party which demanded the immediate application of the essential principle of the Declaration, which comes back to the statement that there was at the outset neither a Republican nor a Democratic party.

When . . . the pact between the nation and the King was definitely broken, experience led the French to apply the consequences of the Declaration, by means of the *régime* of 1792–3—that is to say, by means of Democracy and the Republic.

The men of 1792 and 1793 have been called renegades with respect to the principles of 1789. They certainly violated, for the time being, the liberty of the press and of the individual, and the guarantees of legal and normal justice. They did so because the Revolution was in a state of war against Europe . . . ; they did so to save the essential principles of the Declaration. But what has been forgotten is that they were the first of all to apply these essential principles—equality of rights and the sovereignty of the nation—by establishing universal suffrage and the Republic. . . .[I]n the country itself [they] proclaimed the liberty of conscience, separated Church and State, and sought to govern according to the lights of reason and justice.

The backsliders from the principles of 1789 were not the men of 1793. . . . Logically, there would seem to be no reason why we should not rather apply the term to the men of 1789, who, after having proclaimed the equality of rights, divided the nation into "citizens active and citizens passive," and replaced the ancient ranks of the privileged by a new privileged class, the middle class or *bourgeoisie*.

But it is nearer the truth to say that there were no renegades; only worthy Frenchmen who acted for the best, in different circumstances, and at different moments in our political revolution.

So far I have spoken only of the political consequences of the Declaration of Rights. There were also economic and social consequences, which must be examined and depicted, not with the eloquence and feeling of a party man, but with the impersonality of a historian.

These consequences, which later will be known by the name of Socialism, remained obscure far longer than the political consequences; and even to-day only a minority of Frenchmen have torn this "veil," which the majority seek, on the other hand, to bind more firmly and thickly with sentiments of religious respect and fear.

What is it precisely, this principle or dogma of equality, the object of the first clause of the Declaration?

Did the drafters of the clause wish to say that all men are born equally endowed as to mind and body? No . . . this absurdity was only attributed to them, later on, by absurd adversaries. . . .

The evident sense of this clause is this: that to natural inequalities it is not fair and equitable that institutions should add artificial inequalities. . . . Is it just that there should be, by act of law, men rich by birth and men poor by birth? . . .

Take the *bourgeois*, the man who received, at his birth, an economic privilege and a political privilege; in 1792 the people will strip him of his political privilege. Would it not be logical to relieve him of his economic privilege as well?

Such an idea scarcely occurred, at first, to any one. A first revolution, social and economic, had taken place, or was about to do so, through the destruction of the feudal system, the abolition of the right of primo-geniture, the sale of the national properties. . . . The generality of Frenchmen were satisfied with this revolution, and saw no farther; the most crying injustice, . . . having just been righted.

It was when other sufferings, born of the new order of things, began to make themselves felt, that men began to think of demanding the completest consequences of the Declaration of Rights. And as it was a minority which actually suffered— . . . it was a minority which demanded such consequences and attempted .to rebel; the more so because the *bourgeoisie*, had resumed their political powers. Babeuf preached communism, and, representing only a minority, was easily defeated.

. . . [L]ater on, the development of machinery, the changed relations of capital and labour, were to bring about the movement known as Socialism, a movement which has not yet come to a head, because it has not had the assent of the mass of the nation. . . .

In any case the democratic and social republic is to be found in the Declaration; all the principles of which have not even yet been applied, and of which the future programme passes far beyond the limits of our generation, and it may be of many generations yet to follow. . . .

We have seen how the National Assembly organised the Monarchy. Let us see how it organised the middle class as a class with special political privileges.

The reader will not have forgotten that the philosophers and political writers of the eighteenth century were unanimously—not excepting Rousseau—against the idea of establishing in France a democracy . . . ; and the French had been still further encouraged to repudiate the idea of such a democracy by the example of the American English, who had established in their republican States a property-owners' suffrage.

At the beginning of the Revolution the same state of mind still existed. There were soon voices in favour of universal suffrage, and in favour of democracy, . . . even among those who, like Robespierre, adored Rousseau.

Why?

Because a new factor came into being—the filling of the stage, by the people, who, united to the middle classes, had triumphed over the Bastille, and effected the municipal revolution throughout all France.

Was it just or possible to relegate to the category of proletarians the workers who had beaten back the King's troops in the open streets; the peasants who had triumphed over feudalism; this body of Frenchmen in arms?

This, however, is what the Assembly did. But it was no longer one of those reforms concerning which all patriots are united, and which seem the result of the force of events.

The establishment of the rule of property-holders was effected only after complicated and uproarious debates, and led to a schism between the men of the Revolution. Henceforward there is a democratic party and a *bourgeois* party. . . .

Such was the legal organisation of the property-owners' suffrage; and in this manner the *bourgeoisie* formed themselves into a politically privileged class. . . .

How did the public opinion welcome the property suffrage and the privilege of the middle class?

Let us confess at the outset that there was not at first any very lively protest against the actual principle of the property qualification. People accepted, as a general thing, the distinction between active and passive citizens. It was the qualification imposed upon eligibility to the National Assembly . . . that led to the revolt of a certain proportion of the public.

On the other hand, even among the most democratic of the publicists I find hardly any who demand universal suffrage as we understand it. . . . There are religious prejudices against the Jews; there are social prejudices against actors, and also against executioners. . . .

The National Assembly took no account of social prejudices; it allowed the actor and the executioner to exercise their political rights. But it did, for a certain period, take account of religious prejudice. The decree of December 23 and 24, 1789, which admits non-Catholics to be electors and eligible, provisionally excludes all Jews. The decree of January 28, 1790, admits a portion only of the Jews residing in France: namely, Portuguese and Spanish Jews, and those of Avignon. It was only on the eve of dissolution, on September 27, 1791, that the Assembly decided to assimilate all Jews with the rest of the citizens of France. . . .

Opposition to the property suffrage grew keener every day. It manifested itself in a very lively manner. . . .

To sum up: a democratic party is already becoming visible, especially in the journals. With Marat this democracy is of the Cæsarian type; elsewhere it is mostly of a liberal type. Its programme is to obtain the suppression of the property requirements in general, . . . and an amelioration of the more anti-popular results of the *bourgeois* system which has just been established. . . .

At that very moment Louis was conspiring with other countries . . . with a view to his flight and his *coup d'état.* . . . [O]n the night of June 20th that the King fled in disguise with his family. . . .

The flight of the King was one of the few events of the Revolution which excited the whole country. [I]t was known and felt by every one.

At the first news men were struck with stupor; then followed anger and indignation; lastly, a feeling of fear. The nation was abandoned, orphaned. . . . Terrible dangers were foreseen; France saw herself invaded, and, without her head, lost. But there were brave men, who braced themselves to appear calm. . . . All were up in arms, ready to die for their country.

Then the news of the King's return. Men breathe, think themselves saved. First the sorrow, then this joy, show how loyal France is as yet.

For a moment the republican party seems to triumph in Paris, and to gain a few recruits here and there in the provinces; but France stands aloof, and the republicans . . . are obliged, after one great effort, to yield, to beat a retreat, almost to disappear from view, before the sudden attack of the *bourgeoisie* and the general persistence of royalist feeling.

Let Louis re-ascend the throne, and henceforth let him be better advised: this is the wish of France. . . .

Nevertheless, for nearly three months the royal power is suspended. . . . [T]here is, in very fact, a republic. An object-lesson this, proving that France can, indeed, exist as a republic, despite the opinion of philosophers. Henceforth, the republic is no more a chimera, but a mode of government; nameless yet, but real; it has existed, has *worked*. When Louis becomes definitely impossible, as he will in August, 1792, men will only have to take up the threads of experience, resume the work begun, and the thing will bring forth the word. . . .

The republican movement awoke, in . . . 1792, in almost the same regions . . . of France in which it had awakened a year earlier, on the morrow of the King's flight. But there was one notable difference: in 1791 the republican impulse came above all from Paris, while in 1792 it was spontaneous; and when the Parisians, influenced by Robespierre, seemed to renounce the idea of a republic, a tide of republican opinion arose . . . and drew Paris with it.

It is worth remarking that these . . . republicans in their most vehement declamations did not pronounce the word "republic"; so many apprehensions did this word still evoke. . . . We call them republicans because they demand, either formally or by implication, not only that Louis XVI shall reign no longer, but that there shall be kings no longer. . . .

The Revolutionary Government as a whole is often called the *Government of the Terror*. The phrase, *the Terror,* is also applied to the period when this Government existed in its fullest force. . . . By the Terror we also understand a system of politics which seems to be discernible in the democratic republic.

But we have seen that there was nothing systematic in the creation of the Revolutionary Government. Nearly all the facts hitherto related go to prove that this Government was not the application of any system or any preconceived idea, but that it formed itself empirically, from day to day, out of the elements imposed on it by the successive necessities of the national defences of a people at war with Europe. . . . The Revolutionary Government was an expedient of warfare, and it was always given out that it must come to an end with the war. . . .

The Revolutionary Tribunal fulfilled its office; it terrorised the royalists, the refractory priests who conspired with the . . . invaders, and all agents of the counter-revolution; and in this way it ensured the success of the national defence. But, little by little, it became the instrument of personal ambition and personal revenge. Robespierre made use of it to condemn his personal adversaries . . . as agents of the foreign faction or as royalists. The institution of the Revolutionary Tribunal, once in this manner abased, injured the cause of the Revolution after having done it the most signal service; having chastised the country's veritable enemies, it sent its best friends and servants to destruction. Historically we may say that it worked both good and evil; and we must judge it, not as a whole, but by periods and according to its actions.

When the dictatorship of the Committee of Public Safety evolved into the dictatorship of Robespierre, the Revolutionary Tribunal was modified, in the direction of a greater severity, by the famous law of the 22nd of *Prairial,* . . . drafted by Robespierre. . . . The accused were deprived of their counsel; the hearing of evidence was suppressed; material proofs gave way to moral; and henceforth only one penalty was proclaimed: death; and the jury was completed by the collaboration of Robespierrist fanatics.

The effects of this law may be judged from the fact that before the 22nd of *Prairial* there had been, in thirteen months, about 1,220 death sentences pronounced by the Revolutionary Tribunal; and that after that date 1,376 persons were condemned to death in the space of seven weeks. . . . There was a butchery of innocent and guilty worthy of the rule of the kings, . . . a slaughter which the state of the national defence, by that time assured, leaves absolutely without excuse in the eyes of the historian. . . .

The leaders of this Government have been stigmatised as renegades from the principles of 1789, and they did indeed often violate the principle of individual liberty; they shed blood, they persecuted the French; they stifled the liberty of the press; they established a tyrannical dictatorship; finally they arrived, democrats as they were, at the suppression of nearly all the popular elections. But they only resigned themselves to these violent measures when forced by events, and to ensure the final triumph of the principles of 1789, on whose suppression monarchical Europe was bent. . . . [V]ictory once achieved, they had every intention, as they were continually announcing, . . . of organising the Democratic Republic on a basis of liberty, equality, and fraternity. The most violent among them agreed in presenting the Terrorist rule as a provisional expedient.

None the less, we must confess that this phrase, "a provisional expedient," does not give an absolutely exact and complete idea of this undertaking. It happened that certain measures, entirely fortuitous and empirical, such as declaring all means of subsistence to be in common for the purposes of the national defence, by creating, for the time, collectivist cities of a kind, excited or awoke socialistic theories which later on found expression. On the other hand, certain elements of the Revolutionary Government, at the time when they were decreed, seemed of a kind to enter later on into the society of the future, and the measures taken in view of the success of the armies against the civil enemy were often spoken of as proper to a definite mental revolution. . . .

The cult of a Supreme Being was not merely an expedient of national defence, but also an attempt to establish one of the fundamental essentials of the future State. At the same time schemes for a national education were being elaborated, which ended in tangible results and in foundations; so that we must think of the revolutionists of the year II as preparing to build the future State, while fighting Europe at the same time. . . .

All were not agreed as to the period when it would be necessary to emerge from the revolutionary state. Danton and his friends had wished to relax the bonds of the Terror before Europe had been vanquished, but they were broken. But even those who wished the Revolutionary . . .

who rejected . . . the idea of a committee of clemency, felt the horror of the hideous character which the brutal zeal of ignorant fanatics was engraving upon the face of the Republic. . . .

At last the latent danger of this dictatorship of the national defence was frequently pointed out by Robespierre. At the very moment when everything was being organised with a view to the military victories, the peril of these military victories was denounced. . . . He wished to divert the nation from its taste for war for war's sake, saying in round terms that a warlike people would become enslaved. . . .

This government according to circumstance, created empirically for the immediate present, without system and without plan, in some parts plainly bears the mark of preoccupations concerning the future; and although entirely provisional, it contains the germs, the beginnings, of institutions; . . . contains, in some degree, the France of the future. . . .

Practically no one, even during the Terror, dared to preach socialism openly. . . . But the sum of all the partial and empirical measures . . . which formed the Revolutionary Government, led to a state of things which indirectly prepared men's minds . . . for a new social revolution. . . .

Progressive taxation was one of the measures which effected, if I may use the term, the socialistic education of a certain section of opinion. . . .

The Committee of Public Safety . . . endeavoured to maintain the principle of liberty of conscience. . . . It was in the name of the safety of France that the militant democrats overturned the Catholic altars. It was in the name of the safety of France that the Government that endeavoured to maintain the altars and to protect the Catholics. . . .

In some quarters the cult of the Supreme Being has appeared, retrospectively, to be a solemn reaction against the cult of Reason. But the mass of the French people had no such feeling. To provincial eyes the cult of Reason and the cult of the Supreme Being were very much the same thing. . . .

In reality there was no change in the new national and philosophical religion which the Government had sought to establish in the Catholic places of worship, and to substitute for Catholicism. Under the name of the Supreme Being, as under the name of Reason, it was the *patrie* that men really worshipped; and the cult of Supreme Being, like the cult of Reason, was bound . . . to lose itself in patriotism. . . .

We are now at the end of this narrative, which is long if measured by the number of its pages, but appears curtailed when we consider the

number of facts that have . . . been omitted . . . , or else abridged. . . .
[T]o abridge still further this abridgment, according to that classic custom, under the title of conclusion—what is to be gained by it? Would it
not be useless and pedantic thus to repeat oneself? . . .

Had I had a historical thesis to sustain, or a train of reasoning to
develop, in order to demonstrate the truth of a proposition, a logical
conclusion would have been necessary. But I have merely attempted to
narrate, objectively, and without any preconceived idea, the political
history of the revolution from the point of view of the origin and the
development of democracy and the Republic. . . .

I am content to have uncovered certain facts; let them speak for
themselves.

I wish merely, in a very few words, not to write a conclusion nor a
summary, but to suggest a few ideas which are too general in their nature
to have found a fitting place at any particular point of the narrative . . . .

It seems to me that the facts assembled in this book deprive the
words: *the French Revolution* of their equivocal meaning. People used
to denote, by the same phrase, both the principles which constitute the
French Revolution and the actions consistent with those principles, and
the period during which the Revolution was effected. . . . This confusion was as harmful to the truth as it was useful to the supporters of the
retrograde policy, as it allowed one to attribute to the Revolution, considered as a sort of historical personage, the most grievous or even the
most anti-revolutionary laws or actions. This abusive manner of speaking—"The Revolution did or didn't do so-and-so"—has had the result
that many people see in the Revolution a kind of incoherent power;
capricious, violent and sanguinary. It has been attempted thus to discredit the very principles of the Revolution; especially by the pains and
to the profit of those who regard these principles as *satanic*, and who
would govern society by the reverse of these principles. For the rest, all
the political parties of the nineteenth century have pleaded their cause
by means of arguments drawn from anything or everything that happened between 1789 and 1799; and these facts, taken at random or in-
geniously selected, they have called *the French Revolution*. Now, I
fancy, matters are clearer; the Revolution consists in the Declaration of
Rights drafted in 1789 and completed in 1793, and the attempts made
to realise that declaration; the counter-Revolution consists in the attempts made to prevent the French from acting in conformity with the
principles of the Declaration of Rights . . . .

The French Revolution is, so to speak, a political, social, and rational ideal, which Frenchmen have attempted partially to realise, and which historians have attempted to confound either with its application . . . or with the events provoked by the very enemies of that ideal, with a view to abolishing or obscuring it. This book will, I hope, have contributed to dissipate this dangerous ambiguity. . . .

The Actor Chenard wearing the costume of a "sans-culotte." Boilly, Louis Leopold (School of). Giraudon/Art Resource, N.Y. Musée de la Ville de Paris, Musée Carnavalet, Paris, France.

Marxist Interpretations

Jean Jaurès

The Overthrow of Feudalism by the Capitalist Bourgeoisie

Jean Jaurès (1859–1914), the first Marxist historian of the French Revolution in France was a leader of the first Marxist socialist party, as well. A major purpose of *L'Histoire socialiste* was to familiarize working-class militants with Marx's historical philosophy. As the selection demonstrates, Jaurès also drew inspiration from Jules Michelet, the great republican historian who influenced Alphonse Aulard. Jaurès was committed to the defense of the Third Republic, as well as to the advancement of socialism. In the 1890s he persuaded the party, over the objections of more radical Marxists, to take up the cause of Captain Alfred Dreyfus, whose imprisonment on false charges of treason he saw as a threat to the revolution's legacy of human rights. In

67

the early twentieth century Jaurès became identified with the pacifist movement and was assassinated by a fanatical French nationalist on the eve of World War I.

Socialist History of the French Revolution

It is from the socialist vantage that we shall tell . . . the workers and peasants what happened between 1789 and the end of the nineteenth century. We consider the French Revolution a capital and seminal event; but it is not in our view a definitive event whose consequences are destined to unfold through all subsequent history. The French Revolution indirectly paved the way for the triumph of the proletariat. It established two of the essential preconditions of socialism: democracy and capitalism. On the deepest level, however, it consisted in the political triumph of the bourgeois class.

Little by little everything that transpires . . . paves the way for a new social crisis, a new and more profound Revolution by means of which the proletariat will seize power and transform property and morality.

. . . Between 1789 and 1848 the revolutionary bourgeoisie triumphed and consolidated its power. It used the force of the proletariat against the absolute monarchy and the nobility. Yet despite the prodigious activity of the proletarians, . . . they were no more than a subordinate force, a sort of historical appendage. They sometimes inspired genuine terror in the propertied classes, but for the most part they continued to work for them. They did not have a radically different concept of society . . . nor a clear class consciousness nor . . . even the notion of a different form of property. . . . They hardly went beyond Robespierre's meager thinking: a democratic society of peasant proprietors and smallscale bourgeois artisans, sovereign in its political power but economically stagnant. The marvelous

Jean Jaurès, The Overthrow of Feudalism by the Capitalist Bourgeoisie, selections from his *Histoire Socialiste de la Revolution Francaise*, 8 vols., Albert Mathiez, ed. (Paris, Editions, Editions de l'Humanite, 1927), editor's translation, pp. I, 1–27, 29–33, 56–62.

revivifying sap of socialism, that creator of wealth, beauty, and joy, was not to be found among them. They knew nothing of the seductiveness, the potent sweetness, of this new ideal.

. . . Nowadays confusion is no longer to be feared. The working class and the socialist party are at one in their ideas. . . . If the proletariat seized power tomorrow . . . , it could forthwith make decisive use of its position.

How was it, . . . through what evolutionary changes, did the working class rise to the role which it is destined to fulfill tomorrow? This is the story which we, as militant socialists, intend to tell. . . . At each stage of this narrative we intend to lay bare the economic foundations of human existence . . . the development of property and the growth of industrial and agricultural technology. . . . Nor will we slight the influence of economic conditions on governments, literature, systems of thought. . . . But let us not forget what Marx himself . . . never forgot: it is upon mankind that economic forces exert their power. . . . Moreover, though man lives in and through humanity, he also lives through his senses and his mind, and in a vaster realm, which is the universe itself. . . . Whatever connection there may be between the human soul . . . and man's social and economic systems, the soul reaches beyond the human sphere into vast realm of the cosmos. . . . Contact with the universe rouses deep and mysterious forces, forces of that eternal life which came before the beginnings of human society. . . .

According to Marx, we live as yet in pre-historic conditions. Human history will truly begin only when man, freed at last from the tyranny of impersonal forces, controls production through his reason and his will. At that point his mind will no longer be subject to the despotism of economic forces which he himself created . . . and he will freely face the cosmos. Marx foresees a period of full intellectual freedom during which human thought, no longer distorted by economic servitude, will no longer deform the world. . . . Even now, in the shadows of this preconscious age, certain elevated minds have succeeded in attaining freedom. . . . Our role is to harvest these first fruits of the life of the spirit: they provide us a presentiment of that higher, freer life which mankind will experience under communism. . . .

. . . Our interpretation of history will thus be both materialistic with Marx and mystical with Michelet. . . . [E]conomic life has been the foundation and well-spring of human history, but across the succession of social forms, man, a thinking force, aspires to the full life of thought, to ardent communion with . . . the mysterious universe. . . .

Causes of the Revolution

Under the Old Regime the nation was dominated by the nobility, the Church, and the king. With the development of the French monarchy, the nobles had lost much of their medieval power. . . . But they still enjoyed very extensive privileges. . . . [Their] much-vaunted patriarchal ingenuity . . . allowed them to resort to all the monopolistic maneuvers of bourgeois capitalists in our own day. . . . Feudal law held every natural force in its grip, everything that grows, moves, and breathes. . . . Feudal law irritated and humiliated the peasants . . . interfering with their work . . . by depriving them of full property rights. . . .

With its hand in the public till, the nobility also introduced fraud and disorder into the workings of the great modern State, which must have sound accounts and honest dealings to function properly. Noblemen were in large part responsible for the . . . irregularities which vitiated . . . vast credit operations and . . . audacious capitalist initiatives. . . .

Through its parasitism . . . and its financial immorality the nobility threatened France's very life. But the bourgeoisie and the peasantry will rise against this murderous nobility in a common revolutionary effort and they will bring the monarchy low as well. . . .

No century was ever more attentive than the eighteenth to the details of life, the precise workings of every social mechanism: and never before had such serious study and such thorough documentation set the stage for a Revolution. . . . Never were thinking heads better supplied. . . . M. Taine, who seems to know nothing of the eighteenth century's immense documentary research, makes light of us when he reduces the classical spirit to the genteel art of rearranging impoverished abstract ideas. But the eighteenth century's generous philosophy and vast store of information would have been of little consequence had there not been a new social class which was committed to great changes and capable of bringing them about.

The Bourgeoisie

This social class was the bourgeoisie, and here again one cannot help but be astonished at M. Taine's extraordinary frivolity. In the chapters which he devotes to "the structure of society" under the Old Regime, he fails utterly to study or even to mention the bourgeois class. . . . Nowhere does he show the slightest concern with the economic growth of the bourgeoisie over the previous two centuries, [or] . . . the expanding interests which cast the bourgeoisie in its historic role and endowed the class with the force to fulfill it.

Of what elements . . . was the bourgeoisie composed in the years which preceded the Revolution? At the top were those whom we can accurately term high capitalists . . . the financial bourgeoisie. . . . By its very power, this new aristocracy of money unwittingly thrust the old landed aristocracy into the past.

The military aristocracy ceased to be the primary force in French society. One of the eternal laws of declining societies is that to maintain their position they must seek help from the power which will replace them on the morrow. . . . Thus it was that the Old Regime came to depend upon Finance and Capital.

. . . These financiers and capitalists themselves were torn between two contradictory desires: the wish to prolong a regime from which they profited by virtue of privileged monopolies and the urge to protect themselves against the arbitrariness of the absolute monarchy and that capricious bureaucracy which shut down businesses in which large amounts of capital were invested.

. . . From the first weeks of the Revolution . . . rumors of bankruptcy exasperated the *rentiers* who lived from state bonds, almost all of whom were domiciled in Paris. . . . This needs to be understood if we are to understand either the Revolution's character or the social anatomy of revolutionary Paris. For the artisans and workers of the time the *rentier* class had not yet become what it is for the socialist proletarians of our day — the symbol of parasitic capitalism. They stood in opposition to the Old Regime. They had turned their savings over to the king when pressing public interest required it. Kings, nobles, and priests, in their mindless prodigality, were threatening not to repay them. The *rentier* class was thus an instinctive enemy of arbitrariness, and the poor people of Paris found allies and leaders among the king's bourgeois creditors in their revolt against the Old Regime. . . .

Commercial and industrial activity further enhanced the power of the bourgeoisie in 1789. . . . In the conflict then taking shape between agrarian and mercantile interests the force of its growth gave commerce the last word. . . . In the eighteen century [also] powerful limited liability companies began to come into existence.

Henceforward both capitalist expansion and capitalist organization are to be the rule. The framework through which the bourgeoisie of

Louis Philippe would dominate the country had already been set up. The bourgeoisie is no longer simply a source of savings and a font of common sense. . . . it is the bold conquering force which, after partially revolutionizing the means of production and exchange, now undertakes to revolutionize the political system. . . .

Worker and Peasant Uprisings

In Poitiers workers in manufacturing establishments call for price controls on bread, declaring that anything above three sous a pound costs wage-earners too much. . . . [C]urious disturbances break out in the vicinity of the Nièvre and the Yonne. These are the woodcutters who supply the capital and who now rise up to protest the inadequacy of their pay.

. . . Crudeness and childishness appear at first glance to characterize these disorders; but we glimpse the scene solely through bourgeois accounts. We do not know if these poor woodcutters invoked the Rights of Man to demand the right to live, as the carpentry workers of Paris did during the Great Strike of 1791. . . . The Departmental Directory, which is very hard on the "seditious," and much opposed to "that longstanding policy of leniency which emboldens bad citizens," nonetheless recognizes that they have justifiable grievances against largescale purchasers in Paris. . . . But what stands out most prominently in the Directory's account is the spirit of bourgeois fraternity and conservative solidarity which animated the National Guards of the . . . [vicinity]. Their hearts bleed for their over-burdened "brethren." . . . They all vow to avenge each other's wrongs and to protect order and property. . . .

It was in the neighborhood of Paris that peasant agitation regarding the food supply assumed vast dimensions in 1792. Its character was very distinctive—another fact to which M. Taine . . . remained oblivious. Here we encounter an agrarian offensive against . . . the capitalist agriculture which was already powerful in the region. . . . {It] was directed not only against the largescale farmers of the area, but against the sale of *biens nationaux* to these farmers and to bourgeois. . . . Thence followed, among smallscale landowners and tenant-farmers, who had been . . . pushed aside, a deep resentment of the forms of capitalism which reigned supreme in those rich wheatlands. . . .

This land of big farms, where isolated cottages were few and the rural population was concentrated in rather large villages, is favorable to organized collective disturbances. In some cases the peasants pressured parish governing boards to take the lead. By such means they legalized . . . their actions and when local governments resisted they created new authorities, just as the people of Paris created a revolutionary commune on August 10 (1792). . . . I find it impossible to believe that agitation for controlling the price of sugar and other commodities, to which the people of Paris had resorted in January, found no echo in the countryside. One telling detail is that the insurgents demanded price controls not only for wheat and bread, as was predictable, but for all provisions . . .

Robespierre's Social Policy

Robespierre . . . always put himself forward as the defender of legality and the Constitution. But he asked that legality and constitutionalism be interpreted in a humane and public-spirited sense. He complained that a crime committed against the mayor of Estampes by hard-pressed poor people was being treated by the moderate bourgeoisie as an exceptional crime and that the poor were being overwhelmed with vehement denunciations and implacable investigations, while high crimes of treason, peculation, and hoarding went unpunished. . . . Robespierre denounced the efforts of the bourgeois oligarchy to exploit the natural indignation roused by the murder [of the mayor] in order to consolidate its power. He demanded a more sincere and straightforward interpretation of the law and, with his deep concern for equity, he sketched out a rather vague social plan in which he suggested some general measures which might be undertaken in the people's behalf. He protested concomitantly against the notion of redistributing property—such indeed was his vehemence that he seemed not wholly without anxiety about this matter.

He had no fears of course that communism would find a place on the agenda of the Revolution. But he was afraid that ideas about redistributing landed property would become so widespread in people's minds that the Counter-Revolution might feel itself obliged to take over the repression of the movement. . . . He distinguished two types of men in the revolutionary camp: on the one hand the rich and the propertied, among whom selfishness quickly wins out and who are thus afraid of equality. On the other hand the kind and generous common people. The defense of the Revolution, and the completion of its work, therefore required the people's support. The Revolution would recognize this support by granting equal political rights to everyone, by enacting sound measures for public assistance, . . . but it would not put property in jeopardy or allow anyone to do so. . . .

A singular idea, both democratic and retrograde. It is true of course that in any society the law should help the weak. It should counterbalance the ever active power . . . of property and wealth. But why not look forward to a society in which there would be no "weak"? Why settle for identifying wealth as a corrupting influence instead of making sure that everyone participates in life's activities and satisfactions? To Robespierre selfishness and property seem to turn the privileged away from the Revolution . . . [and] the Rights of Man; yet he makes no provision for making property the common possession of humanity rather than the privilege of the few. He appears to think that "misery" is a prerequisite of the people's civic-mindedness . . . to have pressed the Gospel verse about "the poor inheriting the kingdom of heaven" into the service of the Revolution.

Robespierre seems to have stopped short at the vision of a sad and harsh society in which the ever-growing store of wealth is not abolished but controlled and balanced by the political power of the poor, defiant masses. In Robespierre's thought, as in Rousseau's, we find a confused and bitter mixture of democracy and repressive Christianity. His ideal excludes both communism and great wealth, but this latter is tolerated in practice as an unpleasant necessity.

It is a false and confining vision of mankind's resources which thus stymies the drive of the propertied classes to enrich themselves through vast endeavors . . . and stifles the common people's aspiration to full social justice. Robespierre's thought is a curious mixture of optimism and pessimism: optimism in what relates to the people's moral worth, pessimism about anything having to do with an egalitarian rearrangement of property relations.

Albert Mathiez

Capitalist Revolution and Crucible of Socialism

Albert Mathiez (1874–1932) was the second major Marxist historian of the French Revolution and the first professional historian to interpret it in Marxist terms. He saw himself as a successor to Jean Jaurès and in 1924 published a new edition of *L'Histoire socialiste*. Today, however, Mathiez is remembered not for elaborating on Jaurès' essentially moderate message but for reading into the Bourgeois Revolution in France a prefiguration of the Bolshevik Revolution in Russia. Though he belonged only briefly to the Communist Party, he became an apologist for terrorist violence, which he saw as a positive feature of the revolution. In his own day he was famous for championing Robespierre and denigrating Danton. This position was consistent with Mathiez' politics: He considered Robespierre a protosocialist and regarded Danton as a typically corrupt bourgeois politician. But his choice of sides also reflected his earlier acrimonious relations with his mentor, Aulard, to whom Danton was a hero. His Robespierrist polemics gained Mathiez much greater notoriety than Aulard, but he did not succeed his old antagonist in the Chair of the History of the Revolution at the Sorbonne.

The French Revolution

. . . There was not one avowed communist in the convention. But does this mean, as some have casually stated, that no disagreement in principle existed between Girondins and Montagnards, that they were separated only by personal rivalries and their conception of the role that the capital should play in controlling public affairs? Nothing could be more untrue. . . . The conflict between Girondins and Montagnards was deep-seated, a virtual class conflict. The Girondins, as Daunou observed, included "a great number of property owners and enlightened citizens." They had a sense of social hierarchy that they wished to preserve and strengthen, and felt an instinctive disdain for the coarse, uneducated populace. They believed that the people were incapable of government, and reserved exclusive rights over it to their own class. Whatever might obstruct the freedom of the property-owning bourgeoisie, they considered wrong. . . .

The Montagnards, on the other hand, represented the lower classes, those who suffered from the wartime crisis, who had toppled the monarchy and gained political power through insurrection. Much less swayed by theories than the Girondins were, and greater realists because they had a tighter grip on reality, they understood that the terrible crisis that France was experiencing required extraordinary solutions. In opposition to property rights they readily advocated the right to a decent living, and in place of individual self-interest, they proposed the public interest. They failed to understand how anyone could prefer class to country, under the guise of principles. If need be, they were ready to resort to restricting individual freedom and property if the higher interest of the masses demanded it. . . .

The basic opposition between the two parties appears most strikingly in the writings published simultaneously in October by Brissot on the one hand and Robespierre on the other. Brissot wrote that "the fomenters of disorder are those who seek to level everything: property, comfort, the price of goods . . . [who] want the workers in the field to receive the same wage as lawmakers, who even wish to reduce ability, knowledge and virtue to the same level because they have none!"

Robespierre . . . developed a diametrically opposed program: "Royalty has been destroyed," he wrote. "The nobility and clergy have disappeared; the rule of equality has begun." And he immediately began a harsh attack on false patriots, "who wanted to establish the Republic only for their own benefit," "who sought to govern only in the interest of the rich and public officials." To these false patriots he contrasted the true patriots "who will seek to establish the Republic on the principles of equality and general welfare. . . ."

No one could be under an illusion. Since August 10 the rivalry between Gironde and Mountain had become more than a simple political rivalry. A class struggle was developing. But . . . for many Montagnards, the policy of *rapprochement* and collaboration with the masses was essentially a tactic imposed by the necessities of war. Of course, most of the Montagnards were, like the Girondins, of bourgeois origin.

The class politics that they initiated did not spring from the popular mass. It was politics dictated by circumstances: a plebeian method, as Karl Marx observed, of putting an end to kings, priests and nobles, to all enemies of the Revolution. This was enough to set it in direct opposition to the Gironde's policy.

The Girondins offered no solution to the sufferings of the popular classes. They maintained that unrestricted competition was a cure-all. If goods rose in price, workers needed to secure higher wages. But the workers, who were unorganized, could not put adequate pressure on their employers. They were forced to plead for higher wages and addressed humble petitions to public officials. They could not imagine that the new officials they had elected could be more indifferent to their plight than the old ones, who had intervened in similar situations.

The crisis was more serious in cities than elsewhere. Where they were administered by lower-class [officials], they searched for every possible solution. In Paris the defensive works ordered after August 10 had been both charitable as well as military in their purpose. But these projects were carried out at government expense. Using the pretext of saving money, the Girondins initially ordered that piece work should replace a daily wage. Next they reduced wages, but the workers protested, invoking the high cost of living. The Girondins then denounced the work gangs as "a hotbed of intrigues and plots, the refuge of dangerous agitators." On October 15 the Convention ordered that work should be halted and the workers dismissed. . . .

The government of the Gironde remained unmoved by the workers' complaints. It justified its inaction or hostility by an argument that was repeated a thousand times from the rostrum and in the press: those originating the complaints were simply "anarchists" or deluded individuals who had been led astray.

Yet the workers could contrast their poverty with the luxury of the new rich who insolently flaunted it. This was the moment when complaints against army contractors poured in from everywhere. . . .

The Convention ordered the arrest of some of these suppliers, but most were soon released. The spectacle of the impunity that the new contractors enjoyed could only heighten popular discontent. . . .

How could the mass of workers in the cities and countryside not resent the class policy of the Gironde? But significantly the Mountain itself almost became suspect in the eyes of the obscure leaders who voiced popular demands. When Goujon, chief administrator of the

Seine-et-Oise, appeared before the Convention on November 19, speaking for the electoral assembly of his department, [and] demanded not only controls on prices but also the creation of a central administration for food supplies, his petition won little enthusiasm from the Montagnard deputies. . . . Not one deputy of the Mountain demanded price controls. . . . The Enragés had the personal instincts of the crowd working for them, and the continuation, or rather the intensification, of the economic crisis worked in their favor. In struggling against the Gironde, the Montagnards were compelled to offer them concessions and give them some satisfactions. . . . One of them, the deputy Duroy, announced to the Convention that Roland's economic policy had completely failed: "The price of goods has not fallen . . . , it has only continued to rise." . . . The Girondins themselves defended Roland only weakly. When he resigned . . . , it could hardly be expected that his economic policy of nonintervention would survive him. . . . The high cost of living would contribute substantially to the fall of the Gironde. . . .

Representatives on mission employed both heavy-handed and prudent measures. . . . Fouché was among those who believed that the Revolution could survive only through an energetic class policy that benefitted the sans-culottes. He established in the administrative center of every district in the Niève Department a watch and welfare committee authorized to impose a tax on the rich proportional to the number of the poor. . . . On September 26 he ordered the bakers of Moulins to produce only one type of bread, the "bread of equality," to be sold at the uniform price of three *sous* a pound, subsidized through the allocation of money paid the bakers from taxes imposed on the well-to-do. . . .

Having abolished poverty, he prohibited begging and idleness ordering that "all beggers and idlers shall be jailed." Harvesters who refused to obey requisitions were exposed in the public square. . . . Repeat offenders were thrown into prison until peace was made and their property was confiscated except for what was absolutely necessary for them and their families. . . .

The Committee of Public Safety sought to direct and control the activity of the representatives on mission, not always successfully. Their operations took place far from Paris, and because of slow communications, they did not have time to await instructions from the capital. Only rarely did they report the difficulties that they faced, dealing with these on the spot, relying on their inclinations, good or bad.

Initially the Committee applauded the class policy of Laplanche and Fouché. On August 29 it congratulated Fouché for imposing taxes on the well-to-do. . . . The Committee also approved the policies of imprisonment and removal of officials. . . . But soon it grew unhappy with the anticlerical or rather the antichristian policy of certain proconsuls. . . .

Robespierre had already become alarmed at the decree of October 5 that inaugurated a new calendar. He intended to oppose the enforcement of the law which was to serve as a pretext for dechristianization. How could a class policy that favored the sans-culottes be implemented if their beliefs were violated?

The law of . . . the General Maximum set prices for all goods already subject to the law of July 27 regulating hoarding. Except for grain, flour and forage, tobacco, salt and soap, which were subject to uniform prices throughout France, other goods and essential commodities were to be regulated at the district level. . . .

The Committee had no illusions about the difficulties of applying such a law, which compelled producers to sell at a loss, without compensation, commodities that they had earlier sold at three to four times the price. Even the previous law of May 4, setting a maximum price only on grain, immediately caused markets to empty out. How could the cities and armies be supplied if provisioning them depended on local elected authorities, personally opposed to revolutionary legislation? To enforce the General Maximum would necessarily require a return to compulsion, that is, Terror, and at the same time, a decisive shift towards a stricter, better organized and more dictatorial centralization. . . .

To insure application of the Maximum, an inventory of all the grain in the Republic would be taken, thereby permitting requisitioning to take place with greater certainty. France would be divided into zones for provisioning with Paris supplied for a year from its own region. All resistance would be put down by the Central Revolutionary Army. Detachments from it would be quartered in recalcitrant towns at the expense of the wealthy. Saint-Just also foresaw the creation of a special court that would force suppliers and anyone who had handled public funds since 1789 to disgorge their gains.

All the measures that he proposed were approved without debate. The fears that he had expressed concerning the effectiveness of the Maximum were quickly realized. In Paris and every city in France, once the price controls were posted, shops were immediately emptied out by eager customers. Merchants, who had nothing left to sell, began to shut down their shops. In Paris Chaumette threatened to confiscate their property, and the Commune, at his suggestion, petitioned the Convention to "focus its attention on raw materials and factories so as to requisition them by fixing penalties on those holding or manufacturing goods who allowed them to remain idle, even to put them at the disposition of the Republic, which has no shortage of workers to keep them busy." Collectivism would follow expropriation since the Republic itself would control all agricultural and industrial output. But neither the Convention nor the Committee wanted to go that far and carry out a social revolution to assure the application of the Maximum, which they had unwillingly enacted.

The Commune acted more quickly. It controlled the distribution of available goods by means of requisitioning and rationing by means of goods cards. . . . It empowered the hoarding inspectors to conduct inspections, even of private homes. It worked to secure adherence to fixed prices by police enforcement and by threatening violators with application of the Law of Suspects. Most towns imitated or even anticipated the Parisian example.

But if the distribution of existing goods was carried out haphazardly, resupplying became increasingly difficult. It was no longer in the merchants' interest to replenish their stocks. To revive the circulation of goods and prevent a halt in production and famine, a further step had to be taken toward centralization. On October 22 the Committee created a commission of three members, known as the Committee on Supplies, . . . armed with the widest powers. With its right of seizure it could acquire control of all goods and Maximum prices, distribute these goods among districts and have full control over all agricultural and industrial production, transport, manufacturing, mines, coal, wood, imports and exports. It could call in the armed forces. . . .

Meantime expedients were needed to survive, namely requisitioning and rationing. . . .

For the war's duration, the entire administration of France centered on Paris, as was the case before 1789. The elected officials who still remained were supervised by a national agent appointed by the Committee and invested with the power to requisition, as well as to denounce magistrates and officials. The latter knew that for the smallest deficiency they could be dismissed and then placed on the list of suspects and imprisoned. Elections would no longer be held to replace them, . . . but representatives on mission or national agents confined themselves to consulting the popular society before they drew up lists of replacements.

A decree of 5 Brumaire suspended the election of town governments. For all practical purposes the sovereignty of the people, its electoral power, was concentrated in the clubs—that is, in the party in power. The clubs themselves were purged. The Revolutionary Government became the dictatorship of a party for the benefit of a class, the class of consumers, artisans, small property owners and the poor, controlled by the men of the bourgeois class who had closely allied themselves with the Revolution, and particularly by those members of this class who enriched themselves by the production of war supplies.

The dictatorship of a party or a class is usually only established by force and is a necessity in wartime. The Revolutionary Government was inevitably accompanied by Terror. . . .

To conduct the war, which would prolong the suffering of the sans-culottes, the Committee was compelled to conduct an increasingly daring social policy that would inevitably alienate it from the Indulgents, the usual protectors of the well-to-do classes. The Indulgents paralyzed the law on hoarding from its inception by refusing to vote the amendments necessary for its application. On 2 Nivôse they had succeeded in striking at its weakest point by decreeing that . . . the only penalty provided for—death—would no longer be imposed by judges.

There is little doubt that they hoped that the Law of the Maximum . . . would soon be abrogated, like the law on hoarding. But the Committee would not retreat from its position. It proposed the General Maximum which would regulate prices for all France and correct the defects of the original law, The sans-culottes would consider that they were being protected.

The military campaign was about to begin. The Committees decided to launch a great offensive that would crush their enemies and stir the masses. On 8 Ventôse Saint-Just, speaking in their name, delivered a striking speech that outlined the plan for a new revolution.

Until now the Terror had been considered even by its most ardent supporters as a temporary measure that would disappear with peace. Saint-Just presented it in a completely new way, as the necessary condition for the establishment of a democratic republic. . . . He set forth the principle that the Republic could not be secure unless it was founded on civil institutions that would purify the morals of citizens and make them naturally virtuous. . . .

Until these civil institutions, the plan for which he would soon outline, had been created and had rooted out selfishness from the hearts of citizens, Saint-Just declared that the Terror should continue. . . . After an impassioned apology for the executions carried out by the Revolutionary Tribunal, which were only a feeble response to the barbarities of monarchical regimes, the man whom Jules Michelet called the "archangel of death" threatened with the guillotine all those who talked of indulgence. He referred to their leaders in barely veiled terms. . . . Breathlessly, the Assembly awaited the conclusion of his indictment, which continued. Would he ask that the designated individuals be turned over to [the executioner]? Suddenly, Saint-Just shifted course. He did not demand heads, but rather a revolution in property: "The force of circumstance may perhaps lead us toward consequences that we could not have imagined. Wealth lies in the hands of a rather large number of enemies of the Revolution, while the needs of working people make them dependent on its enemies. . . . The Revolution leads us to recognize the principle that whoever has proved to be an enemy of his country cannot be a property owner in it. . . . The property of patriots is sacred, but the property of conspirators is destined for the impoverished. The wretched are the powerful of the earth. They have the right to speak with authority to governments that neglect them."

Saint-Just secured passage of a bill which provided that the property of individuals who were declared enemies of the Republic would be confiscated. In his eyes, it was not a theoretical act but a definitive measure that would be put into effect, for on 13 Ventôse he won enactment of a new law that required all communes to draw up lists of indigent patriots and watch committees to provide . . . a list of all those imprisoned for political reasons since May 1, 1789, as well as comments on each. Supplied with this mass of information, the [governing] Committees would decide, without any possibility of appeal. . . . [T]he Committee of Public Safety would prepare the list of indigent patriots to whom this confiscated property would be distributed.

The Revolution, after having seized the property of the clergy and that of the émigrés, took what still remained to its enemies. It had put on sale the property that belonged to the first two categories, but its sale had profited only those who had the wherewithal to buy it. It would distribute the property of the newest category to the revolutionary proletariat without charge.

[None of the popular movements] . . . had ever conceived such a radical measure, such a vast transfer of property from one political class to another. There were perhaps 300,000 individuals imprisoned as suspects in the new Bastilles, 300,000 families threatened with expropriation. The Terror was assuming an unforeseen, immense character. No longer was it a matter of temporarily repressing a hostile party by force. It meant dispossessing it forever, destroying its means of existence and elevating in society the eternally disinherited social class at its expense. In addition . . . the Revolutionary dictatorship would be extended as long as it might prove necessary to found the Republic in actuality by means of this immense expropriation and in men's minds through civil institutions. The Terror was no longer ashamed of itself. It was becoming a regime, the red crucible in which future democracy would arise out of the accumulated ruins of everything that belonged to the old order. . . .

His conclusions represented a spectacular attempt to develop a social program out of the confused aspirations of [the popular leader, Hébert]. . . . Strangely, to his amazement, he was neither understood nor followed by the very individuals he sought to satisfy. . . .

The Committee maintained regulations and price controls. It controlled all foreign commerce by means of its agencies and the requisitioned merchant marine. But it made legislation more flexible and instituted measures to stimulate production. It encouraged manufacturers by means of subsidies and bonuses, and merchants by monetary advances. Shortages diminished.

Now manpower caused the most serious concern. The first requisition reduced the labor available, at the very time when the increase in workshops and factories which served the military multiplied demand tenfold. Workers took advantage of the situation to secure wage increases in greater measure than the cost of living. The establishment of the Maximum on wages certainly displeased most of the working class. But it particularly angered the numerous laborers engaged in war production who were subject to rigorous discipline. . . . In Paris ordinary laborers, porters, coachmen and water carriers earned 20 to 24 *livres* a day while trained workers in first-class arms factories received only 16 *livres*, those in the second class 8 *livres*, 5 *sols*, and those in the lowest class 3 *livres*. Thus it is scarcely surprising that workers in the numerous war industries in Paris lived in a virtually permanent state of unrest. The Committee, which had urgent need for their services, increased their wages and allowed them to choose representatives to negotiate with its agents, but never succeeded in satisfying them, for the difference between their demands and legal levels was too great. The Committee realized that if it yielded on the Maximum on wages, it would also be forced to yield on the Maximum on commodities and that the economic and financial structure it had so painfully erected would collapse. It therefore took a hard line toward the working class.

It would seem that worker unrest was widespread throughout the country. Labor shutdowns were so frequent that Barère secured passage . . . of a law which provided that all those engaged in handling, transporting and selling merchandise of primary necessity were requisitioned. [The law also] threatened with the Revolutionary Tribunal those who, by their inactivity, formed a criminal conspiracy against the provisioning of the people.

"The system of the Maximum," as Georges Lefebvre so correctly observed, "was conducive to developing a spirit of class and solidarity in the proletariat. It set property owners against wage earners." It also did more: it tended to ruin small merchants and craftsmen by forcing them down to the level of wage earners. . . .

Peasants burdened by requisitions and cartage duties, workers exhausted by chronic malnourishment and determined to win wages that the law denied them, merchants nearly ruined by price controls, and bondholders devastated by paper currency, seethed with discontent beneath their seeming calm. Only the enlarged band of agents of the new bureaucracy and military producers profited from the regime.

Those in power were under no illusion and threw themselves into a supreme effort. All the same, they would found the Republic in which they had placed their faith and loved all the more since they were uncertain about its future. They recalled that the monarchy had been undermined by the revolt of the poor driven by hunger.

The application of the Ventôse decrees which distributed the wealth of suspects to the poor sans-culottes demanded an extensive inquiry that would take several months. On 22 Floréal, Barère announced that the Revolutionary Committees had already transmitted decisions concerning 40,000 prisoners. But 300,000 cases remained to be decided. Barère proudly claimed that within six weeks the list of the indigent population would be completed. It never was. . . . These partial measures, in the minds of those in power, were merely a prelude. "There should be neither rich nor poor," wrote Saint-Just. "Opulence is infamous." He proposed to make the state the beneficiary of those who died without immediate relatives, suppress the right to make wills, and require all citizens to report annually on how they used their fortunes. . . .

These projects remained dreams and collided not only with the individualistic spirit of the time but also with the demands created by the war. How could the Committee resolutely conduct a class policy when . . . it endeavored to reassure all interests? The illiterate and wretched crowds over whom it watched so solicitously were a burden rather than a support. They watched dumbfounded at the events that they did not comprehend. Essentially the entire policy of the government was based on the Terror, which only the war made tolerable. Yet the Terror destroyed people's respect for the regime.

The Committee focused its attention on the younger generation. Barère declared . . . that it was necessary to revolutionize youth just as the armies had been. Inspired by the happy experience of schools for arms production . . . , which drew young men from all over France and then dispatched them as supervisors in the various workshops, it created a War College intended to provide military and civic instruction for 3,000 youngsters chosen, half from among the children of small farmers or craftsmen, half from the sons of volunteers wounded in battle. . . .

Plans were laid for creating, on the same model, a teachers' training school to produce professors and instructors inspired by the new faith, but the school would not be established until after Nine Thermidor. Meanwhile, a sincere effort was made to apply the law of 5 Nivôse which made attendance at primary schools compulsory and paid public teachers out of taxpayer funds. But faculty were in short supply and the schools opened only slowly. . . . Saint-Just wanted to endow the schools using state owned land. He set forth the principle that, before it belonged to its parents, a child belonged to the state, and drafted a plan for common education on the Spartan model. . .

The Committee, which at the outset had been unwilling to see dechristianization as anything more than a foreign maneuver, did not consider reversing it, making it acceptable to the masses by infusing it with positive content. . . . It celebrated liberty, country and reason, but uniform organization and common doctrine had to be added. Men of the period, even those freest of Christian dogma, even the atheists . . . , did not believe that the state could dispense with credo and ceremonies. Like the old Church, the state was responsible in spiritual matters. . . . The political morality inculcated at the civic ceremonies had to be linked to a philosophical morality that induced private virtue. It was the general conviction that faith in God was the basis of society. . . . Robespierre was delegated to report out the expected decree on festivals. . . . He prefaced it . . . with a moving speech that stirred the Assembly and the country. In it he affirmed that the Revolution, now possessing a philosophical and moral doctrine, had no need to fear an aggressive revival of the old traditional religions. He predicted the approaching end to all priests, with all Frenchmen being reconciled around the pure and simple worship of the Supreme Being and of Nature. In his eyes, Nature and God were one. . . . The Republic would also celebrate the four great anniversaries of July 14, August 10, January 21 and May 31.

Elected president of the Convention . . . by unanimous vote, one that had never been greater—485—Robespierre, bouquet of flowers and ear of wheat in his hand, presided over the magnificent festival devoted to the Supreme Being and Nature that took place on 20 Prairial, the day of Pentecost, before an immense crowd. Throughout France similar festivals were held that same day with equal success. Everywhere there were republican temples with the inscription over their portals reading: "The French people recognizes the Supreme Being and the immortality of the soul." It seemed that the Committee had attained its aim of rallying all Frenchmen around the common feeling of reconciliation and brotherhood. Men of all parties sent Robespierre their enthusiastic congratulations. . . . The impression felt abroad was extraordinary, "It was truly believed," noted Mallet du Pan, "that Robespierre had healed the divisions that the Revolution had created." This feeling was all the more true because France's armies were victorious everywhere. But the sarcasm and threats that some deputies had hurled at the president of the Convention during the very Festival of the Supreme Being were not known. Beneath the brilliant splendor of garlands, flowers, hymns, addressees and speeches, were visible neither the hate nor the envy of those special interests, threatened by the Terror, and indifferent to virtue, which were waiting for an opportunity to exact their revenge. . . .

Revolutionary France would not have accepted the Terror if it had not been convinced that victory was impossible without the suspension of liberty. It became resigned to the dictatorship of the Convention, then that of the Committees, in the hope that its sacrifices were not made in vain and that it was not misled.

In the spring of 1794 it could be proud of the army that had been created in its name. The army was one: all distinctions between regulars and volunteers, including uniforms, had disappeared. . . . With the general staffs purged, confidence now reigned between officers and troops. The former, many of whom had sprung from the ranks, set an example by enduring hardships. . . . The old friction between generals and deputies on mission had disappeared. Carefully selected, the deputies could make themselves obeyed without being overbearing. They preoccupied themselves with the well-being of the troops while inspiring them with their own civic enthusiasm. . . . Harsh punishments had restored discipline. The women who burdened the camps and consumed provisions were driven out. Contractors were closely supervised. Government regulation replaced private enterprise, and inspectors general of transport, who operated in pairs, ended pilfering. The purified army, stirred by ardent patriotism, became a pliant and docile instrument. . . .

Robespierre soon provided his opponents with a highly dangerous weapon by his participation in the drafting and passage of the law of 22 Prairial concerning the Revolutionary Tribunal. . . . Their prime consideration, expressed in the laws of 8 and 13 Ventôse, was to make use of the Terror to dispossess the aristocrats whose property would be distributed to the poor. Saint-Just had inserted into the law of 27 Germinal an article that ordered the creation . . . of "popular commissions" charged with selecting from among the imprisoned . . . a list of those whose property would be confiscated after they were deported or condemned to death by the Revolutionary Tribunal. But the [governing] Committees were in no hurry to establish these commissions, on which the new social revolution would depend. . . . Should it be supposed that Couthon and Robespierre, irritated by the delay of the Committee of General Security in applying the Ventôse laws and considering it criminal, determined to break the logjam and confront it with a *fait accompli* by preventing it from any preliminary examination? Robespierre would later reproach the Committee with recruiting its agents from highly suspect individuals. . . .

Couthon therefore introduced the new legislation in the name of the Committee of Public Safety alone. Accused individuals were deprived of attorneys, for allowing the accused a defender would offer a forum for royalism and the enemy and favor the wealthy at the expense of the poor. . . . The preliminary examination of the accused was eliminated. In the absence of written proof or oral testimony, juries could henceforth be satisfied with "moral proof." The definition of "enemies of the Revolution" was broadened to include "all those who have sought to mislead public opinion, obstruct the education of the people, deprave morals, and corrupt the public conscience." Finally the Revolutionary

Tribunal was reorganized and its number increased. Couthon did not conceal the fact that the intent of the law he proposed was less to administer justice than to exterminate. . . .

A wave of public outrage rose against this orgy of murder. The time had passed when the crowd hastened to the scaffold as to an entertainment. Shops along the route now closed when the sinister carts passed, rolling along the cobblestones. The site of the guillotine . . . had to be moved. Public opinion, disgusted with the bloodshed, was undoubtedly the best weapon in the hands of Robespierre's enemies. Behind the scenes they undermined the Revolutionary government. . . .

The new Indulgents naturally profited from the succession of victories. Fraternal banquets were organized in the streets to celebrate them. . . . The rapid success of these fraternizations disquieted the Commune and the government.

But how would it be possible to maintain the Revolutionary government, resist the pressure exerted by the Indulgent and the corrupt, whom public opinion supported, if the Committees remained divided and if Robespierre continued his opposition . . . ? Word of the internal quarrels among those in power had even spread into the provinces, alarming the representatives on mission . . . , the Revolutionary Government and the Republic. The members of the Committee of Public Safety . . . sought an agreement with Robespierre. Barère repeatedly declared the need to continue the Terror. . . .

Robespierre . . . also believed that the Terror should continue until the property of counter-revolutionaries was finally distributed to the poor and civil institutions, for which Saint-Just was drafting plans, had been established and implanted. . . .

The [governing] committees met in plenary session on 4–5 Thermidor. To demonstrate, by means of a striking action, their firm desire to continue the Terror and extend its social consequences, they at last created the four popular commissions that had remained in limbo but were indispensable for executing the Ventôse laws for the sorting out of suspects and the allocation of their property. The decree, drafted by Barère, dates from 4 Thermidor. . . .

That very evening, thoroughly pleased that he had restored harmony, Barère announced to the Convention that only the vindictive could have spread the rumor that divisions and misunderstandings within the government, or any variations in Revolutionary principles, existed. . . .

The next day Couthon picked up the theme at the Jacobin Club, praising "the energetic and enthusiastic men" who composed the Committees. "If divisions existed among individuals, none existed in their principles. . . ."

Had Robespierre approved at the plenary session on 5 Thermidor the plan of reconciliation formulated by Barère . . . ? It is doubtful. All his grievances had not been satisfied. He wanted to wrest control over the conduct of the war from Carnot, who had not carried out the decree of 7 Prairial forbidding the taking of English and Hanoverian prisoners and who surrounded himself with a council of experts composed of aristocrats. . . . On previous days cries had been heard in the streets proclaiming the imminent arrest of Robespierre, without the Committee's having taken any action. . . .

The tragic irony was that Robespierre and his followers perished largely because they wished to use the Terror as a means to redistribute property. With them disappeared the egalitarian Republic, having neither rich nor poor, that they dreamed of establishing through the Ventôse decrees. The unconcerned sans-culottes would soon regret the "damn Maximum." They would revolt to restore it, but in vain.

For the time being, the only ones who grasped the importance of the victory that the rapacious Terrorists had won was the enlightened stratum of the lower middle class and craftsmen whom Robespierre had introduced into public affairs and who filled various clubs and revolutionary bureaucracies. They felt profound sadness. . . . At Arras and Nîmes, when the arrest of Robespierre became known, the clubs proposed to take up arms and fly to his aid. Numerous patriots killed themselves in despair. . . .

But the Thermidorians now had the Terror at their disposal. They released their supporters from the prisons and filled them with Robespierrists. Hostages of the reaction that they had unleashed, they would be dragged further than they expected. Many of them in later life would express their regret for having participated in Nine Thermidor. In killing Robespierre, they slew the democratic republic for a century.

Born of war and its sufferings, thrown forcibly into the mold of Terror contrary to its principles, this Republic, despite its amazing accomplishments, was essentially an accident. Resting on an increasingly narrow base, it was not understood by the very individuals with whom its existence was bound up. It had taken the fervent mysticism of its creators and their superhuman energy to extend its life until victory was won abroad. Twenty centuries of monarchy and slavery are not erased in several months. The severest laws are powerless to change human nature and the social order at a single stroke. Robespierre, Couthon and Saint-Just, who wished to prolong the dictatorship to create civil institutions and overthrow the rule of wealth, realized this full well. They would have succeeded only if they alone had exercised complete dictatorship. But the intransigence of Robespierre, who broke with his colleagues in the government at the very moment that the latter were offering him concessions, sufficed to cause the collapse of a structure suspended in a legal void. It was a memorable example of the limits of human willpower struggling against the resistance of material things.

Georges Lefebvre

A Revolution of Peasants and Bourgeois Buccaneers

Georges Lefebvre (1874–1959) is closely identified today with aspects of the Marxist interpretation that were discredited by revisionist historians in the 1960s and 1970s. The prominence he attained in the course of his career explains why he was singled out for criticism. Lefebvre was the first historian appointed to the official chair in revolutionary history at the Sorbonne who subscribed to the Marxist thesis that the revolution brought the capitalist bourgeoisie to power. His history of the revolution—from which the second of these two selections is taken—proved to be the most influential version of the "orthodoxy." As the first selection shows, however, Lefebvre in the 1930s was himself a critic of earlier Marxist historians. What most impressed readers about his history when it appeared was his attempt to reconcile the views of Aulard and Mathiez. The middle ground he tried to find between the two historians reflected his politics. Along with other intellectuals on the left during the thirties, Lefebvre was committed to bringing radical republicans, socialists, and communists into a Popular Front coalition for the defense of the Third Republic against fascism.

The French Revolution and the Peasants

It is not my purpose to retrace even in broad outline the role of the peasants in the events of the Revolution, nor to describe the conditions under which they lived during the last years of the Old Regime and up to the beginning of the nineteenth century. What I am concerned with here is to show that it is necessary to recognize that the peasants hold an important place in the history of the Revolution and thereby not only to extend our knowledge of that event, but also to integrate it more exactly into the historical perspective of the French nation, and by this same means to shed further light on the basic character of our civilization. . . . Mathiez himself has not accorded to the peasants the attention which in my opinion they merit. It has seemed to me not inappropriate that I should present the reasons for my opinion in more detail. . . .

I

The French Revolution has for a long time been presented as the work of the *philosophes*, and in the books of Aulard it still appears essentially as an ideological fact. It was Jaurès who accustomed historians to look on it as a sociological fact and consequently of economic origin. This does not mean, of course, that the ideas of the *philosophes* must be denied any importance whatsoever and are to be looked upon only as a symptom and not a cause. Between the social or economic fact and the historic event it is necessary for the mind of man to intervene if the first is to lead to the second. It is none the less true that the Revolution was only the culmination of a long social and economic development which has made the bourgeoisie masters of the world.

This was not a new discovery on the part of Jaurès. In the first decades of the nineteenth century, Guizot . . . showed in most admirable fashion how the originality of western civilization lay especially in its creation of a strong middle class, the bourgeoisie. A class which had little by little created the framework and elaborated the ideology of a

Etudes sur la Révolution Française by Georges Lefebvre (Paris, 1954), pp. 246–269. Translated by the Editor. By permission of Presses Universitaires de France.

new society, the full flowering of which was achieved by the Revolution of 1789. Tocqueville and even Taine shared this opinion. These historians, in truth, without being in any way ignorant of the fact that the origin and progress of the bourgeoisie was the result of the appearance and accumulation of mobile wealth, nevertheless were scarcely interested in the economic origins of the social movement. . . . Finally, in the *Communist Manifesto* of 1847, and then in the first volume of *Das Capital* in 1867, Karl Marx reaped the fruits of the slow development of that idea and by adding to it his observations on contemporary England, ended by formulating with extraordinary power the economic interpretation of history.

It must be acknowledged, however, that the historians of the Revolution have not retained very much of the Marxian formulation of the theory. It is really Jaurès who has been our teacher and he is the more worthy of that honor in that in restoring to history its social and economic base, he corrected the extremes of self-styled Marxism by maintaining very vigorously that ideas have none the less their own proper function, that they play an essential role in history, that the ruling class is not exclusively dominated by its own selfish preoccupations, and that it was sincere in its conviction that the general good of society depended upon the maintenance of its predominance.

As Jaurès presented it, however, the upheaval of 1789 appeared as a single and simple event. The Revolution was brought about by the power of a bourgeois class which had reached maturity and consequently wished to achieve legal recognition of that fact. This view seems to us today to be too summary. First, it does not explain why the accession of the bourgeoisie took place at that moment rather than at any other, nor why in France it took the form of a violent change, while it might have happened, as it did elsewhere in fact, as the result of a progressive evolution—even if not entirely peaceful. We now are well aware that the Revolution of 1789 came to pass only as the result of a truly extraordinary and unforeseen coincidence of a whole series of immediate causes; a financial crisis of exceptional gravity . . . a crisis of unemployment . . . and finally a crisis of rising prices and misery. . . . But these are not all the factors, and the underlying causes of the Revolution seem to us also to become more and more complex. . . .

One can see that the economic interpretation of history does not succeed at all in achieving for us a simplified view of the past. The mere rise of a revolutionary class is not necessarily the sole cause of its victory and it is not inevitable that this victory take place, or in any case that it take place through violent means. In this instance the Revolution was unleashed by those whom it was to destroy, not by those who profited from it, and it cannot be proved that it was inevitable that this group should have been able to impose its will on the sovereign. It cannot be said that stronger kings might not have succeeded in limiting the progress to power of the aristocracy in the eighteenth century. . . .

What is important . . . is to affirm that the Revolution was a complex event; that there was not one Revolution but several. For it does not even suffice simply to distinguish between first a revolution of the aristocracy and then one of the Third Estate. Jaurès first and Mathiez after him have rightly insisted on the rapid disintegration of the latter group and on the antagonism which promptly manifested itself between the upper bourgeoise, the artisans and the proletariat. . . . (As a result) Mathiez . . . has been led to distinguish a third Revolution, that of August 10, 1792, which was democratic and republican in character, and then a fourth of June 2, 1793 which aimed at the establishment of a social democracy. . . .

. . . The picture in my opinion is still not absolutely complete or accurate because the peasants . . . have not taken their place in it. Let there not be attributed to me, for all that, the pretention of having discovered them! No historian, naturally, has been unaware of the uprisings in the rural areas nor the agrarian reforms of the Revolution. But they have been accustomed to see in the actions of the peasantry simply a repercussion of the revolt of the townsman and especially that which took place on July 14; as if the rural classes had simply obeyed the call of the bourgeoisie. They have thought of the peasants' action as directed exclusively against feudal obligations and royal authority, being thereby in full and perfect accord with the bourgeoisie. . . . These are all conclusions which tend to conserve for the Revolution a majestic and homogeneous appearance—to see it only as the Revolution of the Third Estate. Even if they describe the disintegration of the latter, they appear to believe that it took place under the same conditions and produced the same results in the country as in the towns, the well-to-do peasant making common cause with the bourgeoisie and the agricultural day laborer with the town-dwelling artisan. . . .

I am not unaware, of course, that there is in all this a certain amount of truth: the example of the town did exert a profound influence on the village. There would probably not have been any French

Revolution if hate for the feudal regime had not united peasant and bourgeois, and its destruction was one of the most important and most indestructible of its reforms. Finally, in both town and village social distinctions remained very similar and the classes in each did not diverge completely in interests and viewpoint. To put it briefly, the peasant revolution developed within the framework of the French Revolution.

But it is important to point out, and I am striving to do it, that there was, however, a true peasant revolution which had an autonomy of its own in its origins, development, its crises and its tendencies.

It was autonomous in its origin because the peasant masses stirred spontaneously under the influence of poverty and the hopes to which the convocation of the Estates General had given rise. Furthermore they must have at the same time as their fellow townsman, arrived at the conclusion that there was, in the summer of 1789, an aristocratic conspiracy because without that having happened, the "Great Fear" which swept over France at that time would be inexplicable. It was autonomous also in its actions and in the course it followed because up until the 14th of July the bourgeoisie had had neither the time nor was it disposed to attack the clerical tithe nor the feudal obligations. But the peasants began, as early as the month of March, to rise against their seigneurs and to refuse to pay their seigneurial dues well before the capture of the Bastille. On receipt of the news of the events in Paris, they revolted spontaneously, taking their cause into their own hands—to the great discomfiture of the bourgeoisie who in several places took it upon themselves to suppress the risings. Autonomous also it was in that it had its own crises, because agrarian revolts broke out again in 1793 under conditions that bore no necessary relation to the political development of the Revolution. Furthermore, it was even autonomous in its results, since, without the peasant revolution having taken place, one can be sure that the Constituent Assembly would have not struck such serious blows against the feudal regime, and it is not certain that it would have been finally abolished without indemnity. But that it was, above all, autonomous in its anti-capitalist tendencies, on that I would insist particularly. . . .

II

In 1789 the French peasants already held a significant portion of the soil of France; perhaps 30 to 40% on the average, sometimes very much less, sometimes very much more. That is why in comparing them to the serfs of central and eastern Europe who were forced to render uncompensated labor to their lords and to the English agricultural laborers who were free but who were reduced to living on their wages alone, one can describe the French peasants as small independent landholders.

In general nothing is said in discussions of land distribution about those who actually exploited the land—as if it could be assumed that those who owned the land and those who cultivated it were one and the same! This fact is the more striking in that the arrangements under which land was cultivated in France assuredly helped to establish for the French peasant a certain degree of independence with the result that a study of the system of cultivation seems to have the effect of reenforcing conclusions already drawn from a study of the distribution of land ownership. In central and eastern Europe the lords of the great estates had either kept or built up a very extensive domain which they exploited by means of forced labor imposed on their serfs. In England the great landholders by the process of dividing up and parceling out the common lands which was called "enclosure" had created extensive holdings which they exploited by means of agricultural day laborers. In France, the great landholder very rarely undertook the exploitation of his lands directly nor did he have recourse to the practice of enclosure and as a result he rented out his lands either for a monetary rent or on a sharecropping basis in various sized parcels but usually small, and usually as isolated segments of either tillable land, meadow land, or vineyard. Along with the peasant landholder accordingly there were to be found farm tenants and share-croppers and along with them peasants who supplemented their own holdings with lands . . . which they rented. . . .

But these rather optimistic conclusions must be rather drastically qualified when two sets of facts which are ordinarily neglected are taken into account. From the point of view of its social and economic implications, the mere size of a piece of land either owned or farmed signifies nothing by itself. It assumes significance only if one compares it to the size of the average amount required to support a family of average size and thereby assure it of economic independence. The second fact that must be considered is that the total number of owners or tillers of land has significance only if compared to the total number of heads of families. . . . The proportion of those who tilled the land, and to an even greater degree the number of peasant landowners, who could live independently, without working for others, was very small in all parts of the country. Accordingly there was a very much larger group of peasants who owned or rented land but who did not have enough to live on and therefore were obliged either to carry on a trade or business or to hire out from time to time as day laborers in order to supplement their income. And finally there was a more or less considerable number of rural inhabitants who had only their wages to live on and when there was no work or the price of bread was too high, there was nothing left for them to do but to resort to begging. . . . [H]eads of families lacking any property or rented land whatsoever amounted to an enormous majority (70 to 75%). . . . At the end of the Old Regime, furthermore, the population was increasing very fast and accordingly the agrarian crisis was growing more acute.

This is manifest by the ardor with which the peasants encroached on the common lands or forests in order to build themselves a cottage or to clear small areas so as to add to their tillable land . . . [and] very often demanded the sale or lease of portions of the royal domain or even at least a part of the church lands. In this respect the agricultural proletariat and the peasants who already held land, but only an insufficient amount, were in agreement at least in principle. But the crisis also inspired complaints against the whole system of farm land tenure which seemed to come mostly from renters and share-croppers. They called for the dividing up of the great leaseholds and large blocks of land rented to agricultural entrepreneurs for profit, or at least they demanded that the number of small plots available not be decreased. Also they protested against the aggravation of the terms imposed on the leasers of land made possible by the heightening of competition induced by the greater pressure of need. . . . [A]ll of these practices leave no doubt as to what was the more or less conscious ideal of the peasant masses. Each one was to have his share; a limited inequality does not seem to have been repugnant to them, especially since some of them were already above a condition of dire need, but there was a certain amount of land which was sufficient to support a family and no one ought to have more than that. Accordingly unused lands, those making up part of the royal domaine, those of the clergy (and later on those of the emigrés) were to serve to provide for the most unfortunate of the community.

. . . Still it should be emphasized that the "indigent" and the poor farmers did not think of property in exactly the same way as we do. As they did not have the means to buy the nationalized lands [when they were put up for sale during the Revolution], they demanded that they be leased out at the lowest rent possible, which would have secured for them the free disposition of their share at a small payment fixed once and for all while at the same time the nation would have still held them as ultimate owner, just as we have said the dividing up of common lands often saw the ultimate ownership of them reserved to the community. What mattered to the peasants was that they should enjoy the use of the land, the essential instrument of production.

But one would have a very incomplete idea of the limitations which the "common rights" of the peasants imposed on the rights of property if one stopped only with these observations. It is necessary at this point to recall that the "indigent" and the poor farmer only succeeded in subsisting thanks to the collective rights which, of course, the peasant in easy circumstances or even rich, benefited from as well as they, and even, ordinarily, very much more. There were, for example, the right of grazing cattle on lands where the grain had already been harvested and unenclosed fields; certain rights of usage of the forests; the enjoyment of the common rights of the community, such as the right of gleaning in harvested fields, and the right to collect stubble. Certain of these rights on the other hand could not be conceived of without a corresponding regulation of the actual cultivation of the land, the right of grazing cattle on harvested fields inevitably required that all the fields in a particular section be sown and harvested at the same time with the same crop; it automatically prevented the enclosing of fields. Because the rights of gleaning and gathering of stubble were very much less profitable if the scythe were used instead of the sickle, the owner was limited in the methods he used. And finally since the small farmer tilled the soil in order to gain a bare livelihood and like the people of the towns was always tortured by the fear of a shortage of food, which in view of the periodic shortages is very easy to understand, he frowned on the introduction of new crops in place of the familiar grains. He was no less ready than the townsman to prohibit not only the export and the hoarding of grain or any other device to stimulate a price rise, but also the free circulation of grain within France because there could never be too much grain in reserve in the barns. All the thinking of the poor peasant thus tended to limit the rights of individual property in order to defend collective usages which permitted him to live and which he regarded as a property right as sacred as that of others and one which existed to prevent the provisions necessary for his existence from becoming inaccessible to him. It little mattered to him that new arrangements would have increased production since it was he who would have had to pay the price of that progress, while all the benefits—or at least at the beginning—would have accrued to the large-scale farmers who either rented or owned their land and who produced for the market. In short, he opposed with all the force at his disposal the transformation of agriculture into a more capitalistic enterprise.

. . . Toward the middle of the eighteenth century, however, the example of England and the propaganda of the Physiocrats had given rise to a current of opinion in favor of reorganizing agriculture along more capitalistic lines. In order to do this it was necessary to do away with all regulation of cultivation and to grant the right to sell all products freely. It was necessary to suppress collective rights, especially the right of allowing cattle to graze in harvested fields which prevented their enclosure and to divide up the common lands among the inhabitants of the village to assure that this land would be cleared and utilized. . . . But . . . before attaining this golden age of capitalistic economy it would be necessary to go through a period of crisis which might last quite a long time. What would become of the peasants when they were deprived of a part of their resources? If the number of indigent increased, who would pay the taxes in their place? Were not troubles to be foreseen? The local officials, the municipal authorities and certain intendants, all of whom were in direct contact with the people and who were threatened with being blamed if riots broke out, all expressed reservations or showed themselves hostile to the new ideas. . . .

In general the royal administration visibly inclined, however, in favor of the innovators. There does not seem to be any doubt but that it was the interests of the privileged classes which swung the balance . . . [who] simply sought the best means to augment their incomes. . . . [A]s the rise in prices and the rising requirements for luxurious living stimulated them, they had long ago taken the lead in this direction. . . . [I]t does not appear to be contestable that during the last decades of the Old Regime, these tendencies were accentuated. The need doubtless became more and more pressing, but one cannot help but note that this economic offensive developed simultaneously with the aristocratic reaction against royal authority. . . . The theories of the Physiocratic economists very opportunely furnished the feudal interests with the pretext of serving the public good. . . . If the Physiocrats tended to make sacrosanct beings out of the great landed proprietors it was not just pure theory: these great proprietors were the members of the privileged classes.

But perhaps the most curious and least noted feature of this situation was that the tightening up of the feudal regime which was an indisputable characteristic of the eighteenth century, and especially the second half, stemmed from the same source. To free himself from the bother of managing his estates and to assure himself of an increasing or at least a constant income, the seigneur leased out the right to collect the income from his feudal rights just as he farmed out in a block the right to his half of the crop of his share-croppers, or consolidated his leases in the hands of a large-scale leaseholder. This situation was not new, very far from it, but it became more and more frequent. But the one who under this arrangement was to actually collect the payments owed by the peasants, naturally was rigorous in exacting them and attempted to increase them. . . . As a result the intrusion of capitalism into agriculture was made in part under the cover of feudal rights and made them very much more unbearable. It also perverted their very nature because they had been created to support a seigneur who lived in the midst of his peasants and now they passed into the hands of capitalists who thought only of deriving a profit from them.

But they also increased the income of the seigneur and thereby increased the value of his feudal rights in his eyes and his repugnance to abandon them. Even redemption itself would not have been agreeable to him for where could he invest the capital which he would have received from it? And what form of reinvestment would have offered the same security? The rise in prices combined with the new manner of capitalist exploitation of his feudal rights promised an indefinite increase while money loaned was subject to the risk of loss. But there was a basic conflict between the general intrusion of capitalism into agriculture and the maintenance of feudal rights and the payments made for the use of the land. The suppression of the common right to graze cattle in harvested fields, the fencing in of lands, and the freedom to plant various crops at will could only be obtained quickly if all lands were reassigned in such a way that the domain of the great proprietor, instead of being made up of scattered fields, was consolidated into a compact holding. This is what had been done in England . . . There was no longer any obstacle to redivision of the land. In France, on the contrary, the feudal rights and monetary obligations remained in existence; certain ground rents were still collected in kind and the conditions which had permitted enclosure in England did not therefore prevail. On the other hand, the domain lands of the seigneur had in very many villages been reduced almost to nothing with the result that the income from feudal rights constituted his principal revenue . . . And most importantly, very many of the seigneuries overlapped one another and how could one be sure of one's own in the confusion, or hope to carry out successfully such a complicated operation? Moreover, the peasant would have opposed it resolutely and the royal government which had its own interests and which was not as in England and in the monarchies of Eastern Europe subordinate to the aristocracy in law and fact, would never have consented to be constrained by the interests of that class. But it never had to take a stand on the issue because, as we have said, the seigneurs were too attached to their feudal rights to contemplate a general enclosure law. . . . Our rural people wished to be rid of the feudal obligations, but they did not suspect that thanks to them they had escaped the terrible fate which the enclosure movement had brought to the English farmer and still held in store for the Prussian peasant. Perhaps they would not have been able to avoid it if the Old Regime had lasted longer. . . . The events of 1789 saved the French peasant and in spite of appearances his influence was just as conservative as it was revolutionary. He overturned the feudal regime but he consolidated the agrarian structure of France. . . .

The capitalistic transformation of agriculture should not in principle have had the effect of engendering antagonism between the aristocracy and the bourgeoisie, but indeed rather solidarity. One should only note that the former had a very much greater interest in it than the latter because the latter at the end of the Old Regime possessed only relatively few landed estates. The conflict arose when it came to the question of feudal rights and land rents. . . .

. . . [T]he bourgeoisie, in principal, were hostile to them. They presented an obstacle to the introduction of capitalist modes of production which required freedom for the individual and hence the suppression of serfdom; economic freedom and hence the abolition of . . . seigneurial monopolies; the consolidation of the home market hence the abolition of tolls; the mobility of capital and hence the extinction of primogeniture. . . . Finally, as has been shown, the whole system of feudal rights required the maintenance of tenures as they existed and made impossible the redistribution of lands and hence the large-scale methods of cultivation which are natural to a capitalistic organization of agriculture.

A part at least of the great noblemen and certainly the liberal noblemen who played such an important role in the opening phases of the Revolution, doubtless would not have refused . . . the redemption of feudal rights and even the abolition without indemnity of the more oppressive ones. The resistance to this developed rather among the petty noblemen who lived primarily on their feudal payments and who remained attached to the military character and the traditional idleness of the French nobility. They were frightened at the idea that they, like the bourgeoisie, would have to find profitable investment for the money which they would receive from redemption, which would mean that they would no longer be "living nobly." Besides, once their monetary rights disappeared, how could they hope to retain their honorific prerogatives? The nobleman did not wish to become a citizen like any other; he did not wish to pay taxes like any bourgeois and he wished even less to find himself on a footing of equality with his peasants. It was under these circumstances that combined action by the peasantry and the bourgeoisie became possible on the day when the privileged classes in the Estates General refused to join with the deputies of the Third Estate, that is to say, with the bourgeoisie. But if the bourgeoisie while at odds with both the Court and the aristocracy could not afford to be disdainful of the support of the peasants, it certainly did not think of calling them to a revolt against their seigneurs, nor even to concede to them by legal means the abolition without indemnity of their feudal dues. Among the members of the Constituent Assembly there were many lawyers who looked on these rights as an individual property as legitimate as any other, and one which could not be destroyed without placing the bourgeoisie itself in peril. . . . In addition, the nobles were not the only ones who possessed seigneuries: more than one had passed into the hands of bourgeois owners.

But the peasant took his cause into his own hands, as we have said, and settled the issue by refusing to pay his feudal obligations as well as the clerical tithe, and by burning up the records and even in some cases the *châteaux*. Not being in a position to alienate him, the bourgeoisie along with the liberal members of the nobility, granted him on the night of August 4, the pure and simple abolition of part of the feudal obligations and the redemption of those which represented a rent for the use of land. To the degree that the conflict between the nobility and the triumphant bourgeoisie intensified, the former had to agree to more and more extensive concessions. . . . After the uprising of . . . June 2, 1793 it decreed the complete abolition of all obligations without any reservations.

. . . There was then an autonomous peasant revolution. It must be distinguished from the revolution of the bourgeoisie just as that is differentiated from the revolution of the aristocracy and the popular democratic revolution from that of the wealthy landowner.

With these facts in mind a few reflexions of the greatest importance cannot fail to occupy our minds. The economic interpretation of history (inappropriately designated by the name "historical materialism" which I have never found in Marx) is given too narrow an interpretation when the French Revolution is made to evolve solely from the rise of the bourgeoisie. It arose also out of the resistance which the privileged classes opposed to the rise of a new economic order, or, to put it better, out of their resolve to reap the benefits of it themselves. But it had its origin equally in the opposition of the least favored classes to the capitalistic order which had begun to be established. If they were so bitter against the aristocracy it was not only because the feudal regime had always oppressed them, but also because the capitalistic spirit had little by little penetrated the aristocracy itself and thus had rendered the feudal regime the more hateful. But it does not follow from this that they were to the least degree sympathetic toward capitalism or that they fought in order to establish it. But it happened that the emergence of this new social order provoked hostile reactions, which nevertheless at the same time favored its ultimate triumph. To the extent that the Old Regime was forced to adopt policies favorable to capitalism in order to satisfy the economic aspirations of the bourgeoisie, it contributed very effectively to the preparation of its own ruin.

The French Revolution

The World on the Eve of the French Revolution

. . . The European economy developed steadily through the final centuries of the Middle Ages, then gained momentum from the mercantilist policies of great states and the exploitation of new lands overseas. In England during the eighteenth century economic progress gained revolutionary force, brought in the reign of the steam engine and of mechanized power, and on the eve of the French Revolution gave Britain a superiority which was to play an essential role during the long struggle that followed. With the advantage of historical perspective we label this economic surge the industrial revolution because we can

The French Revolution, Vol. I by Georges Lefebvre. Copyright © 1962–1964 by Columbia University Press. Reprinted with permission of the publisher.

perceive in it the germ of world transformation. Its development was slow, nevertheless, even in the country of its origin, and the fact that England owed its superiority merely to the first stages of industrialism implies that the continent was as yet scarcely affected. Europe's economy in the concluding years of the eighteenth century seemed, despite its relative prosperity, to share much in common with the past. . . .

The old methods of production yielded a slow and meagre output. Agriculture was governed by climatic caprice; industry was restricted by the scarcity of raw materials and the inadequacy of power resources. The peasant laboured for his own consumption and sold none of his produce or sold only enough to acquire the cash . . . demanded of him. The artisan supplied only his local market. Difficulties of transportation forced each district to live off its own produce. Every region jealously guarded its grain crop. . . .

Factors which had stimulated the transformation of Europe's economy over the past few centuries were still at work. The powerful states of Western Europe had begun to practise mercantilism as soon as they came into being, and eighteenth-century rulers abandoned none of the economic aspects of that policy. . . .

Luxury industries were aided by purchases from princes and courtiers, who set the style for the upper classes; metallurgical industries, shipyards, and textile and tanning factories were aided even more by government orders that resulted from expansion of the armed forces. . . .

Furthermore, colonial exploitation regained the importance it had held in the sixteenth century. Once again bullion poured into the Old World, reaching an unprecedented level after 1780. . . . France's coin circulation may have ranged from 2 to 3 billion livres. . . . With an abundant supply of money, financiers had funds at their disposal. They unfortunately followed tradition in offering indebted governments the option on this capital, but some part of it did go into production. . . . Always on the lookout for advantageous speculation, they built up a network of international finance which ignored national boundaries. . . . The increase in specie . . . resulted in a steady rise in prices. A long-term upward movement which began about 1730 and lasted until 1820 replaced stagnation. Despite cyclical fluctuations, a rise of this nature encouraged investment with the allure of unearned income. An increase in population, marked after 1760, acted as a rejuvenating force by augmenting both consumption and the labour force, but the rise in prices remained a major stimulant to the European economy.

Commercial dealings with overseas territories caused a significant expansion in Western trade. On the eve of the French Revolution commerce with their colonies represented 40 per cent of the trade of France and of England. Both countries fed many colonial products into their exported goods. . . . The slave trade too brought profits. . . .

This new money, concentrated in the hands of relatively few individuals, was spent for luxury items, lent to royal treasuries, invested in land, or hoarded. Nevertheless, a significant part was undoubtedly used to finance enterprises. In regard to technical progress, perhaps the most important stimulus was the introduction of cotton into European industry. . . .

It was maritime commerce which, by the boldness and risks it involved, had produced the first economic innovators. . . . A mentality foreign to the conventional economy inspired these traders. Their attitude, characterized by a hazardous quest for profit, transformed the warring spirit into a ruthless determination to vanquish competitors and made speculation the mainspring of their activity. With them appeared certain characteristics of what we call capitalism—concentration of capital and of business concerns so that exploitation could be rationalized, a development that gave this economic technique cardinal importance in the rise of European civilization. By the end of the eighteenth century domestic trade and even financial transactions were less risky, but maritime commerce was still subject to the hazards of fortune. . . . In recompense, these investments built up huge fortunes. Rationalization of business procedures had long been evident in methods of financial exchange. . . . But this process was in its early stages, and functions were still mixed— the shipowner was also a merchant, the merchant was also a shipper, both were commission agents, underwriters, bankers. Business methods were perfected in slow stages. The exchange was little more than a convenient meeting-place; trading in futures was rare. . . .

Commercial capitalism, the master of distant markets, had soon begun to exploit the artisanry and to develop a rural industry which paid low wages and did not have strict regulations. The importation of cotton stimulated these home industries through all Western Europe. . . . But rarely was the number of workers thus employed large.

The rise of commerce and industry did not overshadow agriculture as the mainstay of the economy. Everyone was in one way or another involved with land: the individual, rich or poor, who aspired to become a man of property; the statesman who knew that population increase depended upon more food and hence meant more taxpayers and prospective public servants. Yet mercantilism often sacrificed agriculture to industry by curtailing export of raw materials. . . . A free grain trade meant high bread prices and would cause starvation and riots. The farmer therefore was forbidden to sell his produce on the spot; instead he had to deliver it to the local market. . . . Shipments abroad were strictly prohibited. . . .

The economy of continental Europe thus remained essentially what it had been for centuries. . . . [E]xtensive cultivation was relied on to increase production: new land was drained and cleared. . . . In the fertile plains, village lands were split up into separate fields, which lay fallow. . . . Each farmer had at his disposal scattered strips of land within the fields. . . . The peasant was burdened with obligations and either did not possess the means to introduce new methods or else used his savings only to buy another plot. He was usually uneducated and clung to the security of traditional routine. . . .

These are the general characteristics of Europe's economy. Yet the eighteenth century witnessed decisive economic events. The development of a banking organization, of new business methods, of machines and mechanized power, was to entail a radical change in production, replacing commercial capitalism with industrial capitalism as the driving force within the economy. Similarly, aspects of modern agriculture were beginning to appear.

These innovations were at work in England, a nation which outstripped the rest of the Western world while its continental neighbours were only awakening to new developments.

. . . The states of Western Europe lagged noticeably behind Britain, not excluding France, which nevertheless led the rest. Stagnation increased proportionately as one travelled eastward.

Europe's first banks had been established in Italy and then in Holland. . . . But these were still little more than deposit houses. . . . France alone had founded a Bank of Discount in 1776. . . . There were few private banks. . . . In France an abundant money supply was available only at Paris, where tax collections accumulated; in the provinces credit was rarely offered, and then only at high rates. . . . Entrepreneurs generally used personal capital. . . . State authorization was needed to establish a joint-stock company. . . . Sleeping partners and shareholders lacked the legal protection of limited liability. . . . In contrast with England, continental Europe lacked a banking apparatus that could accumulate savings and use them to finance new companies. . . .

Business, particularly maritime commerce, was traditionally of primary importance to the French economy. . . . Several industries, particularly sugar refining, brought new wealth to the ports. Finance in the service of the king had always been responsible for the accumulation of large fortunes. Commercial capitalism had begun to expand, employing the artisanry. . . . Domestic industry spread. . . . There were also factories in the true sense of the term. Some were founded by the king for production of luxury goods; others manufactured munitions, anchors, and cannons for the navy, guns and sidearms for the army. . . .

The French did not lack an inventive spirit. . . . Industrialists were interested in new machinery, and a few Englishmen provided workers for cotton. Yet in 1789 France had only an estimated 900 spinning jennies, as compared to 20,000 in Great Britain. . . . Metallurgy had undergone little change and, dependent upon wood for fuel, remained widely scattered.

Agricultural production in France slowly continued to improve. . . . [V]ineyards spread throughout the nation, potatoes and fodder crops were cultivated. The government endeavoured to improve the breeding of stock. . . . Yet traditions persisted. . . .

France remained a nation of agriculture and of handicrafts. The development of capitalism and of economic freedom met strong resistance on French soil, a fact which was to be of major importance during the Revolution: within the Third Estate, disagreement broke out between the upper bourgeoisie and the lower classes; the controlled economy of the Committee of Public Safety was thwarted by inadequate transportation and scattered sources of production. . . .

By the end of the eighteenth century the economic revolution inaugurated by Great Britain seemed to confirm Europe's supremacy, although an observer fifty years earlier might well have been dubious. He might have noted that the wood supply was diminishing while industrial production increased but little, that agriculture appeared incapable of supporting the labour force; and that if the West did not succeed in supplying its overseas territories, colonial exploitation might soon exhaust them. Europe, it had seemed, might suffer the same fate as Rome, whose purely commercial and financial capitalism had ultimately ruined its conquered territories. Now, however, optimism was justified. Wood was being replaced by coal and iron, the steam engine and power-driven machinery were augmenting production, and Europe's agriculture fed its labouring population. The continent had not yet shifted to a new economy, but this was only a matter of time. . . .

In any case Europe was growing increasingly wealthy, especially in the West, as was to be expected. The precise rate of enrichment is not known. It is believed that the national income of England and of France had more than doubled during the eighteenth century. . . . Ease of material existence and refinement in human relations reached new and higher levels, although, naturally, improvements affected the upper classes most of all.

Ostentation has never been confined to any particular period, but an outstanding trait of the eighteenth century was the pursuit of well-being and of pleasure, enhanced and moderated by a more refined comprehension. . . . Manners grew more polished in salon society. . . .

. . . A spreading thirst for knowledge led to more and more academies, reading rooms, lectures, and courses. Sentiment and sensitivity, charity and philanthropy lent new aspects to the enjoyment of life. . . .

The new wealth filtered down to the artisans, to shopkeepers, and to well-to-do peasants. This was evident in a greater consumption of certain commodities. . . . Coffee, chocolate and tobacco, beer, wine, and brandy were articles in popular demand.

The rise in population is the most noticeable fact concerning the condition of the wage-earning classes, and the rate of increase continued to rise during the last decades of the century. France gained 3 million inhabitants after the Seven Years War. . . . Fewer famines, plus the additional resources offered by industrial progress, lowered the mortality rate.

There are, of course, many qualifications necessary. In Central and Eastern Europe aristocrats continued to inflict physical punishment on their "dependents." In Western Europe aristocratic manners were growing more refined, but not necessarily more moral. The nobility thought itself born to live on a plane above the common man and too frequently displayed its extravagant and libertine nature. Among the lower classes, poverty and ignorance often encouraged drunkenness and violence. The petty bourgeoisie, the artisanry, and the wealthier peasantry were the most attached to restrained conduct, but were not exempt from crudeness and cruelty.

It is none the less true that Europe's enrichment was the basis of an optimism whose intellectual expression was the idea of progress and which encouraged the men of that era confidently and boldly to undertake the reforms that concomitant changes in social and intellectual life seemed to demand. . . .

The social structure on the European continent still bore an aristocratic imprint. . . . Priests and nobles had become royal subjects, but they had not lost their privileges. . . . [A]lmost the whole population was lumped into a third "order," called in France the Third Estate. Aristocratic prerogatives condemned this order to remain eternally in its original state of inferiority.

The social hierarchy was divided not only into . . . "estates." . . . [T]he state was always . . . maintained a corporate structure with the governing principle from top to bottom resting on inequality of rights.

Throughout Western Europe, and especially in France, this ordering of society was being challenged by a long-term change which increased the importance of mobile wealth and of the bourgeoisie, emancipated the lower classes, and highlighted the leading role of productive labour, inventive intelligence, and scientific knowledge.

Socially, as in other ways, Britain differed from the continent. Partly because of its insularity, historical events of the past centuries gave British society certain unique characteristics which a burgeoning economy promised to intensify. . . .

In no country did the clergy constitute more than a small minority of the total population. In France it is usually estimated at approximately 130,000 members. . . . The wealth of the Catholic clergy was a liability to its social importance, compromising both the influence and the cohesion of the Church. . . . Nobles disposed of their children by setting them up in bishoprics, chapters, and abbeys, while the lower clergy and the faithful complained that Church revenue was diverted before reaching its proper destination.

The clergy was an order, not a class, and included nobles as well as commoners. The true aristocracy was the nobility. . . . The nobility of continental Europe constituted an order. . . . Its members were registered; its leaders forestalled derogation from noble rank and defended aristocratic privileges. . . . The nobility preserved its customary laws, chief among them the law of primogeniture. There were numerous survivals of the authority commanded by the lord of the manor: . . . honorific prerogatives; monopolies. . . . The lord also retained a portion of land for his own use, either leasing it or cultivating it for himself.

Nobility was hereditary. In principle it could be conferred only by birth, and noble blood was to be kept free from contamination through misalliance. The aristocrat considered himself racially distinct from the 'ignoble' commoner. . . . He wore the sword; his profession was that of bearing arms. . . . A changing economy which associated power with money had injured the feudal nobility. War . . . exhausted the nobleman's patrimony, already eaten away by rising prices, increasing extravagance, and division of lands through inheritance. As a result, great disparities in wealth and in manner of living had developed within the nobility. But as members of the aristocracy fell behind, their places in the ranks were filled by members of the bourgeoisie.

The ruler of a state had long ago assumed the right to ennoble his servants . . . [through the sale of] certain administrative, judicial, . . . positions. . . . [This] nobility of the robe [was] an administrative or municipal nobility whose titles were either hereditary or personal. . . . These nobles . . . formed a separate oligarchy. Their wealth and influence gave the nobility new force. They eagerly espoused aristocratic manners, affecting snobbery and disdaining the excluded; in turn they changed the noble mentality, making it more bourgeois. The accepted aristocratic profession was still that of bearing arms, but nobles . . . went to war more from duty than from taste for combat. . . . [I]n the West, particularly in France, the nobility competed with both royal authority and the bourgeoisie, nourishing a strong resentment against the throne that had relegated it to an inferior position and jealously guarding its separate existence against the encroaching ascendancy of the middle class.

The nobility, like the clergy, constituted no more than a small part of the population. . . . The bourgeoisie formed neither an order nor a corporate body, but was the richest and most capable part of   the Third Estate. . . . [E]conomic changes had made them singularly powerful in France. . . . At base they were recruited from the artisans and the peasants employed in trades; some had risen to affluent positions by means of hard work and frugality, but for the most part they had found success through the favourable odds offered by commercial speculation, no matter how modest the activity: the middleman was always able to acquire wealth with greater ease and speed than was the producer.

The composition of this class was anything but homogeneous. Those who considered themselves the true bourgeoisie were a small number of commoners who had enough resources to dispense with manual labour and to live "nobly off their possessions," that is, principally off revenues from land. . . . The bourgeois condescended . . . to associate with members of two "labouring" groups. . . .

The first of these two groups was the civil service of the throne, the most coherent, stable, and best-educated body in the nation. Its members were more numerous and influential in France, where "officers" . . . owned their positions. . . . Lawyers of varying positions . . . were also connected with administrative offices and also purchased their offices. . . . This administrative bourgeoisie formed a sort of intermediary class through which social advancement, assured by money, had always been possible. Members of other liberal professions rarely entered this class. . . .

The other group, less respected but often more wealthy, included financiers and directors of the economy. Of the financiers, those who served the state. . . . had considerable prestige. A few sooner or later moved up into the nobility. . . . Shipowners, merchants, and manufacturers were noted more for their numbers than for their influence. . . .

This portion of the middle class under the Old Regime formed what we term the upper bourgeoisie. Like the aristocracy, it was small, but its corporate organization fostered the same exclusiveness it resented in the nobility. . . . The traditional aspiration of these bourgeois was to insinuate themselves one by one into the ranks of their superiors. Nevertheless, in France their rise had been such that they were starting to be ranked by the government, along with those nobles who had managed to retain their wealth, as "notables." This was a social category based on money and transcending the legal classification of orders or corporate bodies. It was the embryo of the modern bourgeoisie.

Future events decreed varying fates for these bourgeois groups. Like the aristocracy, the true bourgeoisie of the Old Regime, those who lived like nobles, were to suffer from the Revolution. The "officers" and members of the liberal professions . . . laid the intellectual foundation of, and then guided, the Revolution. But . . . they were not always spared by the cataclysm. In any case they did not profit as much as the financiers and the businessmen. These, driven only by a blinding passion for profit and power, failed to comprehend anything higher than their class interest. They selfishly used new ideas and revolutionary changes only to serve the bourgeoisie, yet upon their taste for enterprise, speculation, and risk depended nothing less than the development of capitalism and the fate of their class.

What we call the middle class or the petty bourgeoisie was disdainfully referred to by notables as "the people," a term which was to be applied to the same group, but in affectionate tones, by the revolutionary democrats. . . . Whatever his rank, the petty bourgeois was frequently irritated at the airs put on by the bourgeois properly speaking, yet in turn he looked down upon proletarians. . . .

In the eighteenth century intellectual ability tended to compete with moneyed power and to compose a social hierarchy of its own. Professors, men of letters and journalists, scholars and artists, musicians and singers, actors and dancers lived apart from those assured of material security. They constituted a varied and unstable milieu, often poor, sometimes morally loose. . . . [A]mong them were to be found not a few individuals able to speak correctly and to write with ease. The impecunious "men of talent." . . . were understandably champions of equality of rights. A constant and ubiquitous source of ferment, they were to furnish an important part of the revolutionary leadership.

Finally, it should be noted that although birth, corporate status, profession, and sometimes talent influenced social classification, there existed, in addition, a subtle gradation relegating each man, from the wealthiest to the meanest, to his own niche. This gradation implied a marked division of labour and indicated both a widespread desire to move up the social ladder and an increasing individualism. . . . The nobility and bourgeoisie of Europe shared the belief that proletarians were destined by Providence to engage in manual labour and were thereby relegated to an inferior level of civilization. Religious sentiment encouraged the practice of charity, and common sense advised that the masses be treated with discretion. . . . [P]hilosophy introduced the concept of social obligation. . . . As capitalism spread across the continent it carried the idea that to be poor was a just punishment for laziness and vice. . . . [T]he upper classes nurtured repugnance . . . for those whom fortune spurned, and everyone lived in constant fear of individual crimes or collective revolt at the hands of . . . "the rabble."

Apart from the many domestic servants, proletarians were spread throughout rural as well as urban areas. . . . The poorest were agricultural day labourers employed only in season. They were scattered through the towns as well. . . . The labour force was not rigidly specialized — . . . and was not concentrated in certain sections or in large factories. It lacked class spirit. . . . It was not clearly distinguished from the artisans in France, with whom it sided when the Revolution began. A rupture between bourgeoisie and nobility would have been less likely, one suspects, had not the events of 1789 preceded the rise of industrial capitalism and the appearance of a proletarian opposition.

Although economic development may have aided the condition of the proletariat by reducing the occurrence of famine, a growing population added to the unemployed and held wages down while food prices rose. . . . Economists explained that, in the nature of things, a worker's remuneration could never exceed his minimum requirement for existence and for procreation. . . . Resistance was, however, manifested by boycotts and strikes. . . . During the eighteenth century unions appeared in English industry. . . . Yet on the continent as in England, many workers sought the intervention of public authorities, who on occasion acted as mediators to restore public order but were in general antagonistic towards the proletariat. . . .

Indigents formed one-fifth of the French population, and their number swelled with each economic depression. Poor relief was notoriously deficient. . . . Begging was a scourge in some regions, and fruitless efforts were put forth to reduce the number of mendicants through confinement. . . . Swarms of men wandered about in search of work. . . . When crops failed and the inevitable industrial depression followed, workmen, sharecroppers, and holders of land were all reduced to begging. Fear of brigands spread through the country. . . . This fear, easily converted into a "great fear" marked by terror and panic, was shared by the lower and upper bourgeoisie. It was a source of unrest tending towards disintegration of the Third Estate; outside France it was to work against the spread of the Revolution. . . .

The World at the Advent of Napolean

. . . The French Revolution was still far from the bourgeois goals of 1789. The new order began to assume definitive form only under the tutelage of Bonaparte. For this reason his work appears as the conclusion of the crisis. . . .

The principles that the Constituent Assembly attributed in 1789 to the order that the bourgeoisie claimed to be establishing have already been stated. They have continued to inspire most of the nation, but great difficulties developed in interpreting them and in shaping institutions and public life accordingly. . . . To elucidate the historical significance of [the Revolution's end] it is necessary, therefore, to summarize, on the one hand, the upheaval in the structure of society and the character of the reconstructed state; on the other, the variations to which circumstances, divergent class interests, and different currents of thought subjected the reorganization of institutions and impeded it, without succeeding in stabilizing it to the satisfaction of the bourgeoisie . . .

Once the principles of the new order had been proclaimed, the revolutionary bourgeoisie continued to maintain that emancipation of the individual implied the ruin of the hierarchical and corporate structure of society, founded upon birth and privilege. . . . [A] compromise solution would have shown a greater appreciation of many features of the old society. Civil war led the bourgeoisie gradually to eliminate the aristocracy entirely, without even considering the possible danger to themselves.

The clergy suffered most. . . . [T]he "Church" . . . lost its legal existence and became simply a spiritual community. Nonetheless the memory of it . . . persisted in public opinion.

. . . Religious orders were abolished; and on July 12 the Civil Constitution disestablished chapters as well. . . . Church property . . . passed to the nation. . . . [Priests] were reduced to the status of ordinary citizens, partly pensioned by the state. . . .

The French nobility . . . likewise lost . . . its existence. . . . The Constituent Assembly . . . abolished hereditary nobility, titles, and coats of arms. It was the disappearance of the seigneurs that was appreciated above all by the majority of Frenchmen, the peasants whom they had held in subjection. . . .

Since the nobles, like the priests, had become ordinary citizens, their property lost its special status. The distinction between noble land and that of the commoners . . . primogeniture, . . . all disappeared along with feudalism. The wealth of numerous families dwindled, in many instances because manorial rights had provided the greater part of their revenue. . . .

Emigration resulted in still harsher treatment of the nobility. . . . The property of émigrés . . . was put up for sale by the Convention. . . .

The future seemed equally dark to families who had escaped these penalties, because the revolutionaries were taking steps that tended to break up the large estates. Undoubtedly the bourgeoisie felt that the new economic order required mobility of property, and that social stability would be enhanced by increasing the number of owners. But the desire to diminish the influence of the aristocracy, and the passion that the civil war . . . [led to] the decree . . . [which] required equal division of intestate inheritances. . . . [T]he decisive blows came with the Convention . . . [which] condemned entails. . . . and primogeniture. . . .

The inheritance laws of the Montagnards . . . confirmed the equal division of inheritance among heirs, with unlimited power to protest. . . .

[N]atural children were permitted to inherit, and . . . granted them a share equal to that of legitimate children. . . . [T]he nobility suffered as well from the constitutional and administrative reforms. . . . No one dared demand any favours whatsoever because of birth.

Among the nobles most severely affected were those of the robe . . . , who held the highest ranks in the state. With purchase of offices made impossible, they remained unemployed. . . .

The situation of the nobles gradually became worse. Increasingly suspect, they became fewer in public office. . . .

In discussing the increasingly effective measures against the clergy and the nobility, attention must be paid to the popular massacres, the terrorist executions, and "revolutionary vandalism" — chateaux laid waste or burned, churches despoiled and demolished. . . . [T]he loss was irreparable. . . . [I]n this destruction of the corporate society . . . [the] bourgeoisie of the Old Regime were seriously affected as well. . . . Many officeholders were commonerers . . . and the suppression of the organized bodies on which their social rank and part of their income depended, hurt them as it did the others. The notaries became functionaries. . . . Even . . . liberal professions that were not venal experienced some loss. With the lawyers dissolved as a body, the role of "public defender" was open to all. Physicians ceased to be an organized group. . . . [T]he Convention, by suppressing the academies and universities, deprived some of the artists, scientists, men of letters, and professors of their claim to status. . . .

During the Montagnard period the commercial middle class in turn found its future compromised. . . . [T]he Convention eliminated the joint-stock companies, the most advanced form of capitalism. . . .The advent of the controlled economy, taxation, and requisitioning slowed the rise of capitalism even more abruptly by regimenting business activity and limiting profits.

Nor did the "people" — the artisans, retail merchants, and employees — emerge unscathed. . . . [T]he Constituent Assembly suppressed the craft guilds. . . . [and] permitted wage earners to profit thereby through opening their own shops. Nonetheless it deprived masters of their monopoly . . . [and] wounded their pride. . . .

Finally, the private life of the Third Estate was affected. The inheritance laws applied to commoners as well as to nobles, and occasionally ruined their legacies. . . . [M]any bourgeois emigrated. . . . [T]he great majority of those harmed by terrorist repression were neither priests nor nobles. It was essential, however, for the revolutionaries to loosen the bonds that subjected child and wife to the discretionary power of the paterfamilias under the Old Regime; and this applied to the Third Estate as much as to the aristocracy. . . .

Paternal authority was greatly diminished. Henceforth the family court . . . shared disciplinary authority with the father. At age twenty-one . . . children were "liberated" and regained control of their property. No longer need a wife fear imprisonment by means of *lettres de cachet*; her consent was required for the marriage of her children, and like her husband, she could seek a divorce. . . . The rehabilitation of "natural" children heralded a still more formidable disruption of family solidarity. Every social revolution tends to carry its attack to the point where it seems fitting that individuals . . . be released from traditional conformity, so that, whatever the risks, they may adapt themselves to the new order because restraints have been removed. Once the goal is attained, however, discipline must be re-established within the remodelled society.

To stop here would be to leave an inadequate impression of the social upheaval. No less far-reaching were the effects of inflation, which, despite the return to metallic currency, continued its ravages until 18 Brumaire. . . . Inflation was devastating to acquired wealth. . . . But the bourgeoisie willingly invested their savings in mortgage loans. . . .

. . . Finally, the bourgeoisie held the greatest part of the public debt. Thus it bore the brunt of . . . the continued decline of income . . . [from state bonds] and of the payment of dividends in worthless notes.

The number of these changes, and the infinite variety of their repercussions, greatly influenced men's thinking. They alienated the aristocracy from modern society, rallied some members of the bourgeoisie of the Old Regime to counter-revolution, and caused others to desire a conservative reaction. . . . Only those who speculated on the purchase of national property and provisions recovered their losses; but the principal benefits of these operations did not go to the bourgeoisie of the Old Regime. As is usually the case, the war and the monetary disorder produced *nouveaux riches*, whose intrusion into the ranks of the impoverished bourgeoisie added to the social upheaval a quality that had not been anticipated. . . .

At the end of the Old Regime the state, embodied in a divine-right monarch, still retained a personal character. Since the seventeenth century, however, a centralized administration had been tending to make its bureaucratic regulations prevail, and it was making the state bourgeois by rationalizing it. . . . The class which dominates a society always regards the state, created to ensure respect for the positive law and to maintain order, as the bulwark of its prerogatives. The rivalry between royal power and the interests of the aristocracy engendered the Revolution, and the bourgeoisie put an end to the contradiction by seizing the state themselves.

They abolished the privileges of the provinces and the towns, as well as those of the aristocracy, and proclaimed the equality of all Frenchmen before the law. . . . Traditional institutions were swept away, and national unity was achieved through administrative uniformity. . . . In this sense Tocqueville was able to say that the members of the Constituent Assembly crowned the work carried on over the centuries by the Capetian dynasty.

But this was only part of their work. In proclaiming the rights of man, with liberty foremost, the bourgeoisie intended to protect them against the state; so they transformed the latter. Substituting popular sovereignty for that of the prince, they destroyed personal power. From an attribute of a proprietary monarchy, the state was transformed into an agent of the governed, and its authority was subordinated to the rules of a constitution. . . .

Thus the Revolution of 1789 did not reinforce the power of the state. On the contrary, it weakened it by associating the elected representatives of the nation with the king, by requiring them to respect individual rights, and by diluting authority through decentralization . . . This tendency toward libertarian anarchy appeared as much among the counter-revolutionaries and moderates as it did among the sansculottes. Its conflict with the indispensable predominance of a central authority . . . reveals one of the eternal contradictions of every society— that of freedom and authority, the individual and the state.

The bourgeoisie were by no means unaware of the difficulty. They were willing to run the risk . . . [A] triumphant class is never embarrassed by so doing. The violent convulsions that the structure of the state underwent throughout the decade . . . stemmed from the struggle of the Third Estate with the aristocracy, from the support which Louis XVI accorded the latter, and from collusion with foreign powers. As had happened so often in the past, the nation had to reawaken to the fact that its power at home and its security abroad necessitated a government with sufficient power to meet the full extent of the danger. . . .

. . . [T]he bourgeoisie did not doubt that they could maintain their position. Since the new state was supposed to protect their economic and social dominance, they did not think that the political and administrative organization should paralyse it; but the rigorous separation of powers and excessive decentralization threatened the executive with this fate. . . . It required the aggravation of civil war and the threat of invasion to force them to choose between compromise (if not surrender) and restoration of the authority of the state. . . .

. . . [I]n the hands of the Jacobins the state once more became authoritarian, but its personnel was democratized to a certain degree. Moreover, it displayed some of the features of a social democracy. During the brief existence of the revolutionary government there could be seen, as in a flash of lightning, the boundless horizon presented by this equality of rights, which the bourgeoisie had proclaimed in 1789 to condemn the privileges of the nobility. The Montagnards made no promise to suppress inequality of wealth, but they undertook to reduce it. They did not expect that equal rights would benefit everyone fully, but they did assign to the democratic republic the responsibility of giving at least some reality to the principle.

This was but an interlude. A number of those in control saw it merely as an expedient for public safety. . . . [E]verything had to be sacrificed to victory. . . . [B]y ceaselessly accentuating centralization, suspending elections, and imposing a ruthless discipline, . . . antagonized libertarian independence and disappointed the ambitions of the popular leaders. Then, when they balked, it broke them.

Moreover, neither Jacobins nor sans-culottes organized anything resembling a true party for imposing their dictatorship. They acted within the framework of political democracy. . . . [D]espite purges, the other citizens were represented. They claimed to command in the name of the Convention; . . . if they lost control of the machinery of state, they would be reduced to impotence. Nor did they represent any one class. They were recruited from all elements of the Third Estate, from the rich bourgeois to the proletarian. For this reason the Maximum sowed division in their ranks; landowning peasants, artisans, and merchants clashed with their workers and with the consumers.

After 9 Thermidor the bourgeoisie (who were more or less sincerely republican) recovered complete power and hastened to remove state control of the economy. . . . [T]hey continued the special measures affecting the partisans of the Old Regime. . . . Even the suspension of the rights of the citizen remained a possibility.

The need for a vigorous executive, at a time when the war was continuing, . . . did not escape the Thermidorians. Not only was the salvation of the Revolution and of their republic at stake, but also their own security. . . .

The men in power maintained themselves solely by tampering with election results or by openly violating their own constitution. . . . [T]he final upsurge . . . prompted the property-owning bourgeoisie to look to Bonaparte in the hope of reinvigorating the executive without damaging their own social supremacy.

The war had committed the Revolution to dictatorship, and the bourgeoisie, terrified by the experience of the Year II, were willing to let it be a military dictatorship. The day had not yet dawned for the government they had dreamed of in 1789, and it would be long in coming. . . .

Compared with the old, one obvious feature of the new society . . . derived from the disappearance of the Catholic clergy. . . . [T]hey were decimated, poor and in part errant, treated as suspects, even as enemies, . . . reduced by the secularized state to a purely spiritual authority. . . .

For the moment the fate of the nobility seemed no better. . . . the aristocrats had not been despoiled of the material sources of their influence to the same extent. . . .[O]ften families . . . lived peacefully among their former tenants and under their tacit protection. . . . [A]t worst, they suffered only imprisonment and passing difficulties that left their landed property intact. . . .

It goes without saying that the Revolution benefited the bourgeoisie, but not all to the same extent. Those who formerly had boasted of "living nobly . . ." had been humbled. . . . Of those who survived, some . . . lost their property. . . . The fortunes of those whose prudence had kept them in the background were ruined by the abolition of corporate bodies and by revolutionary taxes, forced loans, and inflation. . . . [B]usinessmen . . . suffered from the controlled economy. . . . As for maritime trade, the British blockade, the capture of merchant vessels, and above all, the loss of colonies meant decline and . . . ruin. Nevertheless the bourgeoisie retained their pre-eminence. The monetary disaster did not lead to consequences as serious as those of modern times, because personal property constituted only a modest part of an inheritance. Landowners retained their property. . . . [M]ore than one had compensated for his losses by purchasing national property. . . .

Far more favourable opportunities were offered to the businessmen, since their daily practices equipped them for speculation. Their capital, sent or left abroad, returned intact and was used profitably. . . . It might have been expected that bankers . . . and the manufacturers . . . would know full well how to turn a loss into a profit, and even better. . . .

The only conclusions, then, are that the bourgeoisie cut off a number of their representatives, sometimes the eminent ones, and that their internal equilibrium was modified. The group that depended on acquired property or that exercised functions alien to production—*rentiers*, former officeholders, magistrates, lawyers—without actually losing its established position, was . . . hardly better off than before. Having prepared the Revolution intellectually, formulated its principles, and assumed its direction, this section of the populace deemed its prestige to have been damaged by the rise of managers of the economy who were getting rich, investing their assets in land, and increasing their influence and esteem. . . . Further, the bourgeoisie were strengthening themselves by incorporating these new men.

Distinctions should be made among these parvenus. The most numerous . . . were artisans and merchants who took advantage of circumstances. . . . As always, speculation particularly favoured those who played . . . the role of middlemen, especially grain merchants and millers. A few of these men swelled the ranks of trade and industry, but most of them followed the usual path. Having expanded their businesses and increased their property, they were satisfied; whereas their sons . . . crowded into public administration and the liberal professions if they did not succeed their fathers. They would strive to penetrate more and more effectively into the new order through marriage, connections, and manners, and would not disdain the property-based regime, from which they intended to profit.

. . . [T]he governing class . . . became slightly more democratic, but this trend did not fundamentally alter its character; it was merely a stage in the gradual tendency towards middle-class living that constitutes an essential feature of the social history of France.

Those who were styled the *nouveaux riches* were generally of a different type. They were individuals who, disdaining patient work, daily economies, and slow and measured progress, threw themselves as conquistadors into society in order to attain immoderate wealth in a very short time. This temperament is universal, but an age of social or economic upheaval provides adventure for those who, ordinarily, are deterred from risk either by prudence or their own mediocrity. They proliferated after Thermidor. . . . Most of them, owing everything to chance, rapidly dissipated their gains or came to a bad end.

Such was not the case for all: of the pirates who ransomed the Directory . . . a few remained prominent for a long time. The most gifted of these audacious men eventually invigorated trade and industry by investing their capital. They differed from the older bourgeoisie in their lack of culture, felt no taste for disinterested knowledge, and were totally without revolutionary idealism. A narrow . . . utilitarianism was their lot, and they long retained a fierce, unscrupulous, almost naive appetite for profit. Still, those who despised them should have recognized that such recruits always bring strength and new blood to their class. Without them it would have withered. After several generations the descendants of parvenus ceased working in order to be accepted into the aristocracy, as the rich families of the Third Estate continually managed to do.

A similar but even more important development was manifested in rural society, since the peasants constituted the majority of the population and their rebellion had dealt the death blow to the Old Regime. Fiscal equality and the abolition of the tithe and manorial dues ended the revolutionary ferment so far as rural landowners were concerned. The gap widened between them and the disinherited, whose benefits were reduced to the elimination of serfdom and personal services; and the dissolution of the peasant community was accelerated. . . .

As for the sale of national property, it increased the number of cultivators and the extent of their possessions. . . . [T]he ascendancy of what might be called the peasant bourgeoisie was strengthened. These same people were favoured by freedom of commerce. . . . [T]he same conservative interest henceforth united him with the rest of the bourgeoisie.

If the new order was thus attached to a powerful minority, whose support was to consolidate it more and more during the next century, it cannot be denied that for the moment the situation of most Frenchmen had not altered greatly. Below the bourgeoisie there still remained the host of artisans and retail merchants, whose way of life remained unchanged. . . .

As for the proletariat, it profited, like the rest, from the suppression of indirect taxes. . . . Nonetheless the threat of unemployment continued unabated. . . . [I]nsecurity was intensified by the decline in relief. Finally, the legal status of workers had not been improved. . . . [T]he ban on unions (*coalitions*) and strikes was perpetuated without interruption.

On the eve of 18 Brumaire the upper strata of this society still seemed to be a melting pot. The "notables," who desired to recover the reins so as to effect a regrouping and re-establish their primacy . . . were thus not mistaken in their intention to rely on the persistence of national conditions and habits. The nation had no choice but to tolerate the blows dealt the old corporate order so as to be done with the aristocracy.

Hence it also tolerated the striking success of a small number of persons it did not respect, and saw nothing but temporary expedients and regrettable exceptions in so doing. . . . If pessimists considered moral conformity disrupted, it was because of the lapses always provoked by the uprooting of many individuals and by monetary disorder. . . . Divorce . . . did not find favour in small towns and villages. It was resorted to only in the cities. . . . The revolutionaries who were most enthusiastic in demanding liberty and equality in public life for themselves exercised marital and paternal authority at home, as well as authority over those they employed, with as much resolve as before 1789. . . . The Jacobins, hostile to immorality in private life and pitiless towards profligate women, had no intention of dissolving the family or even of emancipating women. Although women played a role in certain "days," they were kept out of politics and their clubs were closed.

Economic Freedom and Equal Rights

Thus there proves to be greater continuity than might be believed from a logical analysis . . . of the principles proclaimed by the Constituent Assembly. Ultimately the progress of capitalist concentration altered the social structure, while the technical innovations of experimental science increased individual independence by transforming the material conditions of life. As a consequence, economic freedom appears as a basic feature of the new order, businessmen subordinated all others to it.

By the end of the eighteenth century, however, the most daring minds had not calculated its scope, and its immediate effects had not even gained general acceptance. Undeniably, it did attract the French in one respect. Each man was satisfied that henceforth he might try his luck if he secured the necessary means to go into business; and the wage earner clung to the right to sell his services where and when he pleased. It goes without saying that the Revolution did not engender these ambitions—they are inherent in human existence—but it did legitimatize them by liberating them. In this way economic freedom became inseparable from the other freedoms; indeed it was the most precious and symbolic.

Opinion proved less favourable towards technical innovations, which were now free of all hindrance. Out of caution, routine, pride, or lack of capital, artisans appeared no more disposed than before to adopt them without serious consideration. Dislike changed to hostility when the adoption of new processes, especially machines and steam, obviously were leading to capitalist concentration. The craftsman was afraid of being transformed into a wage earner; the worker knew that mechanization began by spreading unemployment. . . . As for agricultural methods, the bourgeoisie desired their improvement, since landed wealth remained the most highly valued, and agricultural production supplied the bulk of national revenue.

Such was not the case, however, where industrial capitalism was concerned. The bourgeoisie of the liberal professions . . . valued large-scale enterprise, because it associated science with production and offered the advantage of absorbing some of the indigent. Nevertheless its expansion worried them. . . . Even among businessmen initiative remained limited, and the inadequacy of the banking structure attests their timidity. Nothing better demonstrates the lack of the spirit of industrial enterprise than the virtually universal prejudice of the nation against the English economy. . . .

Taking possession of nationalized buildings, and employing a wretched labour force, . . . several great capitalist entrepreneurs now became prominent. . . . [T]hey continued the tradition of commercial capitalism . . . , directing cottage workers and a rural labour force in addition to their factories, at the same time engaging in trade, commissions, transport, and banking as well. . . . [T]hey did not let it be forgotten that manufacturing enterprise remained on a small scale and widely dispersed. . . . France still remained primarily agricultural.

The stagnation of farming technique also attests particularly the weakness in the rise of capitalism. . . .

The progress of capitalism, then, was not accelerated during the decade; on the contrary, circumstances rather diminished it. . . . Nor did it concentrate the labour force or bring forth a strictly proletarian class. . . .

The eventual contradictions between economic freedom and equal rights had not yet become fully apparent. The bourgeoisie saw none at all, because in their eyes equality meant simply that henceforth the law was the same for all. Yet by proclaiming this principle in order to eliminate the privileges of noble birth, it brought into the open the conflict of interests among the different social categories within the Third Estate; and it particularly accentuated the disintegration of the rural community. In other words, inequality came to the fore. . . .

Since a regime based on the ownership of property gave the bourgeoisie control over the state, they resolved to give priority to the problem of equal rights. Political democracy seemed to provide the answer, but from the outset some democrats went much further. They denounced the omnipotence of the "haves" over the wage earners, and their virulent criticisms were a prelude to those of future socialist theoreticians. They showed the emptiness of equal rights, and even of freedom, to those who lacked the ability to enjoy them.

Still, their thought remained overshadowed by the traditional opposition between rich and poor. They pleaded the cause of the "indigent" skilfully, but they never defined it precisely. Their analysis . . . did not extend to an emphasis on private appropriation of the means of production and on their technical development. . . .

[T]he Montagnards contested neither the principle of hereditary property . . . nor economic freedom, for they accepted the Maximum only as a war expedient. The artisans and retail merchants were of the same opinion: they did not like the rich, but because of a basic contradiction, they did not abhor the idea of raising themselves to the same height. . . . [T]he peasants . . . wished only to acquire property. . . .

[W]hen Babeuf and Buonarroti proposed communism as the indispensable condition for equal rights. . . . their preaching bore the mark of the age. Advocating the "agrarian law," they proposed in effect to divide up the land among those who cultivated it. They had no thought of establishing collective production. Their communism was limited to socializing produce. . . .

Albert Soboul

A Revolution of *Sans-Culottes* and *Montagnards*

Albert Soboul (1914–1987) was Lefebvre's student and succeeded him as Professor of the History of the Revolution at the Sorbonne. His work on the *Sans-Culottes* is complementary to Lefebvre's studies of the peasantry, and provides further proof that Mathiez exaggerated in suggesting that popular movements during the Revolution prefigured socialist movements in the nineteenth and twentieth centuries. His portrayal of Robespierre in this selection shows that he also disagreed with Mathiez' assessment of the

Jacobin leaders. In his politics, however, Soboul was much closer to Mathiez than to Lefebvre. He was the first major historian of the French Revolution to belong to the Communist Party. In the final pages of this selection Soboul suggests that the ultimate significance of the *Sans-Culottes* movement is that it demonstrated the need for a disciplined working class party.

The Parisian Sans-Culottes

From June 1793 to February 1794, the Parisian sans-culotte movement played a major role in the political struggle leading to the consolidation of the Revolutionary Government and the organization of the Committee of Public Safety. . . . [I]t imposed economic measures upon a reluctant Assembly intended to improve the living standards of the masses. . . . [To] study the motives . . . [and] the attitude of the people at this time, some kind of social definition of the Parisian sans-culotterie . . . is required.

This is not an easy task. . . . What little statistical evidence we have is both vague and misleading. It is mainly through the political documents that we can explore the social characteristics of the sans-culotterie. . . . The . . . mentality and behaviour of the Parisian sans-culotte, only emerges by comparing the attitudes of two social groups. Not particularly conscious of class distinctions, the sans-culotte reveals himself most clearly in relation to his social enemies. This absence of class-consciousness is reflected in the social composition of the Parisian population and . . . in the social composition of the political personnel of the Sections.

. . . [To] delimit the social contours of the sans-culotterie, we should, first . . . discover how the sans-culotte defined himself. . . . [H]e . . . was outwardly recognizable by his dress, which . . . distinguish[ed] him from the more elevated classes. . . . Trousers were the distinctive mark of the popular classes; breeches of the aristocracy, and . . . of the higher ranks of the old Third Estate. Robespierre used to contrast . . . those who wore fancy or embroidered breeches with those who simply wore trousers [*sans-culottes*]. The sans-culottes . . . made the same distinction. . . .

With the dress went a certain social comportment. . . . Here again, it is in his opposition to accepted social behaviour that the sans-culotte asserts himself. The manners of the *ancien régime* were no longer fashionable in the Year II; the sans-culottes no longer accepted a subordinate position in society. . . .

The sans-culottes readily judged a person's character from his appearance; his character then decided what his political opinions would be. Everyone who offended their sense of equality and fraternity was suspected of being an aristocrat. It was difficult for a former noble to find favour in their eyes, even when no definite accusation could be levelled against him. . . .

[C]onsumed with hatred for the aristocracy—a hatred they shared with the montagnard bourgeoisie—the sans-culotterie were still not really "class-conscious." Divided into different social categories, sometimes with conflicting aims, it was practically impossible for them to constitute a class: their unity, in so far as it existed, was of a negative kind. One final point emphasizes this. According to popular mentality, a sans-culotte could not be defined by social characteristics alone: a counter-revolutionary workman could not be a good sans-culotte; a bourgeois patriot and republican might very well be accepted as one. The social definition must be qualified by a political definition: they cannot be separated. . . . The word sans-culotte is used as a synonym for patriot and republican. . . .

For the sans-culotte, it was not simply a question of describing oneself as a sans-culotte . . . it was a question of political conduct. [He] had taken part in the great revolutionary *journées*; he had fought for the democratic Republic. . . . The sans-culotte, therefore, is defined by his political behaviour as much as by his place in society. . . .

[One] document . . . attempts to answer part of this difficulty . . . in replying to "the impertinent question—what is a sans-culotte?" The sans-culotte ". . . is someone who . . . lives quite simply with his wife and children . . ." The *Pére Duchesne* wrote, " . . . [To] meet the cream of the sans-culotterie, . . . visit the garrets of the workers." The sans-culotte ". . . knows how to plough a field, how . . . to make shoes. . . . he goes to his Section, . . . not elegantly dressed . . . [to catch] the eye of the citizens in the galleries, but to . . . support . . . sound resolutions. . . . [He] always has his sword with the edge sharpened to give a salutary lesson to all trouble-makers. . . . [At] the first beat of the drum, he will be seen leaving for the Army."

The modest social condition of the sans-culotte is clearly of importance . . . ; but . . . a definition of the sans-culotte would not be complete without a statement of his political conduct. . . .

If we attempt a statistical analysis . . . we are confronted with the same difficulties . . . [of] defining the sans-culotterie, and of establishing its proportion to the population of Paris as a whole. . . . [It] is impossible to say precisely what the population of Paris was at this time: . . . [and] is even more difficult to estimate the proportion of the sans-culotterie. . . . The *Tableau Sommaire* of the population of Paris gives us a total of 640,504 inhabitants: a figure . . . which is doubtless exaggerated. . . . However, it does agree roughly with a statement . . . of the Year III which gives a figure of 636,772 inhabitants.

However approximate . . . they do throw an interesting light upon the pressure which the population . . . exercised on the problem of food supplies. . . . Two thickly populated areas appear in the heart of Paris on either side of the Seine. On the right bank . . . 180,000 people living in . . . the centre; on the left bank . . . over 70,000 inhabitants. . . . [T]hese different Sections were amongst the most politically active in Paris—the shortage of food supplies being felt more acutely there than anywhere else. . . .

The distribution of the working population corresponds to these areas of population density . . . concentrated in the heart of the capital. . . . The . . . working population of Paris as a whole was 293,820 persons: about half the total population of the capital. . . . The most famous *faubourgs* in revolutionary history had fewer wage-earners than the heart of the capital. . . .

If we analyse the composition of the political personnel of the Sections . . . we must conclude that the revolutionary *avant-garde* of the Parisian sans-culotterie did not constitute an industrial proletariat, but a coalition of small master-craftsmen and *compagnons* who worked and lived with them. This explains certain characteristics of the popular movement, as well as certain contradictions, arising from the ambiguous situation in which the sans-culottes often found themselves.

The small master-craftsman, working and living with his *compagnon*, . . . exercised a decisive ideological influence on the latter. Through him, bourgeois influences penetrated into the world of the workman. Even if he was in conflict with him, the small workshop *compagnon* inevitably derived many of his ideas from his employer, and often living and eating under the same roof had basically the same attitude to the great problems of the day. . . . [L]ower middle-class crafts-man . . . fashioned the mentality of the worker. However, . . . we must distinguish between the "independent" . . . and the "dependent" crafts-man. . . . Juridically free and head of his concern, possessing his own machine, even in a position to hire his own labour, the latter has all the appearance of an employer. But economically he is only a wage-earner, strictly dependent upon the merchant who supplies him with the raw material and who distributes the finished article. The interests of the "dependent" craftsman and the *compagnon* are the same—confronted with merchant capitalism they demanded price-controls and a basic minimum wage. But they did not go so far as to work out a direct rela-tionship between the nature of the work and the rate of pay: wages were determined by the cost of living, not by the value of the work done. The social function of labour is not clearly understood. . . .

[T]he wage-earning worker in the large manufacturing concerns, . . . sometimes showed a more independent spirit which . . . foreshadowed that of the proletariat of the great modern industrial concerns. . . . But more often than not the wage-earners in these larger manufacturing ven-tures had begun employment in small workshops. The spirit of the crafts-man which they retained was strengthened by the environment in which they lived—a small minority of factory-workers surrounded by far greater numbers of *compagnons*. Labour as a whole carried the imprint of lower middle-class artisan mentality. . . . [T]he Parisian labour-force shared its bourgeois ideology. Neither in thought, nor deed, could the Parisian workman become an independent element during the Revolution.

There was a serious contradiction in this situation which affected the sans-culotte's attitude to his work, his position in society and his political activity. . . . [C]raftsmen still owned their workshops, . . . [and] equipment, and looked upon themselves as independent producers. . . . [Their] authority over *compagnons* and apprentices accentuated their bourgeois mentality. Nevertheless the system of small production and direct sale was diametrically opposed to the ideas of the merchant bour-geoisie and commercial capitalism. . . . [T]he more articulate section of the sans-culotterie cherished a social ideal which was incompatible with the evolution of the economic system. They campaigned against the concentration of the means of production, but they were themselves property-owners. When the more extreme sans-culottes demanded a maximum of wealth . . . , the contradiction between their own social posi-tion and this demand escaped them. They expressed their feelings in passionate outcries and bursts of revolt, but never in a coherent programme. The same was true . . . even [of] Robespierre and Saint-Just. . . .

Failing to define . . . [themselves] as a working population, the sans-culottes had no clear and precise idea of the nature of labour itself. They did not appreciate that it had a social function of its own; they only considered it in relation to property. The bourgeoisie in a century of enlightenment had restored the arts and crafts to their rightful place . . . [thus giving] an incomparable impetus to the forces of invention; but . . . they had not conceived . . . of labour as part of the social structure. . . . [T]he bourgeoisie had never thought about labour problems in themselves or in relation to the workers, but always with regard to the interests of their own class. . . . If the Convention decreed the General Maximum . . . after constant pressure from the sans-culotterie, it was, as far as the Montagnard bourgeoisie were concerned, simply a tactical move. Price-controls were related essentially to food supplies; salaries were not in any way determined by the amount of work. . . . Divided between a predominantly artisan economy and nascent industrialism, lacking all sense of class-consciousness, how could the Parisian labour-force fail to be influenced by the bourgeoisie into whose hands it had largely entrusted the defence of its interests in the vital struggle against the aristocracy: its attitude to the problems of labour could only reflect prevailing political and social conditions. For the bourgeoisie, property was the key to the problem. The Declaration of 1789, . . . had established it as the first of the imprescriptible Rights of Man, after the abolition of feudalism had made it an absolute right. For the sans-culottes . . . the problem of labour was not their primary social preoccupation. . . . [T]heir interests as consumers, . . . not the question of strike-action or demands for higher wages . . . roused the sans-culotterie . . . [T]he question of food supplies, a rise or fall in the cost of the main products of popular consumption, . . . above all, bread . . . was the decisive factor . . . [in] the wage-earners' budget. The sans-culottes looked for a fixed system or price-controls on basic commodities; the demand for a sliding-scale of prices was exceptional. This perspective reflects economic and social conditions, as well as the ideology of the period.

Price-controls on basic commodities were demanded . . . by the militants because they were subjected to pressure in their respective Sections, not only from wage-earners, but also from . . . thousands of . . . Parisians, tormented by hunger. Hunger . . . was the cement which held together the artisan, the shopkeeper, and the workman, just as a common interest united them against . . . the noble, and the bourgeois monopolist. . . . ['I']he term "sans-culotte" may appear . . . vague, but from the standpoint of the social conditions of the time, it reflects a reality. . . . [T]he political motives explaining popular behaviour must not be excluded—particularly hatred of the nobility, . . . the desire to destroy privilege and to establish equality before the law. How else can we account for the enthusiasm and disinterestedness of the sans-culotte volunteers? But the riots . . . [and] the popular movement . . . do not entirely fit into the general pattern of the bourgeois revolution: to quote Robespierre himself, these events were due to the popular demand for cheap and shoddy goods. The aim of the maximum . . . was to provide the wage-earners with their daily bread, not to facilitate . . . national defence: the permanent motive behind popular action is to be found in the hardship of everyday life. . . . [E]conomic fluctuations provided the rhythm of the revolutionary movement. After the Revolution the sans-culottes could not forget that during the Terror . . . there was no shortage. The political behaviour of the terrorist is intimately linked with the demand for bread, and it was this dual factor which cemented the unity of the Parisian sans-culotterie. . . .

In the final analysis, it is the passion for equality which distinguishes the sans-culotte: "practical equality" was the necessary complement to equality of rights. . . . [T]his passion . . . fired his revolutionary enthusiasm and mobilized him against the aristocracy, then the bourgeoisie. Not only does it set him apart from . . . the moderate; it also distinguishes him from the Jacobin and the Montagnard. . . . By this same passion for equality, the sans-culotte recalls the leveller and anticipates the social democrat.

But was the time ripe for a social democracy? . . .

. . . [T]he 9 Thermidor constitutes a tragic episode in the conflict of classes within the former Third Estate. But, to place it in the right perspective, we need to remember that the Revolution was fundamentally a struggle between the European aristocracy and the Third Estate as a whole. In this struggle, it is hardly surprising that the French bourgeoisie . . . played the leading role. The Revolutionary Government, founded upon an alliance between the Montagnard bourgeoisie and the Parisian sans-culotterie, had been given the task of defending the Revolution against the aristocracy both within France and beyond her frontiers. . . . [For] the Montagnards . . . it was perfectly natural that the Revolution should have placed the bourgeoisie in control of the nation's destiny; but . . . this was not the immediate problem. Solely concerned with victory, the Montagnards—particularly the Robespierrists—realized that the Third Estate would have to remain united. . . . This explains the alliance with the sans-culotterie which made possible the installation of the Revolutionary Government . . . [and] why this government . . . should have been so anxious to arbitrate between the interests of the bourgeoisie and the popular movement; to share . . . necessary sacrifices . . . ; and to intervene immediately either of them threatened to undermine the policy of national defence. It was a question of directing the entire resources of the nation for war.

On the basic issues . . . the Parisian sans-culottes wholeheartedly supported the Revolutionary Government. . . . But differences of opinion on other vital issues rapidly alienated the sympathy of the Parisian sans-culotte. . . . [T]hese differences . . . reveal . . . the incompatible interests of two distinct social categories.

On the political level, . . . war . . . [required] an authoritarian régime. The sans-culottes . . . were fully conscious of this . . . [and] play[ed] an important part in . . . [its] creation. . . . But it soon became apparent that the democratic ideas . . . [of] the Montagnards and the sans-culotterie . . . [did] not . . . meet the particular problems which arose: this was especially true of the [sans-culottes'] . . . exercise of direct government, [which] was incompatible with the conduct of a war. The sans-culottes had asked for a strong government to crush the aristocracy; they never considered the possibility that, in order to do this, it would be forced to discipline the popular movement.

. . . [T]he political ideals of the sans-culotterie . . . did not . . . further the interests of liberal democracy as interpreted by the bourgeoisie, but those of popular democracy. . . . [The] militants had no intention of accepting an empty and formal type of democracy. Their struggle succeeded in giving practical expression to what had originally been only an idea, . . . the Republic as the embodiment of the democratic ideal. For the . . . sans-culottes, liberty and equality had not been offered to the people once and for all in 1789; they were principles which had to be reconquered from day to day . . . . This was the only way in which the happiness of every citizen, . . . universally recognized as the aim of society, could be realized. This process . . . was a fundamental contradiction between the Parisian sans-culotterie and the bourgeoisie, . . . [and their] Revolutionary Government.

From an economic and social point of view, the contradiction was equally insurmountable. Robespierre and many other Montagnards . . .

[said] that the country could not be governed in time of war as in peace, a statement . . . not only politically, but economically valid. The Revo lutionary Government, equally dependent upon both sides, was forced to arbitrate between the conflicting interests of the *possédants*, . . .[who] support[ed] the government, and the wage-earners, instrumental in bringing it to power.

. . . [The] members of the Committee of Public Safety . . . [reluctantly] agreed to . . . a policy of controls and fixed prices. . . . [O]nly the realization that they could not harness the resources of the nation for war without a controlled economy . . . finally convinced them of its necessity as a temporary measure to be discarded once the war had ended. The revolution which they controlled was still, despite its increasingly democratic character, a bourgeois revolution. As such, it would have been absurd to fix the price of manufactured goods without fixing wages. . . . The government . . . had to maintain a certain balance between the owners of business and manufacturing concerns, whose support was indispensable, and the wage-earners.

A controlled economy was also necessary if a complete collapse in the intrinsic value of money was to be avoided. . . . [To] prevent the [currency] from becoming absolutely worthless, . . . the government . . . impose[d] a maximum on wages as well as on manufactured goods. If it had agreed to a rise in wages, this would inevitably have led to a rise in the price of supplies vital to the war effort, since the government had decided not to interfere in private ownership or profits—a policy . . . of a bourgeois revolution. The Committee of Public Safety accepted price-fixing as a means of [preventing] uncontrollable inflation. . . .

This policy depended upon the continuation of the alliance between the Montagnards and the sans-culotterie . . . [A]lthough it adversely affected . . . [their] interests, . . . the bourgeoisie . . . were prepared to play their part in the defence of the Revolution and accepted the dictatorship of the Committees. But, apart from war supplies bought by the State and fodder requisitioned from the peasantry, craftsmen and shopkeepers . . . evaded the provisions of the maximum. A conflict with the wage-earners was inevitable.

The sans-culottes, suffering from . . . inflation and the shortage of food supplies, still looked at the problem . . . of . . . wages and prices as they had done under the *ancien régime*. Their campaign for price-controls and requisitioning does not reflect their concern for national defence so much as their interest in providing themselves . . . with sufficient food. . . . [T]he workers . . . were naturally anxious to take advantage of the relative shortage of labour to demand higher wages without . . . consider[ing] the effect upon prices. . . . [During] Year II, when the sans-culottes were in control of the capital, . . . they were successful in these demands. The government, deciding . . . to act, . . . reviewed the problem of the declining profits of manufacturing concerns, caught between the maximum . . . and an illegal rise in wages. . . . [T]he Committee of Public Safety authorized a rise in the price of goods compared with the scale fixed by the maximum, . . . despite the law. But these higher prices would have had no real effect if wages had continued to rise. The result was the decree. . . enforcing the *maximum des salairies*. Although . . . only . . . introduced to the capital, the Committee of Public Safety. . . had asked . . . [for] a similar drop in wages for agricultural workers. . . . By depriving the wage-earners of the advantages . . . so recently acquired, the [municipality] appeared to be departing from [the government's] mediatory policy. . . . The controlled economy . . . became unbalanced: after Thermidor, the whole structure collapsed.

. . . [I]n a fundamentally bourgeois society the system of arbitration introduced by the Committee of Public Safety would be bound to favour the *possédant* class more than the wage-earners. . . . If it had been . . . possible, the Robespierrists would probably have . . . redress[ed] the balance. There can be little doubt that artisans and shopkeepers would have been less hard on the consumer if, assured of an adequate supply of raw material and food supplies, their sales had guaranteed them a reasonable profit. *Compagnons* and artisans [who] had always maintained that . . . prices should bear a direct relationship to wages, . . . might well have resigned themselves to the maximum if only they could have been sure of receiving the basic necessities of life. . . . But the Revolutionary Government simply did not have the means of regulating the law of supply and demand for manufactured goods and vital food supplies: production methods and transport facilities had not yet been modernized by the capitalist concentration, rationalization, and mechanization of industry. The government had to work within the framework of an outmoded economic structure; war further aggravated the problem of keeping the nation supplied. Insurmountable difficulties arose when the [revolutionary] economic system . . . was introduced to meet the demand for livestock and farm produce. The interests of the peasantry had also to be taken into consideration. Even the regular supply of bread was affected by inadequate means of transport, . . . [and] the absence . . . of concentration in the milling trade—one of the problems which capitalism would eventually solve.

The Revolutionary Government decided . . . that the best it could do . . . was to keep the population of Paris supplied with bread. . . . [L]ocal authorities and consumers had to make what arrangements they could to see that producers and merchants observed the provisions of the maximum. Requisitioning was reserved solely for the benefit of the army. The . . . sans-culottes, discovering that this arrangement did not . . . work . . . in their favour, demanded a rise in wages and resorted to strike action: the Committees, faithful to the tradition of the *ancien régime,* declared such action to be illegal. Thus, at the root of the fundamental contradiction which had arisen between the Revolutionary Government and the popular movement responsible for bringing it to power, lay the failure of an artisanal economy to adapt itself to the demands of a full-scale national war.

The contradictions . . . [of the] sans-culotterie were . . . as important in explaining the collapse of the system . . . as the conflicts which divided the Revolutionary Government and the popular movement. . . . There was a social contradiction between the Jacobins, drawn almost exclusively from the . . . bourgeoisie, and the sans-culottes. . . . But it would be wrong to identify the sans-culotte with the wage-earner despite the fact that wage-earners formed the largest section of the sans-culotterie. The reality is far more complex. The sans-culotterie did not constitute a class, nor was . . . [their] movement based on class differences. . . . [They] joined with a bourgeois minority to form a coalition but there was still an underlying conflict between craftsmen and merchants, enjoying a profit derived from the private ownership of the means of production, and *compagnons* and day-labourers, entirely dependent upon their wages.

The . . . maximum brought this contradiction into the open. Craftsmen and shopkeepers agreed that it was . . . reasonable . . . to force the peasantry to feed the population of the towns; but they protested immediately . . . [when] the maximum began to affect their own interests. . . . By creating a shortage of labour, . . . the war led to a rise in wages: if producers and "middlemen" refused to observe price-fixing, why should the workers. . . ? The . . . revolutionary struggle had welded the unity of the Parisian sans-culotterie and momentarily pushed the conflict of interests into the background: there was no question, however, of suppressing them altogether.

Differences in social outlook complicated the problem. . . . The contradictions within . . . [their] ranks . . . were not simply those which separated the . . . [bourgeoisie] from the salaried workers. Amongst the latter we find . . . those who belonged to the clerical and teaching professions, who . . . regarded themselves as bourgeois. . . . On the other hand, many citizens recognized as . . . [bourgeois] . . . described themselves as "sans-culotte" and acted as such.

The sans-culottes . . . could not, therefore, have been really [class] conscious. . . . Although . . . generally hostile to the new methods of production, it was not always from the same motives—the craftsman . . . [feared falling] to the status of a wage-earner; the *compagnon* detested the monopolist . . . for the rising cost of . . . living. As for the *compagnons*. . . , it would be anachronistic to . . . [call] them . . . class-conscious, since their mentality was still conditioned by the world of the craftsman. . . . The capitalist concentration of industry, by bringing them into daily contact through the factory, had not yet created the mentality which would awaken the feeling of class solidarity.

However, . . . it is possible to detect a certain awareness of class amongst the wage-earners. Entirely dependent upon their employers, they regarded themselves as a distinct social group, not only because of . . . [their] manual . . . work . . . , but also on account of . . . [their] clothes . . . , the food they ate, their pastimes, social habits and . . . living accommodation. . . . [T]hat they were mostly uneducated—education being reserved solely for citizens privileged by birth and wealth—also tended to distinguish them from their fellow citizens, creating a feeling of inferiority, and . . . powerlessness. . . .

. . . [D]evoid of class-consciousness, the Parisian sans-culotterie . . . lacked a really effective weapon of political action—a strictly disciplined party which could only have been created by a drastic purge followed by recruitment on a class basis. This was equally true of the Revolutionary Government, since the Jacobins themselves were not representative of any one social class. The entire régime . . . rested upon an abstract conception of political democracy which largely explains its weakness. The consequences of this were particularly disastrous for the popular movement.

Although . . . many militants . . . tried to discipline the general assemblies and popular societies, leading figures in a number of the Sections aggravated the situation by disputing power amongst themselves. . . . As for the mass of the sans-culotterie, apart from hatred of the aristocracy and the summary methods envisaged for dealing with . . . [them]—chiefly massacre—they . . . [had little] political insight . . . [and] simply wait[ed] to receive the benefits which the Revolution would inevitably bring. They . . . believed that price-controls would help to maintain their standard of living. When they realized that . . . a controlled economy did not meet this requirement, they abandoned it in favour of a new policy. Would the sans-culottes have agreed to drop their demand for higher wages if . . . [the bourgeoisie] had agreed to respect the provisions of the maximum by accepting a margin of profit which the Revolutionary Government considered . . . reasonable[?] The possibility appears . . . extremely remote. The war made certain sacrifices inevitable. . . . [N]o section of the community should try . . . to profit from the circumstances it created . . . to further its own particular interests.

. . . [T]he 9 Thermidor [thus deceived] the sans-culottes. Disillusioned by the effect of the maximum, discontented with the Revolutionary Government, they failed to realize that its collapse would also involve their own ruin. Ten months later . . . , realizing at last what they had lost, they demanded a return to a controlled economy, rose in insurrection for the last time only to be completely crushed and swept from the stage of history.

The internal contradictions of the sans-culotterie, however, do not entirely explain the collapse of the popular movement: its gradual disintegration was inscribed in the dialectical march of history itself. . . . It was . . . inevitable that . . . [it] should have lost momentum: its development, its very success, only strengthened those factors which finally contributed to its defeat.

There was . . . [one] reason of a biological nature. Most . . . militants had been actively engaged in the revolutionary struggle since . . . 1789; . . . participat[ing] in every insurrection. Since . . . 1792, they had redoubled their activity. But the enthusiasm and excitement of the great *journées* involved a certain expenditure of nervous energy which, after the victory, increased the tension and strain involved in the daily life of the militant. Five years of revolution had drained the physical resources of . . . the popular movement. . . . [T]his physical exhaustion . . . also . . . affected the militants always in the thick of the battle. . . . [A]s the war dragged on, . . . apathy communicated itself to the popular movement, depriving it of its vigour and initial enthusiasm.

There was also a psychological reason arising . . . [from] events. . . . The end of the civil war . . . and . . . the realization of victory, led to an understandable relaxation of tension. . . . [The] relief felt by the bourgeoisie cannot be explained by the end of the Terror alone—there was also the prospect of an end to the economic policy of controls and fixed prices, as well as the return of administrative and governmental authority into . . . [their] hands. . . . The people were anxious to reap the benefits of all their effort. . . . In the eyes of the militants, the . . . [Constitution] of . . . 1793 was the symbol of social democracy; they had continuously campaigned for . . . public relief and the right to instruction. But the majority of the people were primarily concerned with their right to subsist. . . . [With] victory . . . in sight, they expected . . . at [the] least, less difficulty in being provided with food as well as a guaranteed daily supply of bread. In fact, victory led to the demobilization of the popular movement.

The Parisian sans-culotterie were also weakened . . . by the dialectical effect of the war effort. . . . [C]onscription . . . deprived the Sections of a considerable number of the youngest, . . . most conscientious and enthusiastic patriots who regarded the defence of the nation as their first civic duty. . . . The lists of citizens capable of carrying arms . . . underlines this sapping of . . . armed strength . . . : men of over 50 and, occasionally, . . . 60 . . . represent a large proportion of the companies formed. . . . The popular movement grew old as a result of these successive enrollments: the inevitable effect on the revolutionary enthusiasm and combative keenness of the Parisian masses can readily be appreciated.

Finally, the dialectical effect of success led to a gradual disintegration of the framework of the popular movement. Many of the . . . militants . . . regarded an official position as the legitimate reward for their militant activity. The stability of the popular movement largely depended upon the satisfaction of these personal interests. . . . But, in such cases, success breeds a new conformity. . . . At first, their revolutionary ardour had distinguished them from the other members of . . . [their] political organizations. . . . But since they had been recruited chiefly from the lowest social ranks of the sans-culotterie, it became necessary . . . for them to be paid a salary. The fear of losing their position . . . soon turned them into willing instruments of the central power. Throughout the Year II, many . . . militants were transformed into salaried civil servants as a result of this process, which was not only a necessary outcome of the internal evolution of the sans-culotterie, but also of the intensification of the class struggle within France. . . . The really politically-minded elements of the sans-culotterie became part of the administrative machinery of the State. . . . At the same time, the democratic ideal was being weakened . . . , the process of bureaucratization gradually paralysing the critical spirit and activity of the masses. The eventual outcome was a relaxation of the control exercised by the popular movement over the [increasingly authoritarian] Revolutionary Government . . . . This bureaucratic encroachment deprived the sans-culottes of many . . . channels through which the popular movement had operated.

These various considerations . . . account for the weakening of the popular movement, and clearly precipitated its collapse.

It would be wrong, however, to draw up a purely negative balance sheet of the popular movement. . . . Doubtless it was impossible for it to attain . . . the egalitarian and popular republic towards which the sans-culottes were moving without any clearly defined programme. . . . [C]ircumstances as well as its own contradictions raised far too many obstacles. Nevertheless, the popular movement . . . contributed towards historical progress by its decisive intervention in support of the bourgeois revolution.

Without the Parisian sans-culotterie, the bourgeoisie could not have triumphed in so radical a fashion. From 1789 to . . . [1794], the sans-culottes were used as an effective weapon of revolutionary combat and national defence. . . . [T]he popular movement made possible the installation of the Revolutionary Government and, consequently, the defeat of the counter-revolution in France and the allied coalition in Europe. . . .

[In wider] perspective, its intervention in the course of history does not appear to be less significant. The success of the popular movement . . . led to the organization of the Terror which struck such an irreparable blow to the old social order. The upper bourgeoisie of the *ancien régime*, founded on commercial capital and linked in some ways with the old social and political system of the feudal aristocracy, failed to survive the upheaval. In the Year II, the shopkeeper and craftsman element of the sans-culotterie, . . . became the most effective weapon in the struggle for the destruction of outmoded methods of production and the social relationships founded upon them. . . . The Terror cleared the way for the introduction of new relationships of production. In the capitalist society born of the Revolution, industry was destined to dominate commerce: the function of commercial capital, against which the sans-culottes had fought so bitterly in the Year II, would be subordinated henceforth to the sole productive form of capital—industrial capital.

As for the sans-culottes themselves, . . . economic evolution would eventually lead to a new division of their ranks. Of the small and fairly substantial producers and merchants who had filled the leading positions in the popular movement . . . , some would . . . become industrial capitalists, others would . . . swell the ranks of the wage-earners. Many would retain their interest in the workshop and the store. Economic freedom accelerated the concentration of small concerns, transforming the material conditions of social life, but altering . . . the structure of the . . . "popular" classes. Craftsmen and *compagnons* had a dim awareness of the fate which awaited them . . . , the latter realizing that mechanization would increase the risks of unemployment; the former that capitalist concentration would lead to the closing down of their workshops and transform them into wage-earners. Throughout the nineteenth century, both craftsmen and shopkeepers defended themselves desperately against this threat. It would be interesting to know, in this respect, the part played by the proletariat . . . from the *journées* of 1848 to the Commune of 1871, and that played by the popular classes of the traditional type. . . .

Thus, as we are reminded of the dramatic character of class struggles in the Year II by an examination of their ultimate consequences, so we are able to distinguish more clearly the original characteristics of the national history of contemporary France.

Revolutionary Festival. Demarchy, Pierre-Antoine (Attributed to) Fête de l'Être Suprème au Champ du Mars, 8 Juin, 1794 (Festival of the Supreme Being). Giraudon/Art Resource, N.Y. Musée de la Ville de Paris, Musée Carnavalet, Paris, France.

IV Post-Marxist Interpretations

François Furet

The Beginnings of Modern Mass Politics

François Furet (1927–1997) has succeeded Georges Lefebvre as the foremost authority on the French Revolution. In historiographical perspective, his position was unusual because, unlike earlier authorities, he did not hold the official chair in revolutionary history at the Sorbonne. Furet made his name outside the regular French university system as a leader of the *Annales* school and went on to head an important center of *annaliste* research, the *Ecole pratique des Hautes Etudes*. He then directed the *Institut Raymond Aron* in Paris. Furet's success as a post-Marxist historian followed a major change in his political life. In his youth he was a communist—belonging to the same party cell as Albert Soboul. Like other French intellectuals, he broke with the far left in 1956 after the Soviet suppression of a democratic rebellion in Hungary. His abandonment of communism led to a rejection of

Marxism and eventually to a disillusionment with revolutionary politics that is apparent in these selections.

Interpreting the French Revolution

The French Revolution is over.

Historians engaged in the study of the Merovingian Kings or the Hundred Years War are not asked at every turn to present their research permits. So long as they can give proof of having learned the techniques of the trade, the discussion of their findings is a matter for scholars and scholarship only. . . . The historian of the French Revolution, on the other hand, must produce more than proof of competence. He must show his colours. . . . [W]hat he writes about the French Revolution is assigned a meaning and label even before he starts working: the writing is taken as his *opinion*, a form of judgment that is not required when dealing with the Merovingians but indispensable when it comes to treating 1789 or 1793. . . . He is labelled a royalist, a liberal or a Jacobin. Once he has given the password his history has a specific meaning, a determined place and a claim to legitimacy. . . .

What is surprising here is not that the history of the Revolution, like all histories, involves intellectual presuppositions. There is no such thing as "innocent" historical interpretation, and written history is itself located in history, indeed *is* history, the product of an inherently unstable relationship between the present and the past. . . . But if all history implies a choice, . . . it does not follow that such a choice always involves a preconceived opinion about the subject chosen. For that to happen, . . . the subject must arouse in the historian and his public a capacity for identifying with political or religious passions that have survived the passing of time. . . . The passing of time may weaken that sense of identification, or on the contrary preserve and even strengthen it, depending on

François Furet, The Beginnings of Mass Democracy, selections from *Interpreting the French Revolution*, Elborh Forster, translator, (Cambridge, U.K., Cambridge University Press, © 1981) 1–6, 8–17. Reprinted with the permission of Cambridge University Press.

whether the subject treated by the historian does or does not continue to express the issues of his own times, his values and his choices. The theme of Clovis and the Frankish invasions was of burning interest in the eighteenth century because the historians of that era saw it as the key to the social structure of their own time. They thought that the Frankish invasions were the origin of the division between nobility and commoners, the conquerors being the progenitors of the nobility and the conquered those of the commoners. Today the Frankish invasions have lost all relevance, since we live in a society where nobility has ceased to act as a social principle. No longer serving as the mirror of an existing world, the Frankish invasions have lost the eminent place in historiography that [the] world once assigned to them, and have moved from the realm of social polemic to that of learned debate.

. . . Beginning in 1789 the obsession with origins, the underlying thread of all national history, came to be centred precisely on the Revolutionary break. Just as the great invasions were the myth of a society dominated by the nobility, the saga of its origins, so 1789 became the birth date, the year zero of a new world founded on equality. The substitution of one birth date for another, . . . the . . . definition of a new national identity, is perhaps one of the *abbé* Sieyès's greatest strokes of genius. [His *What Is the Third Estate?* tells] us not only that the nobles' proprietary claims over the nation are fictitious, but also that, even if those claims were well founded, the Third Estate would have only to restore the social contract in force before the conquest, to . . . obliterate centuries of violent usurpation. . . . It is a matter of constituting a "true" origin for the nation by giving a legitimate date of birth to equality: that is what 1789 is all about. . . . But Revolutionary historiography has had the function of keeping alive that account of society's origins. Consider, for example, the manner in which studies are divided for the teaching of history in France. "Modern" history ends in 1789 with what the Revolution christened the "Ancien Régime." . . . Thereafter, the Revolution and the Empire form separate and autonomous fields of study. [T]he quarter-century separating the storming of the Bastille from the Battle of Waterloo . . . is both the end of the "modern" era and the indispensable introduction to the "contemporary" period, which begins in 1815, the period of transition that gives meaning to both, the watershed from which the history of France either flows back to its past or rushes toward its future. By remaining faithful to the conscious experience of the actors of the Revolution, despite all the intellectual absurdities implicit in such a chronological framework, our academic institutions have invested the French Revolution and the historian of that period with the mysteries of our national history. The year 1789 is the key to what lies both upstream and downstream. . . .

But it is not enough to say that the Revolution explains what lies downstream—the period beginning in 1815 that the Revolution is supposed to have created. . . . The Revolution does not simply "explain" our contemporary history; it *is* our contemporary history. . . . The Revolution has a birth but no end. . . . It contains a promise of such magnitude that it becomes boundlessly elastic. Even in the short term, it is not easy to "date": . . . the historian . . . may encapsulate the Revolution within the year 1789, seeing in it the year in which the essential features of the Revolution's final outcome were fixed . . . or he may go up to 1794 and the execution of Robespierre, stressing the dictatorship of the Revolutionary committees and of the *sections*, the Jacobin saga and the egalitarian crusade of the year II. Or he may use 18 Brumaire 1799 as the terminus. He may even integrate the Napoleonic adventure into the Revolution. A case can be made for any of these time frames.

. . . One could also envisage a much longer history of the French Revolution, extending even farther downstream, and ending not before the late nineteenth or early twentieth century. For the entire history of nineteenth-century France can be seen as a struggle between Revolution and Restoration. . . . Only the victory of the republicans over the monarchists at the beginning of the Third Republic marked the definitive victory of the Revolution in the French countryside. . . . Integration of France's villages and peasant culture into the republican nation on the basis of the principles of 1789 was to take at least a century. . . . Republican Jacobinism, dictated for so long from Paris, won its victory only after it could count on the majority vote of rural France at the end of the nineteenth century. . . . But its electoral "victory" did not mean that it was honoured or assimilated as a value, something so unanimously accepted as to be no longer debated. The celebration of the principles of 1789, the object of so much pedagogical solicitude, or the condemnation of the crimes of 1793, which usually serves as a screen for the rejection of those principles, has remained at the core of the set of notions that shaped French political life until the middle of the twentieth century. Fascism, by its explicit rejection of the values of the French Revolution, gave an international dimension to that conflict of ideas. . . . France in the 1940s was still a country whose citizens had to sort out their history, date the birth of their nation, choose between the Ancien Régime and the Revolution. . . .

The reference to 1789 disappeared from French politics with the defeat of fascism. Today the discourse of both Right and Left celebrates liberty and equality, and the debate about the value of 1789 no longer involves any real political stakes or even strong psychological commitment. But if such unanimity exists, it is because the political debate has simply been transferred . . . from the Revolution of the past to the one that is to come. By shifting the conflict to the future, it is possible to create an apparent consensus about the legacy of the past. But in fact that legacy, which is one of conflict, lives on by dominating the representations of the future. . . . For the French Revolution is not only the Republic. It is also an unlimited promise of equality and a special form of change; . . . not a national institution but a matrix of universal history. The nineteenth century believed in the Republic. The twentieth century believes in *the* Revolution. The same founding event is present in both images.

The socialists of the late nineteenth century conceived of their action as both coordinated with and distinct from that of the republicans. Coordinated, because they felt that the Republic was the prerequisite of socialism. Distinct, because they saw political democracy as a historical stage of social organisation that was destined to be superseded. They perceived 1789 not as the foundation of a stable State but as a movement whose logic required it to go beyond that first stage. The struggle for democracy and the struggle for socialism were the two successive forms assumed by a dynamic of equality originating in the French Revolution. Thus was formed a linear history of human emancipation whose first stage had been the maturing and the dissemination of the value of 1789, while the second stage was to fulfill the promise of 1789 by a new . . . socialist revolution. This two-pronged mechanism, implicit in Jaurès's socialist history of the Revolution, was unable to give an account of the second stage which was still in the future.

All that changed in 1917. . . . [T]he socialist revolution had a face. [T]he French Revolution ceased to be the model for a future that was possible, . . . but as yet devoid of content. Instead, it became the mother of a real . . . event: October 1917. [T]he Russian Bolsheviks never . . . lost sight of that filiation. But by the same token the historians of the French Revolution projected into the past their feelings or their judgments about 1917, and tended to highlight those features of the first revolution that seemed to presage those of the second. At the very moment when Russia . . . took the place of France . . . as the vanguard of history, because it had inherited from France . . . the idea that a nation is *chosen* for revolution, the historiographical discourses about the two revolutions became fused and infected each other. The Bolsheviks were given Jacobin ancestors, and the Jacobins were made to anticipate the communists. . . .

[F]or almost two hundred years, . . . the history of the French Revolution has been a story of beginnings and so a discourse about identity. In the nineteenth century that history was virtually indistinguishable from the event it purported to retrace, for the drama begun in 1789 was played over and over, generation after generation, for the same stakes and around the same symbols, an unbroken memory that became an object of worship or of horror. Not only did the Revolution found the political culture that makes "contemporary" France intelligible, but it also bequeathed to France conflicts between legitimacies and a virtually inexhaustible stock of political debates. It was not until the end of the century with the founding of the Third Republic, that the Revolution began to acquire academic respectability. . . . [T]he Sorbonne offered in 1886 a "course" in the history of the Revolution, taught by Alphonse Aulard. . . .

Did the Revolution, once it was officially taught, become national property, like the Republic? As in the case of the Republic, the answer is . . . yes and no. Yes, because in a sense, with the founding of the Republic on the vote of the people . . . the French Revolution was finally "over" sanctioned by the legal and democratic consent of citizens. Yet, on the other hand, the republican consensus built on the political culture born in 1789 was conservative and obtained by default from the ruling classes, . . . and from the peasants. . . . However, a victorious French Revolution, finally accepted as a closed chapter of history, as a patrimony and a national institution, contradicted the image of change it implied, for that image involved a far more radical promise than lay schools and the separation of church and State. Once the Revolution had succeeded in imposing the Republic, it became clear that it was much more than the Republic. It was a pledge that no event could fully redeem.

That is why, in the very last years of the nineteenth century, . . . socialist thinking seized upon the notion of the Revolution as prefiguration. Aulard had criticised Taine for reconstructing the "Origins of contemporary France." Jaurès saw the French Revolution as the beginning of a world that would give birth again. . . . The Russian Revolution of October 1917 seemed made to order to fulfill that expectation of a renewed beginning. Henceforth—as Mathiez made quite explicit—the inventory of the Jacobin legacy was overlaid with an implicit discourse for or against Bolshevism, a development that hardly made for intellectual flexibility. In fact, the overlap of those two political debates extended the nineteenth into the twentieth century, and transferred onto communism and anti-communism the passions previously aroused by the king of France and by the Republic. . . . Those passions were re-implanted in the present . . . from the events of 1789 or rather 1793. But in becoming the pre-figuration of . . . communist revolution, in which the famous "bourgeoisie" would not come to confiscate the victory of the people, the French Revolution . . . simply renewed its myth, which became the poorer for it. . . .

I should like to avoid a misunderstanding here: that contamination of the past by the present . . . , which . . . characterises a Revolution conceived as a starting point, does not preclude partial progress in certain areas of scholarship. . . . [S]ince the end of the nineteenth century, each generation of historians has had to do its share of archival work. In that respect, the emphasis on the popular classes and their action in the French Revolution has brought advances in our knowledge of the role played by the peasants and the urban masses. . . . But those advances have not appreciably modified the analysis . . . of the "French Revolution" taken as a whole. . . .

Take the problem of the peasantry, . . . an area . . . in which Georges Lefebvre made his main contribution to historiography. . . . From his analysis of the question and of peasant behaviour, . . . came two ideas: first, that there were several revolutions within . . . *the* French Revolution; second, that the peasant revolution was not only largely autonomous and distinct . . . , but also anti-capitalist, . . . traditionalist and backward-looking. Those two ideas are difficult to reconcile with a vision of the French Revolution as a homogeneous social and political phenomenon opening the way to a capitalist or bourgeois future that the "Ancien Régime" had blocked.

. . . Georges Lefebvre also noted that, in the . . . Ancien Régime, capitalism['s] "spirit" had deeply penetrated the landed aristocracy. Consequently, . . . the same peasantry could successively come into conflict with the seigneurs in 1789 and with the Republic in 1793 without the "Revolution" having changed anything in [its] nature. . . . "The Ancien Régime," [he wrote] "started the agrarian history of France on the road to capitalism; the Revolution abruptly completed the task that the

Ancien Régime had begun." But this conclusion, which sounds almost like Tocqueville, does not lead . . . [Lefebvre] to a critique of the very concept of revolution. He does not try to understand how one might reconcile the idea of radical change with that of an actual continuity. He simply juxtaposes . . . an *analysis* of the peasant problem at the end of the eighteenth century and a contradictory *tradition* that consists in seeing the Revolution, through the eyes of its participants, as a . . . time both qualitatively new and different, as homogeneous as a brand-new fabric. It would not be difficult to show that the twentieth century's greatest university scholar of the French Revolution, the man who had a richer knowledge and a surer grasp of the period than anyone, based his synthetic vision of the immense event . . . on nothing more than the convictions of a militant adherent . . . of the Popular Front. . . .

Scholarship . . . is never sufficient in itself to modify the conceptualisation of a problem or an event. [U]nder the influence of Jaurès, 1917 and Marxism, [it could] take a turn toward social history and conquer new territories in the twentieth century. Yet it remains attached . . . to the old recital of origins, which was both renewed and made more rigid by deposits of socialist thinking. For the takeover of the history of the Revolution by social history . . . has only shifted elsewhere the question of origins: the advent of the bourgeoisie has been substituted for the advent of liberty, but it remains no less an advent. . . . [T]he historiographical shift from a political to a social emphasis shows the lasting power of the notion that the Revolution was an advent, precisely because such a shift is even more incompatible with "revolution." . . . That intellectual contradiction is masked by the celebration of the beginnings. For in the twentieth century . . . the historian of the French Revolution commemorates the event he narrates or studies. The new materials he brings to bear are no more than supplementary ornaments offered up his tradition. . . .

[I]n France the Revolution . . . was dignified as an academic specialty not because it contains demonstrably special problems, but because it allows the historian to identify with his heroes and "his" event. . . . Mother of the political culture into which all of us are born, the Revolution allows everyone to look for filiations. But all those histories, which have bitterly fought each other for the last two hundred years in the name of the origins of their opposition, in fact share a common ground: they are all histories in quest of identity. No Frenchman living in the second half of the twentieth century can perceive the French Revolution *from the outside.*

One cannot practise ethnology in so familiar a landscape. . . . [A]ny attempt to consider it from an intellectual "distance" is immediately seen as hostility—as if identification, be it a claim to descent or rejection, were inevitable. . . . Yet we must try to break the vicious circle of that commemorative historiography. . . . [P]eople of my generation brought up under the double influence of existentialism and Marxism, stress that the historian is rooted in his own times. . . . Continued harping on those truisms—however useful for combating the positivist illusion that "objectivity" is possible—is liable to perpetuate . . . polemics that have had their day. Today the historiography of the Revolution is hampered . . . by mental laziness and pious rehashing. [I]t is time to strip it of the elementary significations it has bequeathed to its heirs, and to restore to it . . . intellectual curiosity and the free search for knowledge about the past. [A] time will come when the political beliefs that have sustained the disputes within our societies over the last two centuries will seem as surprising to men as the inexhaustible variety and violence of the religious conflicts in Europe between the fifteenth and the seventeenth century seem to us. The very fact that the study of the French Revolution could become a political arena will probably be seen as an explanatory factor and as a psychological commitment of a bygone age. . . . But that "cooling off" of the "French Revolution" is not to be expected from the mere passing of time. One can define the conditions needed to bring it about, and even spot the first signs of it, in our own time. I do not claim that those conditions will at last provide us with historical *objectivity*; but they are already deeply modifying the relation between the historian of the French Revolution and his subject, making less spontaneous and therefore less compelling [his] identification with the actors, his commemoration of the founders, or his execration of the deviants. . . .

I can see two routes . . . , which I consider beneficial for the renewal of the history of the Revolution. The first is emerging . . . ineluctably, from the contradictions between the myth of Revolution and the societies that have experienced it . . . the second is inherent in the mutations of historical knowledge. . . .

The impact of . . . the contrast between myth and reality is becoming increasingly clear. I am writing these lines in the spring of 1977, at a time when the criticism of Soviet totalitarianism, and more generally of all power claiming its source in Marxism, is no longer the monopoly . . . of right-wing thought and has become a central theme in the reflections of the Left. . . .

[L]eft-wing culture, once it has made up its mind to think about the facts—namely, the disastrous experience of twentieth-century communism—in terms of its own values, has come to take a critical view of its own ideology, interpretations, hopes and rationalisations. It is in left-wing culture that the sense of distance between history and the Revolution is taking root, precisely because it was the Left that believed that all of history was contained in the promises of the Revolution. . . .

Solzhenitsyn's work has become the basic historical reference for the Soviet experience, ineluctably locating the issue of the Gulag at the very core of the revolutionary endeavour. Once that happened, the Russian example was bound to turn around, like a boomerang, to strike its French "origin." In 1920, Mathiez justified Bolshevik violence by the French precedent, in the name of comparable circumstances. Today the Gulag is leading to a rethinking of the Terror precisely because the two undertakings are seen as identical. The two revolutions remain connected; but while fifty years ago they were systematically absolved on the basis of excuses related to "circumstances," that is external phenomena that had nothing to do with the nature of the two revolutions, they are today, by contrast, accused of being, consubstantially, systems of meticulous constraint over men's bodies and minds. . . .

Thus the exorbitant privilege assigned to the idea of revolution . . . is beginning to lose its standing as a self-evident fact. Academic historiography—in which the communists, almost as a matter of course, have taken over from the socialists and the radicals as the keepers of republican commemoration—still clings to that privilege and does not make light of its traditions. Holding on ever more closely to their short period of "ancestral" history as if it were their social patrimony, those historians are not simply faced with the conceptual devaluation of their patrimony among intellectuals; they have trouble embracing, or even imagining, the intellectual changes that are indispensable to progress in the historiography of the Revolution. . . . In fact, this historiography should be made to show, not its colours, but its concepts. History in general has ceased to be a body of knowledge where the "facts" are supposed to speak for themselves, once they have been established according to the rules. It must state the problem it seeks to analyse, the data it uses, its working hypotheses and the conclusions at which it arrives. If the history of the Revolution is the last one to adopt that method of *explicitness*, it is partly because all its traditions have drawn it, generation after generation, toward the myth of the beginnings; but, in addition, that myth has been taken over and canonised by a "Marxist" rationalisation that does not change its character in any fundamental way but, on the contrary, consolidates the myth by making it appear a conceptual elaboration having the elemental power derived from its function as a new beginning. . . .

That rationalisation does not exist in Marx's writings, which do not include any systematic interpretation of the French Revolution; it is instead the product of a confused encounter between Bolshevism and Jacobinism, predicated upon a linear notion of human progress and punctuated by the two successive "liberations," nested like a set of Russian dolls. The most hopelessly confused aspect of the "Marxist" vulgate of the French Revolution is the juxtaposition of the old idea of the advent of a new age — the seminal idea of the French Revolution itself — with an enlargement of the field of history that is part of the very substance of Marxism. In fact Marxism — or perhaps one should say the kind of Marxism that penetrated the history of the French Revolution with Jaurès — has shifted the centre of gravity of the *problem* of the Revolution toward economic and social matters. It seeks to root in the progress of capitalism both the slow rise of the Third Estate (a theme dear to the historiography of the Restoration) and the apotheosis of 1789. [It] includes economic life and the fabric of society as a whole in the myth of a revolutionary break: before the Revolution, feudalism; after, capitalism; before, the nobility; after, the bourgeoisie. But since those propositions are neither demonstrable, nor in fact even likely, and since, in any case, they shatter the accepted chronological framework, the Marxist approach amounts to no more than joining an analysis of causes carried out in the economic and social mode to . . . a narrative of events written in the political and ideological mode.

[T]hat incoherence . . . underscor[es] one of the essential problems of the historiography of the Revolution, . . . how to fit the various levels of interpretation into the chronology of the event. If one is determined to preserve the idea of an objective break in the continuity of history, . . . one is indeed bound to end up with a number of absurdities. . . . One could say . . . that between 1789 and 1794 the entire political system of France was radically transformed because the old monarchy then came to an end. But the idea that between those same dates the social or economic fabric of the nation was renewed from top to bottom is obviously much less plausible. The "Revolution," then, is not a useful concept for making such assertions even if it is true that some of the causes of the Revolution were not exclusively political or intellectual. . . .

Any conceptualisation of the history of the Revolution must begin with a critique of the idea . . . that it was a radical change and the origin of a new era. So long as that critique is absent from a history of the Revolution, superimposing a more social or more economic interpretation upon a purely political interpretation will not change what all those histories share, a fidelity to the revolutionary consciousness and experience of the nineteenth and twentieth centuries. Nonetheless, the social and economic deposits added by Marxism . . . bring into sharp focus the dilemmas of any history of the Revolution that remains founded on the personal consciousness of those who made that history.

It is here that I encounter Tocqueville, and that I take the measure of his genius. . . . Tocqueville, and Tocqueville alone, . . . wrote a *different* history of the Revolution, basing it upon a critique of revolutionary ideology and of what he saw as the French Revolution's illusion about itself. . . . "So you think that the French Revolution is a sudden break in our national history?" he asked his contemporaries. In reality it is the fruition of our past. It has completed the work of the monarchy. Far from being a break, it can be understood only within and by historical continuity. It is the objective achievement of that continuity, even though it was experienced subjectively as a radical break. . . .

Thus, Tocqueville developed a radical critique of any history of the French Revolution based only on the consciousness of the revolutionaries themselves. . . . If Tocqueville never wrote a real history of the French Revolution it was, I believe, because he conceptualised only one aspect of that history, namely its continuity. He presented the Revolution in terms of its outcome, not as an event; as a process, not as a break.

At the time of his death, he was working on his second volume and was confronting the problem of how to account for that break. . . . But what remains fundamental in the work of this deductive and abstract mind, providentially wandering in a field suffused with the narrative method, is that it escaped the tyranny of the historical actors' own conception of their experience and the myth of origins. . . .

That is why his book is even more important for the method it suggests than for the thesis it advances. Tocqueville constantly examines the discrepancy he discerns between the intentions of the actors and the historical role they played. For Tocqueville, there was a gulf between the Revolution's true outcome and the revolutionaries' intentions. . . . That is why, in my opinion, *L'Ancien Régime et la Révolution* remains the most important book of the entire historiography of the French Revolution. It is also why it has always been, for more than a century now, the stepchild of that historiography, more often cited than read, and more read than understood. Whether of the Right or of the Left, royalist or republican, conservative or Jacobin, the historians of the French Revolution have taken the revolutionary discourse at face value because they themselves have remained locked into that discourse. They keep putting on the Revolution the different faces assumed by the event itself in an unending commentary on a conflict whose meaning, so they think, the Revolution itself has explained to us once and for all through the pronouncements of its heroes. . . . Into this game of mirrors, where the historian and the Revolution believe each other's words literally, and where the Revolution has become history's protagonist, the absolutely trustworthy Antigone of the new era, Tocqueville introduces a doubt that strikes at the very heart of the matter: what if that discourse about a radical break reflects no more than the illusion of change? . . . The answer to that question is not simple, nor would answering it take care of the whole history of the Revolution. Yet it is probably indispensable to a conceptualisation of that history. Its importance can be measured negatively: unless the historian comes to grips with it, he is bound to execrate or to celebrate, both of which are ways of commemorating. . . .

Revolutionary France, 1770–1880

The French Revolution began in 1798, but there is no clear date for its end. It has no American-style definitive close like the 1787 constitution, which became the sacred ark of the nation. Nor does it claim to live on indefinitely, in Soviet fashion, but it falls somewhere between the two extremes. Like the American Revolution, and at almost the same epoch, its desire was to found, within the law, a body politic of free and equal individuals; but the French Revolution was continually revising the terms of the undertaking, deferring its final outcome or success, and so reproducing *ad infinitum* the fear that it has been dispossessed.

One can trace a short-term history of its course, stopping at the fall of Robespierre or the arrival of Bonaparte. The method I have chosen in this book is . . . to write an extended version, spread over [a] hundred years and more. . . . The central theme is that only the victory of republicans

Revolutionary France, 1770–1880, Antonia Nevill, translator, (Cambridge, Mass., Blackwell Publishers, 1992), pp. i–x, 3–4, 6–16, 29–30, 59–61, 71–77, 80–81, 97–98, 142–150, 477–480.

over monarchists in 1876–7 provided modern France with a regime that established in lasting form the full range of the principles of 1789 ensuring not only civic equality but also political liberty. Thus I have attempted to encompass and depict the first century of democracy in France.

This falls into two great cycles, widely commented upon in the nineteenth century. The first covers the French Revolution (in the narrow sense), from the *ancien régime* to the Napoleonic Empire. . . .

In 1814, however, the Empire, vanquished by a European coalition, inaugurated a second chain of events through which the first began anew, in fresh circumstances, but still haunted by the memory of what had happened before. . . .

[B]etween the two cycles of this long period lies an essential difference. At the end of the eighteenth century, the Revolution smashed the entire structure of the *ancien régime*. In the nineteenth century, the prefects survived the revolutions. The country's administrative constitution . . . stood throughout the whole era like an inviolable monument. Thus, in its own way, the centralized state ensured the continuity of public authority and national unity; but at the same time it constantly intensified post-revolutionary civil struggles over the 1789 heritage. Being the vital centre of the nation, it had only to seize control to become the master of society. Paradoxically, the points on which the French were in agreement only inflamed their differences; the conservative in them was also the revolutionary, bound by a common conception of the state. This is exactly what we learn from de Tocqueville, when he remarks that Napoleon "by constructing this powerful hierarchy . . . suddenly made revolutions easier for us, yet at the same time less destructive."

By establishing the state, through universal suffrage in the name of the equality of its citizens, the republicans of the 1870s managed to entrench the law on a lasting basis in the sovereignty of the people. Thus they at last completed the task begun in 1789.

The Monarchy

The French revolutionaries gave a name to what they had abolished. They christened it the *ancien régime*. In doing so they were defining not so much what they had suppressed, but more what they wanted to create—a complete break with the past, which was to be cast into the shadows of barbarism. Of the past itself, its nature and its history, the revolutionaries said scarcely more than the imprecatory phrase they used to describe it, . . . "night," as opposed to the day which was just dawning.

The notion of a past entirely corrupted by usurpation and irrationality was surely one of the paths by which [Sieyès'] pamphlet . . . *What Is the Third Estate?* penetrated public opinion rapidly and deeply. So the historian studying the history of France . . . [asks] this question about the term *ancien régime:* what did the men of 1789 understand by it to damn it so utterly? The enigmatic strangeness of the French *tabula rasa,* which so disconcerted and angered the British Whig parliamentarian, Edmund Burke, in 1790, can still serve as an introduction to the later years of eighteenth-century France.

As of old, the king of France was an absolute monarch. The king was the fountainhead of all public authority, all legislation [and] . . . accountable to God alone. . . . Thus behind the power of kings, however absolute, lay the essential constraints of an even greater power . . . beside which even monarchs were as nothing. This of itself entailed the obligation to behave as a Christian sovereign.

The respect for divine law, however, was not the only law to which the king of France had to submit, for all that he was absolute monarch and not bound by any human law. Over the centuries something had developed which it is perhaps too much to call a constitution, yet which appears in retrospect as a set of custom-based principles . . . primogeniture, the Catholic faith . . . , respect for the liberty and property of his subjects, the integrity of the royal domain. Above the law, yet subject to law, . . . the French monarchy, a state based on law, must not be confused with despotism, which is the unfettered power of a master. . . .

. . . Under Louis XIV it had noticeably shifted toward deification of the king himself. . . .

However, the idea of a king as the sole repository of sovereignty, in keeping with ancient tradition, and the concept of a monarchy both absolute and enshrined in custom . . . had undeniably survived absolutist exaggeration. . . .

However, the nature of royalty changed more rapidly than its image. Dominated by wars, always short of money, the monarchy, while taking care to keep a tight hold on the reins, continued to spread an administrative network throughout the country in order to mobilize men and wealth more effectively. Gradually it [established] . . . the authority of a sovereign set at the heart of a more or less centralized administration capped by a council of ministers. . . . [T]he king had become the head of a government; lord of lords, he was also chief of a burgeoning bureaucracy.

. . . At the precise moment when the king formed the focal point of his vast personal theatre, known as the court, he simultaneously became

the most elevated person in the huge, abstract machinery of administration. . . . The second part of his office overlapped the first the more
easily because absolutism, in making a cult of royalty, tended to weaken
its traditional image, while it firmly established the institution in the fulfillment of its modern functions.

. . . [T]he chief innovation of this development lay in its effects on
society. On the one hand, it certainly tended towards the leveling off of
an aristocratic world inherited from feudal times. . . . [The] top civil servants of the monarchy, had been constantly irritated by the obstacles
raised against royal administration by privileges . . . [T]heir action
aimed at uniting the nation into so many individuals all bound by the
same laws, the same regulations and the same taxes.

It was not enough that the monarchy had gradually deprived the
aristocracy of its political rights . . . ; it was not enough that it had reduced the greatest families in the kingdom to begging for a glance from
the king at Versailles, it had to exercise over all the bodies and orders in
the realm, starting with the nobility, a standardizing process which in
this case was inseparable from the formation of the nation. On the other
hand, at the very time when it was seeking uniformity, the administrative monarchy multiplied the obstacles to it; here lay what is without
doubt its chief contradiction.

. . . [The] kings of France did not build and extend their power over
a passive society; on the contrary, they had to negotiate each increase . . .
with a social world organized on the aristocratic principle. . . .

The king's need for money was immense. . . . [T]he Bourbons . . .
had raised money from all possible sources. . . . [and] gradually set up
a centralized administration. . . . But taxation was not enough to meet
requirement. The monarchy also made money from the privileges . . .
of various social bodies. . . .

The administrative monarchy was therefore an unstable compromise between the construction of a modern state and an aristocratic
society remodeled by that state, . . . [and] reduced to the mere enjoyment of exemptions or honours. On the other hand, it separated the
orders of society into castes by converting them into cash, weighing
each privilege at its highest price. . . .

The eighteenth-century had aggravated the tensions of this mixed
system of absolute monarchy and aristocratic society. . . . None of the
Great King's successors was in a position to control even the court, let
alone Paris. Everything conspired to enfeeble them: intellectual activity,

the growth of wealth, the emergence of public opinion. However, the old French monarchy, simultaneously very ancient and very new . . . remained for a long time the centre of a matchless civilization. . . .

The Nobility

. . . [The] state remained bound to the social compromise carefully developed over the preceding centuries, [but] . . . it was completely destroying the spirit of that society . . . [which] was falling apart under the joint pressure of economic improvement, the increasing number of individual initiatives and aspirations and the spread of culture. Money and merit were coming up against "birth"; in their path they found the state, guaranteeing privileges. . . .

There lay the origins of the social and political crisis of eighteenth-century France, giving rise to a part of the French Revolution and its prolongation into the nineteenth century. Neither the French king nor the nobility put forward a policy which might unite state and . . . society around a minimum consensus. . . . [R]oyal action oscillated between despotism and capitulation. . . . But if the state was unable to point the way, . . . the nobles were equally impotent, since they had lost their identity together with their social autonomy. They had but one principle left to reunify them: to defend their privileges. . . .

Even the crisis of 1789 would be powerless to rebuild their unity, save in the imagination of the Third Estate ideologists. . . . If the French Revolution . . . met with such poorly co-ordinated resistance at its start, it was because the political *ancien régime* had died before it was struck down. . . .

The Enlightenment

What can be said of the intellectual sphere? The society which the monarchy had fragmented was united by the culture of the century: public opinion was burgeoning in the twilight of the court and in the birth of a formidable power—which would last until universal suffrage was achieved—the omnipotence of Paris. The nobles of both Versailles and the capital read the same books [as] the cultured bourgeoisie. . . . : Voltaire's *Lettres philosophiques*, d'Alembert's *Encyclopédie*, Rousseau's *Nouvelle Héloise*.

The monarchy . . . had separated the elites by isolating them in rival strongholds. In contrast, ideas gave them a meeting-point, with special privileged places: the salons, academies, . . . cafés and theatres, an enlightened community which combined breeding, wealth and talent, and whose kings were the writers. An unstable and seductive combination of intelligence and rank, wit and snobbery, this world was capable of criticizing everything, including and not least itself; it was unwittingly presiding over a tremendous reshaping of ideas and values. . . .

The new intellectual realm was the workshop where the notion of *ancien régime* would be forged. . . . What characterized it in the political field was . . . the forcefulness of [its] condemnation . . . [of] contemporary life—including the Church and religion. There was a violently anticlerical and anti-Catholic side to the philosophy of the French Enlightenment which had no equivalent in European thought. . . .

France had her religious wars, but no victorious Reformation. . . . [T]he Church and the absolute monarchy together formed an almost natural target for the attacks of a "philosophy" which was all the more radical for not being built, as in England, on the foundation of a previous religious revolution.

. . . [The] Revolution . . . did not deliberately seek conflict with the Catholic Church; but . . . the century's culture had borne it in that direction, and it had taken that path as if naturally, without, however, having . . . weighed the consequences.

. . . [The] other great culprit was the absolute monarchy, . . . incapable of appearing before the court of reason. . . . [A] monarchy per se, . . . encumbered with "gothic" prejudices, the distributor of arbitrary privileges, reigning over a kingdom filled with vestiges of feudalism. It mattered little that France was in reality the least feudal country in Europe, as a result of the very activities of the administrative state, and that it was also the country where criticism of the state by reason was the most systematic: suddenly the remains of feudalism . . . were perceived as all the more oppressive precisely because they were residual. . . .

Royalty, which was too modern for what it had preserved and refashioned of the traditional, and too traditional for what it already had in the way of modern administration, tended to turn itself into the scapegoat for an increasingly independent society, which was nevertheless still bound hand and foot to the government, deprived of political rights and representation, trying to work out its autonomy in terms of government by reason. . . .

The monarchy had lost its authority over opinion. . . . Paris produced an ever-increasing number of pamphlets and debates, dominated by the writers, orchestrated by the salons and cafés. . . . The Versailles bureaucracy, by not associating the elites of the city with the government of the kingdom, transformed the literary life of the capital into a forum for the reform of the state. . . .

At the beginning of the twentieth century, Augustin Cochin's great contribution was to grasp . . . [that] the 1789 elections . . . revolved around a small committee which worked out the "Patriot" platform: doubling of the Third Estate, voting by head, and also exclusion of the ennobled and seigneurs' agents from commoners' assemblies. . . . From this starting-point, the Patriot committee infiltrated all established bodies . . . members of the legal profession, doctors, guilds, finally the town hall. In the end, the document concocted in a small committee had become the unanimous wish of . . . [several] towns, where . . . [an] outflanking of constituted authorities by . . . lawyers took place. In December, the nobles organized themselves. They intended to resist the egalitarian exaggeration of their erstwhile allies, the barristers, but they were excluded from the Patriot camp, which held sway over the . . . elections.

Most of the history of the 1789 ballot has still to be written. . . . A whole network of propaganda and manipulation had an almost obvious but still little-known hand in it. The historian can pick out certain leading figures, . . . but details of intrigues and their results are unknown. . . .

For want of procedures and institutions, the dawning egalitarian democracy developed by way of circuits of enlightened opinion . . . : clubs, Freemasons' lodges, groups of thinkers. There was more deliberate and concerted action towards the incipient revolution than history has recorded, yet no one imagined . . . the unprecedented nature of what was happening. . . . [The] *ancien régime* still appeared to be in place. . . . [The] king of France . . . was banking on regaining his authority through the very division of his subjects. But it was only a matter of time. . . .

Between May and August 1789, the entire *ancien régime* came to grief. In three months, the space of a season, in the most extraordinary summer in French history, nothing was left standing of what the centuries and the kings had constituted. The French had turned their rejection of the national past into the principle of the Revolution. A philosophical idea had become incarnate in the history of a people. . . .

The Third Estate's large number of deputies was remarkable for its social and political homogeneity: no peasants, artisans or workmen, but a group of bourgeois, educated and earnest, unanimous in the desire to transform both state and society. The lawyers, . . . the most numerous, were not conscious of any distinction between themselves and the merchants and shopkeepers; the local celebrities from the French provinces . . . were not intimidated by Paris. . . .

Under the anonymous greyness of costume and origin was concealed the strongest collective will ever to have moved an assembly. . . . Enthusiasm for civic equality, however, did not rule out a certain amount of calculation . . . [for] converting the old seigneurial due into a sound bourgeois contract. . . .

Abandoning the feudal principle was such an important step that the Assembly was gripped by a kind of magic of transformation: they vied with one another to be the first at the tribune to renounce the privileges of the old world, amid general applause. . . . The feudal regime was obliterated. . . .

Despite the wariness and long-windedness, there was something in the Assembly's . . . perception which, for the historian, remains fundamentally true: the notion of a break with the old society and the foundation of a new one. . . . The peasant felt himself victorious over the seigneur. The bourgeois had broken aristocratic privilege. What disappeared in 1789—and for ever—was a society of corporate bodies defined by shared privilege.

What came into being was a modern society of individuals, in its most radical conception, since everything which might come between the public sphere and each actor on the stage of social life was not only suppressed, but also roundly condemned. The Revolution rediscovered an idea put forward by Sieyès . . . [in] *Qu'est-ce que de Tiers État?* Within the modern individual there are two legitimate sides: the private one, which keeps him apart from others in enjoyment of himself, his family and his private interests, and that of the citizen, which he shares with all other citizens and which, in aggregate, forms public sovereignty. But the third side, that of the social individual who tends to create inter-social coalitions on the basis of particular interests, must be ruthlessly excluded from the state. Hatred of aristocratic society had led the men of the French Revolution to ban associations, in the name of radical individualism. . . .

[T]he new law . . . [established more than] that property-owning society dreamed of by the monarchy's enlightened reformers in the eighteenth century. Nevertheless such a definition is not completely erroneous: provided "property-owner" is not confused with "capitalist"— France was an agrarian country. [The Assembly] by making all equal before the law, instituted the universal nature of the property contract: not a new economic society, but a new legal society. . . .

. . . [H]ow was the divergence between social man and the citizen to be dealt with? . . . That was the chief question of the summer for the Constituent Assembly; by destroying the "feudal" regime, it had redefined the French people as individuals . . . free and equal in the eyes of the law. It then had to constitute them as . . . a corporate political body. Two debates were crucial in this respect. The first concerned the Declaration of Rights of Man. . . .

The American Declaration of Independence in 1776 was present in all minds, but so was the chasm which separated the situation of the old kingdom from that of the American ex-colonies, who from the start had cultivated the spirit of equality, unhampered by external enemies or a feudal or aristocratic heritage. As in the American example, the French declaration had to have as its aim the foundation of a new social contract within natural law, in keeping with the century's philosophy, and the solemn enumeration of the imprescriptible rights possessed by each contracting party. . . .

In France, however, those rights had not been in harmony beforehand with the social state: on the contrary, they would be proclaimed after a violent break with the national past, and against the corruption of an old society. . . . This aroused many fears among the more moderate . . . revolutionar[ies] [who were] afraid of the anarchy which might spring from the contrast between the proclamation of theoretical rights possessed equally by all individuals and the actual social situation of those individuals—poverty, inequality, class distinctions. From that arose the compensatory demand for a declaration of the citizen's duties in order to underline his obligation at the same time as his liberty.

These debates, well known for their abstract quality, show . . . that the deputies recognized quite clearly the scope of the problem. . . . They had just declared the complete emancipation of the individual: what then would become of the social bond? . . . The idea that affirmation of the subjective rights of individuals as a foundation of the contract carried the risk of social breakdown has haunted European political thought ever since Burke. . . . It was already fully present in the debates of 1789. . . .

However, it was the Patriots who easily won the day, and a simple Declaration of Rights of Man, a preamble to the coming Constitution, was adopted on 26 August. It was a noble and well written text, often close to the American model. . . .

What most clearly differentiated the French declaration from the American text concerned the coupling of these natural rights with written law. In the American example, those rights were perceived as having preceded society and also being in harmony with its development; moreover, they had been inscribed in its past by the jurisprudential tradition of English Common Law. In the France of 1789, however, . . . the law, produced by the sovereign nation, was established as the supreme guarantee of rights. . . .

So it was society's responsibility, through the intermediary of the law, to ensure the rights of individuals; that law which was constantly referred to in the articles of declaration as the "expression of the general will." The dominant inspiration of the Constituent Assembly was centered on the law: its immediate highlights were the idea of "general will," intended to define the extent and the exercise of rights, and the refusal to recognize any authority other than . . . the sovereign.

Now this "sovereign" . . . people, or . . . nation, needed to be given a form, . . . an extraordinary difficult problem. France was a modern nation, too vast for its citizens to be summoned together in a public square to vote on laws. It was also a very ancient nation, whose heritage included a hereditary king, at the head of what one of the deputies called "the gothic colossus of our ancient constitution." In three months, all of the complete sovereignty which he had held . . . had entirely disappeared. In its place was a society composed of free and equal individuals, on the one hand; on the other, a people who had reappropriated sovereignty: how was that to be organized? [The] problem . . . was now being posed for the first time in the existence of one of the oldest European monarchies.

To understand how the men of the Revolution tackled it, let us turn to the beginning of the great constitutional discussion. Having made the Declaration of Rights, they now had to organize the new public authorities by way of a real constitution. This could not be a shaky monument made up of ancient customs and haphazard revisions, like the *ancien régime* monarchy, but an ensemble of institutions based on the new principles . . . of reason.

That definition already left outside the Patriot camp a small minority of former revolutionaries. . . . They were . . . hostile to the reconstruction of a political society on the basis of will or reason. They believed that the extraordinary summer could be turned into no more than a fertile incident if it led to the reform, in a liberal, English sense, of what they called "monarchic government," the heritage of the national past. Their vision was a joint sovereignty of the king and two chambers. . . .

A political and intellectual chasm separated them from . . . the overriding spirit of the Revolution. They were men who stood for continuity and the adjustment of institutions: this was the nearest that French political tradition came to Burke, and gives some idea of their political isolation in 1789. They battled in vain for a bicameral system, without realizing that, for an assembly which had struggled so hard to join three Estates into one alone, it was hopeless to try to recommend a return to a division between an upper and a lower chamber. The spectre of aristocracy would still stalk the Constituent Assembly without any need of them, but it had marked them out in advance as losers.

. . . [S]overeignty . . . belonged to the Assembly, which had been delegated by the nation to create a constitution; afterwards, once the authorities had been constituted, it would be embodied by the legislative power, of which the king, as head of the executive power, would merely be the secular arm. . . . Reading the debates, one is struck by the obsession with legitimacy which runs through them, the stress laid on the absolute transfer of sovereignty and the indivisible. . . . nature of that sovereignty. . . .

The words of the *Contrat social* permitted the naming of the new realities, while concealing what they were unwittingly borrowing from the past: the indivisible and limitless nature of sovereignty was an absolutist inheritance which the "general will" transposed in terms of the autonomy of individuals producing a collective autonomy. . . . Rousseau had excluded representation as incompatible with the very principle of will. . . .

[Among the] Patriots in the Assembly . . . the common feeling was certainly to give the vote to those citizens who were enlightened and capable of autonomy, so as to make will and reason coincide, and together to resolve all the problems posed by Rousseau. . . . The general will of the Constituent Assembly went no farther than the sovereignty of a body which was supposed to concentrate in its bosom both free individual wills and the evidence of reason. . . .

To finish with . . . 1789, . . . something has to be said on the Revolution's relationships with the Catholic Church and the traditional religion of the French, through with the Revolution added a major element to the unprecedented break it introduced into national history.

That break, however, had not been brought about deliberately. . . . French philosophy of the Enlightenment was anticlerical in spirit, sometimes antireligious. . . . [I]n the act of inaugurating its reign, demo-cratic civilization substituted the rights of man for a world regulated according to divine order. . . . But if, for that reason, it was inevitably wounded in the destruction of the *ancien régime*, the Catholic religion as such was not threatened by the revolutionary majority of the Con-stituent Assembly.

. . . [T]he 1789 Revolution did not intend to substitute a new reli-gion for the old. Its ambition was limited to the radical rebuilding of the body politic on universal principles. In that it included, at least formally, features which gave it similarity to a religious movement. . . . [It] had quickly given rise to a crisis with incalculable consequences between revolution and Catholicism. . . . By uprooting the Catholic Church from society, depriving it of its stability and possessions, it had violently sepa-rated French democracy from Catholic tradition. Here began a conflict which was fundamental yet circumstantial, from which France is barely emerging two hundred years later. . . .

During 1790 something began to evoke an "English-style" fusion be-tween the revolutionary great nobility, which had maintained its social prestige, and the bourgeois revolution. The Festival of Federation, which celebrated the "national" spirit as opposed to the vanished "feudalism," was the outstanding testimony. It was the year of a very temporary . . . reign of an Enlightened society which had been formed by the entire cultural evolution of the century, in which liberal nobles and success-ful bourgeois could share ideas. . . . Here was a France of notables and property-owners replacing that of the seigneurs.

Was this the France that innumerable reformers of "abuses" . . . [had] so tirelessly mapped out? . . . Yes, . . . to some extent: the idea of a property-owners' monarchy was older than the Revolution. But the way in which it had finally come to pass, in the abstractness of principles and a social storm, enveloped its birth in the ephemeral on both the monarchic and property-owning side.

What had been most spectacular and profound about the event was related to the universality of its message, which had made it resemble a new religion. The 1789 Revolution had wanted to rebuild society and the body politic on the idea that the essence of man, and therefore com-mon to all men, was liberty. . . .

It had in fact combined two inspirational sources: liberal individu-alism on the one hand . . . ; on the other, a very unitarian conception of the sovereignty of the people, through the idea of the . . . "general will." Those two sources had been violently separated by French philosophical tradition, since Rousseau's *Contrat social* can be read as a criticism of the first by the second. . . .

In the Constituent Assembly's debates . . . and . . . laws . . . one may thus endlessly follow that tension between the universal principles on which it prided itself and their adjustment to the current situation of the old kingdom, which was a product of its "gothic past." The idea of *"ancien régime"* explained what it could not yet do. . . . "[R]evolution," by contrast, meant being torn away . . . [from] that accursed past by the advent of rational legislation. . . .

The universality of civil laws encompassed all Frenchmen without exception. The Constituent Assembly had wavered a little before the questions of Alsatian Jews, who were less "assimilated" than the Bordeaux Sephardim and were the victims of a strong local anti-Semitism, which had its spokesmen in the Assembly. . . . Even the "Mosaic religion," that cement of Alsatian ghettos which seemed so strange in this old Catholic country, was in the eyes of the law no more than a private affair of individuals, to be absorbed into the legal equality of citizens, which was a constituent of national unity. . . .

On 14 September 1791 Louis XVI . . . solemnly swore an oath of loyalty to a revised Constitution which he accepted no more sincerely than before, and the Constituent Assembly proudly proclaimed before parting: "The end of the Revolution has arrived." But its words were firmer than its convictions. . . .

The historian who seeks to understand why can begin from the extraordinary case with which the fate of the old society had been sealed and civil equality inaugurated. . . . [W]hat had been accomplished in the civil sphere in 1789 was irrevocable. . . . [In] the political sphere, there was an end to the absolutism of divine right, which was swept away with the whole of the *ancien régime*. On the other hand, the Revolution came up against the reconstruction of public authority: no one could believe that this *de facto* republic, accompanied by a former absolute sovereign, instituted by the constitution, could be destined for an easy future. . . .

1794 was the hour of the Committee of Public Safety's absolute dictatorship. . . . The Convention, as the prisoner of the Terror, . . . obeyed the Committee of Public Safety, whose members it had elected and re-elected. . . . Robespierre was . . . the head of the Republic's government. . . . In this personal dictatorship, the old revolutionary dilemma of "representation" of the sovereign people found an unprecedented solution: the source of Robespierrist power lay both in the Convention and in the sovereignty of the people . . . : the Incorruptible had ended up by personifying the Revolution. . . .

It was an immense, though fleeting, victory . . . enough to isolate Robespierre from the politicians of the epoch and make him a figure apart, which he remains to this day. As Michelet understood so well, the French Revolution had not had any really great men . . . since 1789, it had involved many actors, but swept them along in its wake, and not one of them was capable of taming its fearsome advance. . . . [I]t had cast into the void all those who had come forward in succession to put an end to it. . . . If . . . the historian wants to single out certain men . . . , he can cite Sieyès and . . . Robespierre. . . . Robespierre's greatness in the French Revolution . . . was to have gradually assumed power and, for a few months, exercised it. . . .

The Robespierre of the Revolution put no energy into private intercourse with his fellow men. . . . Maximilien Robespierre, lacking any other private existence than that which he had received willy-nilly, had found himself truly at home among the principles of the French Revolution. From the emptiness of his private life he derived the strength of his political action. . . .

For Robespierre . . . political ideas and . . . principles . . . were deeply rooted in universal morality, itself based on the existence of a "Supreme Being." . . . His reasoning never emerged from a world where a kind of transparency had to exist between history and morality: a patently absurd supposition, but extremely potent in revolutionary France, which had inscribed it on its banner. That was Robespierre's "*Rousseauism*," far more than his admiration for the *Contrat social*. . . .

The influence over opinion . . . he drew from the inevitable tension between those rights proclaimed as belonging equally to all and the true state of society. His words tirelessly returned to that flaw, a component of democracy itself. . . .

. . . [Robespierre] also possessed immense talent as a tactician . . . [his] second secret. . . . [H]e was not a true thinker . . . , [but] he was a great strategist and a profound politician. . . . [H]is moralistic turn of mind had instilled in him a veritable obsession with suspicion. . . . [He] ceaselessly mapped out his route to power by continually denouncing power. . . . His doctrinal purity was bound to be fictitious. . . . His power came from the representatives of the people, but also from the people themselves. Such was the strange chemistry which allowed the two features of his talent to combine. . . . [It] lets us understand the secrets of his dominance. . . .

. . . Through . . . [the] Festival of the Supreme Being, . . . Robespierre tri[ed] to terminate the Revolution in his own way and to his own advantage—in the utopia of a social harmony in tune with nature. . . . Was the public at the fête . . . laying the first stone in the building of the future? . . . [The] spectacle presented was that of the religion of the century, . . . its repertoire in advance, the idea of an end and a fresh beginning. . . . Nothing was left. Here . . . was the cornerstone of a nascent society.

. . . [T]he illusion did not last very long—the bloody law of Prairial followed in a couple of days. The Supreme Being did not have the same hold . . . as the Committee of Public Safety. War and fear remained the political and psychological mainsprings of the revolutionary dictatorship. War . . . was beginning to loosen its stranglehold. . . .

Victory abroad was a defeat at home for Robespierre and the Robespierrists. For if France was victorious, why the guillotine and why the dictatorship? . . . [T]he Terror was detested by public opinion, . . . [but] it could be overturned only by the Convention, which had given it life before becoming imprisoned by it.

There was no other power left standing which could confront Robespierre: the generals were under close supervision and the army had not yet entered politics. Within the country, fear prevented any public demonstration of opposition. Because of this, the *journée* of 9 Thermidor (27 July) which, in the days that followed, met with such spectacular assent, established the victory of parliamentary conspiracy hatched amid intrigues of which . . . no trace has been preserved. . . .

Who was the conductor of this orchestra? Probably no one. The essence of the matter is that when two oppositions united, they became a majority in the Convention. . . . Everyone wanted some breathing space to ward off the fear that stalked abroad—in short, to enjoy life. . . .

[Jules] Ferry was a decentralizer, who preached the Anglo-Saxon example, both British and American—a new point of reference in [the Republican] political family. . . . [T]he administrative nature of imperial despotism had spread the conviction, often expressed by Tocqueville, that it was virtually impossible to graft parliamentary freedom on to centralization. A decentralization campaign had been launched by liberal conservatives. The idea was taken up again in 1865 by Jules Ferry who gave this piece of advice: "If you want to . . . [be] industrious, peaceful, and free . . . , you have no business with a strong power. . . . France needs a weak government."

. . . The later Jules Ferry, he of the Republic, would forget this state reform. But he would retain and apply the idea of balancing departmental authority with municipal democracy. . . . That was the only way in which the existence of a national government could be reconciled with the sharing of power with an enormous municipal democracy. . . .

Jules Ferry had . . . [an historical] way of putting it. . . . In the French Revolution, he would be a man of the Constituent Assembly, against the Convention. Or, in the Convention, he would be a Girondin, against the Montagnards.

A great book made its appearance in 1865, precisely on this topic, written by a republican writer, Edgar Quinet who had been engaged in a long reflection on the downfall of the French Republic. Like all his contemporaries, he had believed he was reliving the French Revolution in its nineteen-century version. . . . His problem therefore was not to celebrate the Revolution, . . . but to try to understand and explain its failure. By doing so, he found eager listeners among the young republican generation. . . .

Two ideas formed the basis of his book. The first was that the Revolution, the sublime promise of a new political and moral order, had been unable to fulfil its mission because it had lacked the daring to conceive and found a new religion, following the example of Protestantism in the sixteenth century. This idea held no interest for Jules Ferry, who was too anticlerical . . . to want to base democracy on even a renewed Christianity. On the other hand, Ferry was fascinated by Quinet's second thesis. Quinet . . . saw the true spirit of the Revolution, the emancipation of the free individual, in the work of the Constituent Assembly, which had left nothing standing of the old monarchy. . . .

The Convention, on the contrary, brought about the spectacle of its destruction only to revive its spirit: . . . the Jacobin dictatorship, under the pretext of public safety, linked up again with the ancient "reason of state" and the worst traditions of absolutism. . . . By reincarnating Richelieu, Robespierre foretold Bonaparte. In the Revolution he was the first to create national servitude; Napoleon would be the second. Like Tocqueville, but in a different way, Quinet was seeking the secrets of Bonapartism in the tyrannies which had preceded it. . . . His book thus opened a vast Parisian polemic within the republican party. . . .

The debate deserves to be quoted at length, by virtue of what it reveals of the passions . . . which still made up the history of the Revolution, and because of what it discloses about the developments taking place inside republican ideology. . . . Quinet was accused of undermining . . . the "democratic party," the heart of opposition to the imperial regime. To challenge his book was consequently a duty.

. . . Jules Ferry replied . . . with . . . [a discussion of] the relations between Jacobinism and democracy, the central theme of republican philosophy: is what is at stake . . . as important today as it once was? Does it merit the abdication of critical consideration in the name of loyalty to the republican fight? No. The Jacobin religion . . . came about as . . . [a] necessary reaction . . . against the return of the kings [after Napoleon's fall]. . . . But half a century later, when the French Revolution has conclusively triumphed, they no longer have a *raison d'être*.

This . . . [summarizes] a vital distinction of French liberal thought: the Revolution has founded a society, not a government. This society, democracy, is so deeply rooted that its enemies no longer have any strength: the aristocracy is dead. But, in its triumph, it also has its flatters who lack a *raison d'être*: by this Jules Ferry means those who adhere to Bonapartism. . . .

The dictatorship no longer had the excuse of the counter-revolution. . . . What was it that still divided French society from the government of democracy, . . . the Republic? Precisely that "Jacobin religion," the adversary and yet the accomplice of the Bonapartist religion which had been built and cultivated around the two ideas of public safety and dictatorship.

During those years when he expected the fall of the Empire . . . , what Ferry wanted to give to the republican left for the future was governmental credibility. He therefore . . . had to exorcize the spectre of the Terror from . . . the country. . . . There followed a theoretical discussion on the dictatorship and the Terror, in which Ferry wanted to demonstrate that the two phenomena, born of a spontaneous reaction . . . of the people to invasion, had very soon constituted a system of absolute power, independent of the circumstances which had facilitated its formation, . . . propelled by its logic of domination, not by national safety. . . .

Thus, between Edgar Quinet and Jules Ferry was formed a common interpretation of the Revolution.

Mona Ozouf

The Transfer of the Sacred

Mona Ozouf (1931–) is a director of *Le Centre national de la Recherche scientifique* in Paris and was a close collaborator of François Furet. Unlike Furet, who made his name with his studies of revolutionary historiography, Ozouf owes her reputation to her archival research. Ozouf also figures as a pioneer among the many women scholars who have risen to prominence in her field. Her major work, *Festivals and the French Revolution*, excerpted here, is the most influential book on the French Revolution to be written by a woman since the publication of Madame Germaine de Staël's *Considérations*, the first major liberal interpretation, in 1818.

Festivals of the French Revolution

. . . Traditional festivals had become enigmatic to the "enlightened" sensibility. For one Diderot who still marveled at the Corpus Christi celebrations, how many were there who, like Marmontel, had to restrain his laughter at a passing religious procession in Aix; like Boulainvilliers, rendered speechless by the "giants" of Douai; or like Voltaire, pouring scorn on the Flemish Christmas! It seems that there were only two ways of looking at the popular festivals at this time. They were seen either as bizarre (but with no trace of curiosity: their predicted demise aroused no regrets, no nostalgia, not even a scholarly description) or as barbarous. . . .

Finally, and most important, the traditional festival was the realm of distinctions. This was true of the royal festivities, which, with exemplary rigidity, articulated the hierarchy of rank between corporate persons and bodies. It was just as true of religious celebrations, in which the ceremonial had become "arrogant and despotic, almost an opera," and had taken on an ostentation that many found scandalous. It was also true, finally, of theatrical performances, which concentrated in themselves the defects of other sorts of festivities, all of which tended toward the spectacular. Treatises on architecture had for decades denounced the theater as a place in which social hierarchy and an intoxicating display of social stratification had reached their apogee. The theater was the "dark little place" that Diderot judged incapable of "holding the attention of an entire nation."

. . . Far back in the mists of time, a festive assembly had been held in which the participants found their satisfaction simply in the fact of being together. There had been a primitive, a primordial festival; it would be enough to return to it. But the model seemed to have been lost.

Fortunately, it had not been entirely lost. Athens and Rome had just been "unveiled" through their customs, and although the practices of ancient people were themselves . . . merely a decadent version of a more primitive—hence even truer—mythology, at least their proximity to history's origins gave them status as models. The collective imagination compensated for the mediocrity of latter-day festivals by emigrating to Greece, . . . or to Rome, where, according to Bernardin de Saint-Pierre, the civic crown was the object of public homage. The desire for new festivals was projected not only into the future of the French people but also into the past. Time opened up in both directions, forward and backward. It was with images of chariots, athletes, gymnastic competitions, palms, and laurel crowns that the man of the Enlightenment climbed onto the stage of the Revolution.

Furthermore, when temporal exoticism failed, this century of voyagers could call on space to feed its dreams. There were the Abbé Mallet's Danes, who held pure religious festivities in the woods to worship a God who was already a "Supreme Being." There were Mirabeau's Chinese, who had invented symbolic festivals in which the emperor himself bowed low "before the nourishing plow" (and who were recalled by the organizers of the Revolutionary Festival of Agriculture). . . . Then there were the civilized nations of the New World, who, Mably declared, had returned to the principles of Nature herself; Raynal added that they were capable of renewing the world a second time; Grégoire later recalled that they already had their own civic festivities and their Liberty Trees as a focus for community rejoicing. . . .

In the clean-swept world that the Revolution seemed to offer the utopian dreamers, the suppression of hierarchies and the homogenization of the human condition left men alone. Men were individuals, in theory all identical, all equal, but solitary. It was now the task of the legislator to connect them, a task that all the utopias of the century took up with meticulous relish. The men of the Revolution also took on the task of finding an efficacious form of association for beings whom they thought of as having returned to the isolation of nature. The festival was an indispensable complement to the legislative system; for although the legislator makes the laws for the people, festivals make the people for the laws. According to Michel Foucault, there were two great mythical experiences in the eighteenth century: the person blind from birth who regains his sight and the foreign spectator who is thrown into an unfamiliar world. We might add to the list the individual who is rebaptized as citizen in the festival.

This is the source of the extraordinary interest—particularly extraordinary in view of all the other things that required their energies—that the men of the Revolution took in festivals. Through the festival the new social bond was to be made manifest, eternal, and untouchable. Hence nothing about festivals was unimportant: neither the objects proposed for general contemplation and admiration, which had clearly to appear as common property; nor the pictures portraying Revolutionary history, in which the founding event had to be celebrated quite unambiguously; nor the repetition of the choruses or the intoning of invocations in which a common will found expression; nor the spectacle created by processions, restructuring the huge crowd of isolated individuals into an organized community; nor the publicity given to private engagements or the solemnity lent to public engagements; nor, finally, the search for transcendence. The elaboration of the festival—where desire and knowledge met, where the education of the masses gave way to joy—combined politics and psychology, aesthetics and morality, propaganda and religion.

Little wonder, then, that the Revolutionary festival, for so long neglected, is not attracting the attention of historians. This is undoubtedly because their study of the work of folklorists and ethnographers has shown them the importance of the festival. It is also because the festival has now become a multiform reality for us, as it was for the men of the Revolution: one has only to think how our various vocabularies—in political essays, in literary commentaries, in theater criticism—have been invaded by the notion of the festival. . . .

So we cannot avoid the issue of what precisely the Festival of the Supreme Being represented in the mind of its creator. This is an old question that recurs whenever Robespierre is discussed. Was the Festival of the Supreme Being an ingenious brainwave, an ill-intentioned trick meant to establish the fortune of the possessors (as suggested by Daniel Guérin), or a well-meaning plot to reconcile patriotic Catholicism with the Revolution (as suggested by Mathiez)? Or was it, on the contrary, the culmination of a religious project, the effusion of a naturally religious soul (as suggested by Aulard)? In short, by establishing this festival, did Robespierre show himself to be a clever politician or a truly devout man? A strategist or a pontiff?

None of these interpretations is short of supporting evidence. If one chooses to opt for Robespierre the politician, one may obviously argue, as Mathiez does, that the Revolution, which had just recovered from defeating the double opposition of the Hébertists and the Dantonists, was now eager above all to avoid new divisions and saw the ability of the festival to promote social integration. One may also, like Dommanger, see the Festival of the Supreme Being as Robespierre's greatest—and almost only—political project, planned and implemented by a consistent series of actions. On November 21, 1791, it is true, Robespierre assured the Jacobins that it would be better not to risk a head-on collision with "the religious prejudices so adored of the people." In March 1792, in opposition to Guadet, he repeated that one should be careful not to confuse the cult of the deity with that of the priesthood. From this position one passes, without the slightest contradiction, to the blows delivered in Frimaire, Year II, to the policy of de-Christianization, to the theory of Floréal, and to the practice of Prairial.

If we are determined to reveal the extent to which Robespierre's beliefs were deeply held, there is no shortage of arguments either. What we find is the classic portrait of a man in whom character and the personal coincide absolutely, in whom the reflections of Rousseau nourished a spontaneously religious outlook. The coherence of Robespierre's thinking serves to show once again, as Aulard was so keen to demonstrate, that "from 1792 he had a concerted design where religious matters were concerned, a strong determination to resist popular enthusiasm, a remarkable firmness in confronting almost the whole of Paris, whose philosophical unbelief was amused by Hébert's childish pranks."

Indeed, the two interpretations are not mutually exclusive. It is perfectly possible at one and the same time to see the Festival of the Supreme Being as a political maneuver and as a serious belief, the latter justifying the former. This is all the easier since neither belief nor maneuver was original at the time. If one wishes to interpret the Festival of the Supreme Being as an instance of the cunning of reason, it is clear that Robespierre expected it to complete the closure of the revolution, for it is possible to reread the Floréal report with a view of seeking, and finding, at least as obsessive a presence of the vocabulary of established power as that of the "divine names." It is simply a question of "securing" (morality to eternal bases), of "fixing" (faith and happiness), of "establishing" (on the immutable foundations of justice). But that is precisely what all the successive leaders of the Revolution tried to accomplish, one after another. Neither the purpose pursued nor the means adopted—the festival as a force for conservation—are therefore peculiar to Robespierre. Whether Robespierre is admired or cursed, he did develop the most widely held of the Revolutionary ideas, and this conformity almost dispenses with the always thorny question of sincerity.

As much might be said if one wanted to see the Festival of the Supreme Being as the culmination of a wave of religious enthusiasm. There is nothing about that faceless God imagined by Robespierre, that "Great Being," that "Being of Beings," that "Supreme Being," that is peculiarly his. There is nothing there that was not repeated endlessly in the catechism of a deistic century. It might even be said, if we follow Jean Deprun on this point, that the terms used by Robespierre, which he borrowed from both the Christians and the philosophes, at the meeting point of "the traditions of Bérulle, Rousseau, and Voltaire," were even more ecumenical than is usually supposed. All the intellectual and moral authorities of the century, then, are to be found around the cradle of Floréal, with the exception of the Encyclopedists, who are indeed singled out for opprobrium. Only those "ambitious charlatans" are chased from the temple for their militant radicalism, their particular mistrust of deistic talk, and surely, too, for their "persecution" of Jean-Jacques. It scarcely needs to be added that this exclusion functioned, as one might expect, as the condition for a general reconciliation. Once the "sect" was set aside, the Floréal report and the two speeches made by Robespierre at the festival itself would have no trouble bringing together the elites on the basis of a Rousseauist proposition that "atheism is a naturally distressing system." For the rejection of original sin, a view that atheism is a perversion symmetrical with superstition, the demand for a cult liberated from the narrowness of the sanctuary and the rigidity of dogma, the distance placed between God and the priest, the supposed closeness of God to men, the abandonment of the historical religions to the benefit of natural religion, and lastly and above all, the transfer of religious feeling from the sphere of individual existence to that of social existence—all this, which is developed with admirable rhetorical flair in the Floréal speech, is, beyond individual divergences, the true ground of understanding of the eighteenth-century philosophes. . . .

Here, as elsewhere, Robespierre is no more than an echo. But the strength and beauty of the Floréal speech prevent one from seeing it as simply a work of plagiarism. The intellectual consensus of the century found in Robespierre emotional conviction. If there is a constant in his sinuous, manipulative interventions in the Jacobin debates, it is a hatred of display. . . . The festival of the winter of Year II shocked him on three counts, by combining darkness, masquerade, and violence. None of that could be tolerated by the cautious conformist who described himself as "one of the most defiant and most melancholy patriots to appear since the Revolution." . . .

There is, therefore, in the report of Floréal, Year II, a combination of an existential disposition and a circumstantial politics, both — and this is the secret of its strength — working for the embodiment of a century-long dream: for if all enlightened opinion could accept the project of Floréal, if so many enthusiastic men believed that 20 Prairial would see the end of the Revolution, it is because they found in the festivals the consecrating image of the "new Philadelphias," the "happy nations" that had haunted their dreams.

. . . Robespierre linked the age-group festivals less closely to the seasons, abandoned the Festival of Marriage and Fraternal Love, extended the list of virtues, adding justice, modesty, stoicism, frugality, and, incorruptible as ever, disinterestedness. He gave up celebrating the allied peoples to the advantage of the French people, abandoned the Constitution for the Republic. There was nothing very radical in all this. The most important change, perhaps was that Reason had disappeared from Robespierre's list of festivals. This is hardly surprising. The project of Floréal does have one touch of militant defiance: it makes provision for "a festival to the hatred of tyrants and traitors," the only allusion to the redoubled work of the guillotine, a fleeting admission that nothing was over yet. But at the time, nobody noticed it in the joy of the rediscovered utopian festival. . . .

The Festival and Time

. . . The men of the Revolution were very well aware of the irrational hold that the calendar had over people's minds; for them, the calendar was a sort of talisman. In this sense, as Joseph de Maistre saw very clearly, the new calendar was a "conjuration." Both Romme and Fabre d'Eglantine, convinced that inclusion in the calendar "consecrated," wanted to oppose one talisman with another. They were anxious reformers for whom everything still remained to be done. The first thing to be done was to manifest the discontinuity brought about by the Revolution in the flow of time, to signify, quite unequivocally, that the era of the Republic was no longer the era of kings, and to make this absolute beginning. The next stage was to divide time up with new festivals: this required choosing objects or events worthy of being celebrated. Lastly, they had to invent a guarantee against unforeseeable change and therefore to find a means, against time, of making the Revolution eternal. The festival lay at the heart of all these enterprises: it began, divided up, commemorated, and closed. It did so with unequal success.

. . . The legislator's first task was to begin the Republican era with a festival, thus placing the new time beyond dispute and showing that history derived from a founding act. It was necessary to have "a fixed point to which all other events might henceforth be related." There was hardly any dispute as to the need for this. Of course, in the Committee of Public Instruction, there was a moment when good reasons were presented why no new beginning should be made: by making all the calculations backwards, by changing all the names, one might make the old era accord with the rhythm of Republican time. But however attractive this recovery of the past might have seemed to men anxious to make evil serve good, "retrograde computation" did not prevail against the magic virtue of a fresh beginning, against the imperious need to stress a break, against the conviction that one was living through an exceptional history: the time opened up by the Revolution seemed new, not only in the way it was broken up but almost in its very texture. In such circumstances, how could one imagine that one could move at a steady pace from old time to new time? . . .

So the organization of festive time was in the grip of an obsession with security. In all the animated debates concerning the new Revolutionary calendar and the choice of its festivals, there were very few voices pleading for an open Revolution, very few minds capable of conceiving that the Revolution had not yet "come to the end marked by philosophy." This opinion . . . found no support. Yet Duhem . . . demanded that the Convention should abstain even from commemorating those undisputed times that Republicans "hold so dear to their hearts." How, indeed, could one legislate for posterity? How could one know if what one had chosen to include in the calendar was really "the greatest achievement of the Revolution"? This uncertainty as to history's verdict, and also the danger of idolatry that he detected in any solemn inclusion, led Duhem to demand a calendar that had the equitable neutrality of numerical order.

But . . . to adopt the dryness of numerical order would be to renounce "the moral and Revolutionary cachet" that results from a commemorative calendar. And, worse still, there would be nothing left to convey the Revolutionary message to future generations. This was the fundamental aim; this was the obsession with this whole organization of time. Its purpose was to instruct: the festival had to have a future in its own image. . . .

With what was one to replace what had been destroyed, and what could be substituted for Catholicism? How was the new religion to be established? The true answer, the leitmotif of the Revolutionary assemblies, was given by the imitation encouraged by the syncretic euphoria of the Revolutionary dawn. To replace was first of all to imitate—or to copy, said the critics. The new religion, like the old, had to have its sacred center, the altar of the fatherland, a place that was both religious and civic, on which one might, as Benoist-Lamothe suggests, expose the bread of fraternity. There, too, there would have to be the sacralizing presence of a book, the sole receptacle of all moral precepts. This book would be the Declaration of Rights, which would be all the more capable of replacing the missal on the altar in that it contained the sacred statement of origins, that of the unchallengeable principles (a "children's alphabet" according to Rabaut Saint-Etienne, a "national catechism" according to Barnave), often preciously kept in an "august tabernacle," an ark of the Constitution. There would be a need for prayers and singing; hence the flood of patriotic anthems, "civic" sermons, "divine and constitutional" prayers, such literary confections as the "Village Sheet" intended to supplant "the old, superstitious prayers." A liturgical calendar would be needed, and ceremonies: thus a civil baptism was imagined, in which someone, say the godfather, wearing his cockade, [would] unstop a bottle, pour a few drops on the forehead of the newborn child, moisten his lips as the Republican Decalogue was recited, or someone [would] read the commandments of the perfect member of the people's club. And there would be a civic Lent, during which people would fast for the sake of liberty. There would be priests, who would be chosen not from among the "celibates" but from among family men. Apart from a few conditions—white hair and an upright life—they would perform exactly the same functions as Catholic priests, presiding at weddings, witnessing births, comforting the sick.

In all these suggestions there is a desperate wish to compete with religion—even to the extent of such physical features as the columns of the law and the altars of the fatherland. This furious rush of imitation is particularly apparent in the religious impregnation of vocabulary, a study of which has hardly begun. The mountain is "holy," the assemblies are "temples" and families "churches," a father is a "pontiff" and a mother his "loving and beloved vicar," the history of the Revolution is the "gospel of the day" and Paris the "true Rome," the "Vatican of Reason." The projects for a Republican liturgy, of which there was a proliferation at this time, illustrate this to the point of pastiche: there were, for example, suggestions that the Easter communion should be given twice a year, under the species of a cake at harvest time and wine from a ciborium at the wine harvest, that the rogation procession be kept under the innocent name of "tour of the territory"; that Christmas be celebrated as the Festival of Birth (if the mother of the household had a male child in that year); that All Saints' Day commemorate the great men who had died in the family; that on Good Friday, the wishes of the community be brought to those persons who, during the year, had suffered the most physically or morally.

We may laugh at the poverty of imagination of men condemned to reproduce a banished religion. This would not be entirely fair, for, in their conviction of the necessity of rites, the men of the revolution were not content to borrow from what lay to hand. Antiquity provided them with at least as many models. There was, for example, the funeral ceremony. . . . Before the corpse the public officer would deliver the funeral oration. Then honey would be poured around the coffin in homage to the dead man's sweetness of character, then milk in memory of his candor, wine to commemorate his strength, and, lastly, incense so that "his good actions may fill the tableau of his life" like smoke. In their looting of ancient practices, the festival organizers and the authors of projects also found the powerful drama of the oath, with the curses that would befall the perjurer and the invocations that were not only a rhetorical resource but an attempt to equal the Romans, who, these men had read hundreds of times, believed that they were under a serious obligation only when they had sworn by Jupiter. It would seem, then, that in their obsession with ceremonies, they drew their models from different sources in quite unprincipled imitation.

And in fact there were no principles, or rather there was only one. By drawing on a mass of practices, wherever they were to be found, Revolutionary creation obeyed only a single law, that of the purge, which dominated both Revolutionary thought and Revolutionary action. Abolishing coats of arms, burning papers, striking out names, removing crowns and miters: a whole enterprise of subtraction and purification was directed at Catholic worship, with what was regarded as its excessive ornamentation and superfluous regulations. All this was regarded as so much bric-a-brac that needed to be swept away. . . .

Here we come to the type of history being taught in schools. The ancient authors then being taught . . . described their present against the background of a republic of their dreams, and used a double palette, a dark one for their present and a bright one for their past. This has the result, which is of crucial importance for us here, of dehistoricizing early ancient history, utopianizing it as a simple, frugal, equitable life. The antique was scarcely historical, and we can understand why the century that . . . invested so little in the past invested so much in antiquity. Antiquity seemed to the men of the Revolution to be a quite new, innocent society, in which words were a perfect match for deeds; when they did have to confront the theme of the decline of ancient society, they defused it by moralizing it, attributing the decadence of history to a taste for wealth and the loss of virtue; and they tried to see that decline occurring as late as possible.

A very fine text by Billaud-Varenne . . . shows us what the men of the Revolution wanted from antiquity: the image of an ideal Republic, purged of despotism, in which the most obscure citizens enjoyed personal liberty and were protected from arbitrary rule. It does not seem to have been very important whether the model was more Spartan or more Athenian, whether a Spartan Mountain was to be contrasted with an Athenian Gironde, whether the dramaturgy of the oath was copied precisely from the antique ceremonial or whether it was young Anacharsis who provided its distorted image. There is not a great deal of scholarly application here. What matters is being able to conceive of a society in which the instituted is still not too far removed from the instituter. Indeed, it is in this sense that the festival is itself, for the men of the revolution, their great borrowing from antiquity, for the festival is instituting. When Saint-Just tried to copy Sparta in his *Fragments sur les institutions républicanes*, he borrowed two things: the school and the festival, that is to say, the two teachers of the nation.

This also helps us to understand why those men tried to bypass their own history. The obsession with decadence drove them to eliminate the mediocrity of those intermediary states that could not, in any case, be founding moments. Their minds were still in the grip of the omnipotent idea of beginning, and for them the initial was also the founding moments. Even Condorcet, who was more susceptible than anyone else to the cumulative effect of human knowledge, transmitted from generation to generation, considered that the American Revolution, which escaped the radicalism of the French Revolution, had not been a true revolution. The good fortune of the French Revolution was that it broke with all tradition. The ancient festival was seen, therefore, not as a tradition to be rediscovered and copied but as an eternal model of communal togetherness, simplicity, and joy. . . .

Festival, law, origin: what we have here is an association suggestive of a sacralization. The great figure invoked by the festival organizers was . . . that of the legislator, the possessor of the power to institute, capable of bringing about a mutation of the savage world into the civilized world. Solon or Lycurgus: it hardly mattered which for such men, seeking in antiquity a model that had . . . the whole generation, which seemed to sense that the career that was open to all the talents in a period of revolution was that of the lawyer, played not as "if I were king" but as "if I were legislator"—so sighed Manon Philipon (not yet Madame Roland) at the age of twenty-four. The need for sacrality was concentrated entirely on the figure of the lawmaker. Jesus was not only a man, he was a legislator. . . . The humanization of Jesus was compensated . . . by the sacralization of the man who began or began again, placed his energies at the service of social happiness, and seemed by the same token endowed with supernatural powers. One is no longer surprised by the arrogance of certain orators, such as Camus, declaring at the session of January 1, 1790, "Assuredly we have the power to change religion."

So we may risk this conclusion: recourse to antiquity in the Revolutionary festivals expressed not only the nostalgia of the aesthete or even the moral need to replace the great examples that had disappeared with the old order. It expressed also, and above all, in a world in which Christian values were declining, the need for the sacred. A Society instituting itself must sacralize the very deed of institution. If one wishes to found a new order, one cannot be sparing of the means to do so; beginning a new life cannot be imagined without faith. This is the key to the paradoxical victory that the Revolution accorded the ancients over the moderns. To opt for the moderns was obviously to opt for the instructive accumulation of experience, for the beneficent continuity of the generations. To opt for the ancients was to say that in going back to origins, no purpose is served in pausing at the intermediary stages. Thus each generation conquers its autonomy and its capacity to break with the past. Antiquity itself is not at all a moment in human history like other moments. It has an absolute privilege, for it is conceived as absolute beginning. It is a figure of rupture, not of continuity; and the fervor that it arouses is not diminished but enhanced by this.

The myth of origin is also the instrument of a teleology: to make conceivable and credible the transition to the New Jerusalem presupposes a memory of the past Eden. Indeed it is by no means certain that the memory can coexist in men's minds with the belief in human perfectibility. . . .

The function of the festival for the men of the Revolution, whatever political tendency they belonged to was to demonstrate to man the transcendence of mankind and to establish mankind in his humanity.

So the Revolutionary festival referred to a world of perfect intelligibility, order, and stability. In this it was faithful to its utopian aim of redeeming society from the obsession with decline that had haunted the entire century. There were few thinkers who, like Condorcet, considered with lucid pessimism that the ancient legislators, who had aspired "to render the constitutions that they presented eternal, in the name of the gods, to the enthusiasm of the people," had, by that very fact, placed "a seed of profound destruction" in those perpetual constitutions. His was an isolated voice, so strong did the connection between origin, law, and the sacred then seem. The Revolutionary festival, which saw itself as establishing an eternal society, was an immense effort to conjure away decadence, that sickness of society, to regularize the time of the Revolution, and to conceal its false starts and sudden changes.

After this, one would hesitate to call the festivals of the French Revolution "revolutionary," since such a charge of emotion and subversion has been invested in the adjective of social turbulence. One may agree that these festivals were "revolutionized": their break with the ancient rituals and their contempt for the traditional, popular religious festival are sufficient evidence of this. Whether they were "revolutionizing" is another matter: their organizers did not expect them to be. Once the immense event had taken place (which they obstinately conceived in terms of order, not of disorder), they saw the festival as doing no more than strengthening the Revolution, expected of it no subversion, and attributed it to no more than a power of conservation. . . .

Must we, then, at the end of this book on the "revolutionary festival," abandon the magic of the adjective and be content simply to speak of the festivals of the French Revolution? One would be tempted to adopt this solution, which would avoid any suggestion of contempt, were it not that the men of the Revolution, already struck by the abuse of the adjective, had themselves taken the trouble to say exactly what they meant by "revolutionary": "A revolutionary man is inflexible, but sensible; he is frugal; he is simple, but does not display the luxury of false modesty; he is the irreconcilable enemy of all lies, all affection. A revolutionary man is honorable, he is sober, but not mawkish." . . . The virtues listed by Saint-Just in defining the private man may also, when magnified, define the public festival. That was certainly how the festival was seen and was intended to be. So why not dare to call it revolutionary?

Furthermore, if it was revolutionary in the eyes of the men of the Revolution, it was because it seemed better equipped than anything else to reconcile the rational and the sense perceptible, time and eternity, the savage and the civilized. The festival announced the advent of that unified man of whom Diderot declared that he had traveled through the history of the centuries and nations and failed to find. He had seen men "alternately subjected to three codes: the code of nature, the civil code, and the religious code and forced to transgress alternately each of those three codes, which were never in agreement; hence it is that there has never been in any land either man, citizen, or religion." What the festival tried to do was to demonstrate the compatibility of the codes, and its result seemed to be the emergence at last of the reconciled man.

Yet it will be said, it failed to create him. But Brumaire, which saw this astonishing system of festivals disappear, nevertheless did not see the disappearance of the new values that it had sacralized. Rights, liberty, and the fatherland, which the Revolutionary festival bound together at the dawn of the modern, secular, liberal world, were not to be separated so soon. The transfer of sacrality onto political and social values was now accomplished, thus defining a new legitimacy and a hitherto inviolate patrimony, in which the cult of mankind and the religion of the social bond, the bounty of industry, and the future of France would coexist. How can it be said that the Revolutionary festival failed in that? It was exactly what it wanted to be: the beginning of a new era.

Lynn Hunt

A Revolution in Political Culture

The interest of Lynn Hunt (1945–) in the French Revolution grew out of her study of historicist literary criticism at the University of California at Berkeley. Her work also reflects the influence of Furet and other historians of the *Annales* school. *Politics, Culture, and Class in the French Revolution,* the book from which this selection is taken, established her as an authority in the field among both American and French historians. Hunt is also a specialist in women's history, the philosophy of history, and the comparative study of revolutions.

Politics, Culture, and Class in the French Revolution

. . . [The Revolutionaries] took Rousseau as their spiritual guide, but Rousseau was vaguest precisely where they faced the most momentous decisions. Given the unique opportunity to renegotiate the social contract, what form should it take? What was the general will in France in the 1790s? What was the best government possible, taking government, as Rousseau did, "in its broadest sense"?

The Revolution showed how much everything depended on politics, but it did so in ways that would have surprised Rousseau had he lived fifteen years longer. Revolutionaries did not just debate the classical questions of government, such as the virtues of monarchy versus republic or aristocracy versus democracy. They also acted on them in new and surprising ways. In the heat of debate and political conflict, the very notion of "the political" expanded and changed shape. The structure of the polity changed under the impact of increasing political participation and popular mobilization; political language, political ritual, and political organization all took on new forms and meanings. In ways that Rousseau prophesied but could himself only dimly imagine, government became an instrument for fashioning a people. . . .

Out of the remarkable experience shaped by this goal of reconstitution and regeneration came most of our ideas and practices of politics. By the end of the decade of revolution, French people (and Westerners more generally) had learned a new political repertoire: ideology appeared as a concept, and competing ideologies challenged the traditional European cosmology of order and harmony; propaganda became associated with political purposes; the Jacobin clubs demonstrated the potential of mass

Lynn A. Hunt, *A Revolution in Political Culture*, selections from *Politics, Culture, and Class in the French Revolution*, University of California Press, 1981, pp. 2, 10, 12, 13, 15, 16.

political parties; and Napoleon established the first secular police state with his claim to stand above parties.

. . . [T]he focus on origins and outcomes has made the revolutionary experience itself seem irrelevant.

As a consequence, revolutionary innovations in the forms and meanings of politics often seem either predetermined or entirely accidental. In the Marxist account, liberal constitutionalism, democracy, terror, and authoritarian rule all appear as the handmaidens of the consolidation of bourgeois hegemony. In the Tocquevillian analysis, they all serve the progress of centralized power. Revisionist accounts are less consistent in this regard, because revisionists do not refer to a common original text, such as the works of Marx or Tocqueville. . . . Whereas in the Marxist and Tocquevillian interpretations, the politics of revolution are determined by the necessary course from origins to outcomes, in revisionist versions, politics seem haphazard because they do not fit into the origins-outcomes schema. The end result, however, is the same; politics lose significance as an object of study.

This book aims to rehabilitate the politics of revolution. Yet it is not at all a political history. Rather than recounting the narrative of revolutionary events, I have tried to uncover the rules of political behavior. Historians cannot simply add up all the professed intentions of individual actors in the Revolution to get a sense of what they thought about what they were doing. If there was any unity or coherence in the revolutionary experience, it came from common values and shared expectations of behavior. These values and expectations are the primary focus of my account. The values, expectations, and implicit rules that expressed and shaped collective intentions and actions are what I call . . . political culture. . . .

. . . Revolutionary political culture cannot be deduced from social structures, social conflicts, or the social identity of revolutionaries. Political practices were not simply the expression of "underlying" economic and social interests. Through their language, images, and daily political activities, revolutionaries worked to reconstitute society and social relations. They consciously sought to break with the French past and to establish the basis for a new national community. In the process, they created new social and political relations and new kinds of social and political divisions. Their experience of political and social struggle forced them to see the world in new ways.

One of the most fateful consequences of the revolutionary attempt to break with the past was the invention of ideology. Hesitantly, even reluctantly, revolutionaries and their opponents came to see that the relationship between politics and society was deeply problematic. Tradition lost its givenness, and French people found themselves acting on Rousseau's conviction that the relationship between the social and the political (the social contract) could be rearranged. As disagreement over the nature of the rearrangement became apparent, different ideologies were invented in order to explain this development. Socialism, conservatism, authoritarianism, and democratic republicanism were all practical answers to the theoretical question raised by Rousseau. Rather than expressing an ideology, therefore, revolutionary politics brought ideology into being. In the process of revolution, the French recast the categories of social thought and political action.

This is not to say, however, that the Revolution was only intellectual or that politics had primacy over society rather than vice versa. The revolution in politics was an explosive interaction between ideas and reality, between intention and circumstance, between collective practices and social context. If revolutionary politics cannot be deduced from the social identity of revolutionaries, then neither can it be divorced from it: the Revolution was made by people, and some people were more attracted than others to the politics of revolution. A better metaphor for the relationship between society and politics is the knot or the Möbius strip, because the two sides were inextricably intertwined, with no permanent "above" and "below." The politics of revolution appealed to certain individuals and groups, who in turn shaped the uses of revolutionary politics. The new political class (using class in a broad sense) was formed by its relationship to revolutionary politics as much as it formed them.

In order to reconstruct the logic of revolutionary action and innovation, it is thus essential to examine both the politics of revolution and the people who practiced them. My contention is that there was a fit or affinity between them, not that one can be deduced from the other. The political culture of revolution was made up of symbolic practices, such as language, imagery, and gestures. These symbolic practices were embraced more enthusiastically in some places and by some groups than in other places and groups. In many ways, the symbolic practices—the use of a certain rhetoric, the spread of certain symbols and rituals—called the new political class into existence; talk of national regeneration and festivals of federation, for instance, gave the new political elite a sense of unity and purpose. On the other hand, the differences in reception of the new practices also had their impact on the way revolutionary politics worked, and especially on its successes and failures. . . . The investment of symbolic actions with political significance gave specific policies, individuals, and organizations greater impact than they would have had in nonrevolutionary times.

This method of proceeding relies on the work of three French historians who have pioneered in the study of revolutionary political culture. . . . The first is François Furet, who has done more than anyone else to revive the historiographical debates and point them in new directions. In a more specific vein Maurice Agulhon showed how images of the Republic on seals and statues actively shaped French political perceptions. Similarly, Mona Ozouf demonstrated how revolutionary festivals were used to forge a new national consensus. The studies of Agulhon and Ozouf show that cultural manifestations were part and parcel of revolutionary politics, and Ozouf in particular shows that there was a logic to revolutionary rituals. Historians can no longer assume that politics exists in a clearly separate realm from culture.

The chief accomplishment of the French Revolution was the institution of a dramatically new political culture. The revolution did not startle its contemporaries because it laid the foundations for capitalist development or political modernization. The English found more effective ways to encourage the former, and the Prussians showed that countries could pursue the latter without democracy or revolution. Revolution in France contributed little to economic growth or to political stabilization. What it did establish, however, was the mobilizing potential of democratic republicanism and the compelling intensity of revolutionary change. The language of national regeneration, the gestures of equality and fraternity, and the rituals of republicanism were not soon forgotten. Democracy, terror, Jacobinism, and the police state all became recurrent features of political life.

. . . [T]he new tradition of revolution, with its values and expectations, did not disappear. Even outside of France, it continued to have a vigorous life in the underground, and its specter was kept alive in the fears and writings of the defenders of that new ideology—conservatism. Even in the new police powers developed to contain it, the memory of revolution continued. Once revolutionaries acted on Rousseau's belief that government could form a new people, the West was never again the same.

Robert Darnton

A Conflict Between "Possibilism" and "The Givenness of Things"

Robert Darnton (1939–) is one of a small number of American scholars who have collaborated with François Furet and other historians of the *Annales* school at the *Ecole pratique des Hautes Etudes* in Paris. In the United States he has worked closely with the eminent cultural anthropologist Clifford Geertz. Like Taine, Darnton did extensive research on the Enlightenment before he began writing about the French Revolution. His particular interest was eighteenth-century "print culture." This selection reflects the influence of Crane Brinton, an earlier American historian who was the first to study the impact of changes the French Revolution made in names, terms of address, and other "little things" of daily life.

What Was Revolutionary about the French Revolution?

The French Revolution at Street Level

What was so revolutionary about the French Revolution? The question might seem impertinent at a time like this, when all the world is congratulating France on the 200th anniversary of the storming of the Bastille, the destruction of feudalism, the *Declaration of the Rights of Man and of the Citizen*. But the bicentennial hoopla has little to do with what actually happened two centuries ago.

Historians have long pointed out that the Bastille was almost empty on July 14, 1789 . . . that feudalism had already ceased to exist by the

Robert Darnton, A Conflict Between "Possibilism" and "The Givenness of Things," selections from *What Was Revolutionary about the French Revolution?*, (Waco, Texas, Baylor University Press, 1990), pp. 1–6, 10–19, 24–41. Reprinted by permission.

time it was abolished, and few would deny that the rights of man were swallowed up in the Terror. . . . Does a sober view of the Revolution reveal nothing but misplaced violence and hollow proclamations— nothing more than a "myth," to use a term favored by the late Alfred Cobban, a skeptical English historian who had no use for guillotines and slogans? . . . [But] myths can . . . acquire a rock-like reality as solid as the Eiffel Tower, which the French built to celebrate the 100th anniversary of the Revolution in 1889. France will spend millions in 1989 . . . producing concrete contemporary expressions of the force that burst loose on the world two hundred years ago. But what was it?

Although the spirit of '89 is [not easy] to fix in words . . . , it could be characterized as energy—a will to build a new world from the ruins of the [Old] Regime. . . . That energy permeated everything during the French Revolution. It transformed life, not only for the activists trying to channel it in directions of their own choosing but for ordinary persons going about their daily business.

The idea of a fundamental change in the tenor of everyday life may seem easy enough to accept in the abstract, but few of us can really assimilate it. We take the world as it comes and cannot imagine it organized differently, unless we have experienced moments when things fall apart—a death perhaps, or a divorce, or the sudden obliteration of something that seemed immutable, like the . . . ground under our feet.

Such shocks often dislodge individual lives, but they rarely traumatize societies. In 1789 the French had to confront the collapse of a whole social order . . . the Ancien Régime . . . and to find some new order in the chaos surrounding them. They experienced reality as something that could be destroyed and reconstructed, and they faced seemingly limitless possibilities, both for good and evil, for raising a utopia and for falling back into tyranny.

To be sure, a few seismic upheavals had convulsed French society in earlier ages . . . But no one was ready for a revolution in 1789. The idea did not exist. . . .

The French did not have much of a political vocabulary before 1789, because politics took place at Versailles, in the remote world of the king's court. Once ordinary people began to participate in politics— in the elections to the Estates General, . . . and in the insurrections of the streets—they needed to find words for what they had seen and done. They developed fundamental new categories, such as "left" and "right," which derive from the seating plan of the National Assembly, and "revolution" itself. The experience came first, the concept afterwards. But what was that experience?

Only a small minority of activists joined the Jacobin clubs, but everyone was touched by the Revolution because the Revolution reached into everything. . . . [It] recreated time and space. According to the revolutionary calendar . . . , time began when the old monarchy ended, on September 22, 1792—the first of the Vendémiaire, Year I.

. . . [T]he revolutionaries divided time into units that they took to be rational and natural . . . ten days to a week, three weeks to a month, and twelve months to a year. The five days left over at the end became patriotic holidays, given over to civic qualities: Virtue, Genius, Labor. . . .

Ordinary days received new names, which suggested mathematical regularity: primidi, duodi, tridi, decadi. Each was dedicated to some aspect of rural life so that agronomy would displace the saints' days of the Christian calendar. . . .

The adoption of the metric system represented a similar attempt to impose a rational and natural organization on space. According to a decree of 1795, the meter was to be "the unit of length equal to one ten-millionth part of the arc of the terrestrial meridian between the North Pole and the Equator." Of course, ordinary citizens could not make much of such a definition. They were slow to adopt the meter and the gram, the corresponding new unit of weight, and few of them favored the new week, which gave them one day of rest in ten instead of one in seven. . . .

. . . [The] revolutionaries stamped their ideas on contemporary consciousness by changing everything's name. . . . Fourteen hundred streets in Paris received new names, because the old one contained some reference to a king, a queen, or a saint. The Place Louis XV, where the most spectacular guillotining took place, became the Place de la Révolution; and later . . . the Place de la Concorde. Notre Dame became the Temple of Reason.

The revolutionaries even renamed themselves. It wouldn't do, of course, to be called Louis in 1793 and 1794. The Louis called themselves Brutus or Spartacus. Last names like Le Roy or Lévêque, very common in France, became La Loi or Liberté. Children got all kinds of names foisted on them—some from nature ("Pissenlit" or Dandelion . . . for girls, "Rhubarb" for boys) and some from current events, "Constitution." . . .

Meanwhile, the queen bee became a "laying bee" . . . ; chess pieces were renamed, because a good revolutionary would not play with kings, queens, knights, and bishops; and the kings, queens, and jacks of playing cards became liberties, equalities, and fraternities. The revolutionaries set out to change everything: crockery, furniture, law codes, religion, the map of France itself, which was divided into departments—that is, symmetrical units of equal size with names taken from rivers and mountains—in place of the irregular old provinces.

Before 1789, France was a crazy-quilt of overlapping and incompatible units, some fiscal, some judicial, some administrative, some economic, and some religious. After 1789, those segments were melted down into a single substance: the French nation. With its patriotic festivals, its tricolor flag, its hymns, its martyrs, its army, and its wars, the Revolution accomplished what had been impossible for Louis XIV and his successors: it united the disparate elements of the kingdom into a nation and conquered the rest of Europe. In doing so, the Revolution unleashed a new force, nationalism, which would mobilize millions and topple governments for the next two hundred years.

Of course, the nation-state did not sweep everything before it. It failed to impose the French language on the majority of the French people, who continued to speak all sorts of mutually incomprehensible dialects, despite a vigorous propaganda drive by the revolutionary Committee on Public Instruction. But in wiping out the intermediary bodies that separated the citizen from the state, the Revolution transformed the basic character of public life.

It went further: it extended the public into the private sphere, inserting itself into the most intimate relationships. Intimacy in French is conveyed by the pronoun *tu* as distinct from the *vous* employed in formal address. Although the French sometime use *tu* quite casually today, under the Old Regime they reserved it for asymmetrical or intensely personal relations. Parents said *tu* to children, who replied with *vous*. The *tu* was used by superiors addressing inferiors, by humans commanding animals, and by lovers. . . .

The French Revolution wanted to make everybody *tu*. . . . That may sound laughable today, but it was deadly serious to the revolutionaries [who] wanted to build a new society based on new principles of social relations. . . . So they redesigned everything that smacked of the inequality built into the conventions of the Old Regime. . . . They substituted Citizen and Citizeness for Monsieur and Madame. . . .

And they changed their dress, [which] often serves as a thermometer for measuring the political temperature. To designate a militant from the radical Sections of Paris, the revolutionaries adopted a term from clothing: *sans-culotte*, one who wears trousers rather than breeches . . . trousers, . . . an open shirt, a short jacket, boots, and a liberty cap over a "natural" crop of hair, which dropped down to his shoulders.

Women's dress on the eve of the Revolution had featured low necklines, basket-skirts, and exotic hair styles, at least among the aristocracy. Hair dressed in the "hedgehog" style rose two or more feet above the head and was decorated with elaborate props. . . . After 1789, fashion came from below. Hair was flattened, skirts deflated, necklines raised, and heels lowered.

At the height of the Revolution, however, . . . virtue was a fashion [and] the central ingredient of a new political culture. It had a puritanical side, but it should not be confused with the Sunday-school variety preached in nineteenth-century America. To the revolutionaries, virtue was virile. It meant a willingness to fight for the fatherland and for the revolutionary trinity of liberty, equality, and fraternity.

At the same time, the cult of virtue produced a revalorization of family life. Taking their text from Rousseau, the revolutionaries sermonized on the sanctity of motherhood and the importance of breast feeding. They treated reproduction as a civic duty and excoriated bachelors as unpatriotic. . . .

Saint-Just, the most extreme ideologist on the Committee of Public Safety, wrote in his notebook: "The child, the citizen, belongs to the fatherland. . . . Children belong to their mother until the age of five, if she has [breast] fed them, and to the Republic afterwards . . . until death."

It would be anachronistic to read Hitlerism into such statements. With the collapse of the authority of the church, the revolutionaries sought a new moral basis for family life. They turned to the state and passed laws that would have been unthinkable under the Old Regime. They made divorce possible, . . . accorded full legal status to illegitimate children, [and] abolished primogeniture. If, as the *Declaration of the Rights of Man and of the Citizen* proclaimed, all men are created free and equal in rights, shouldn't all men begin with an equal start in life? The Revolution tried to limit "paternal despotism" by giving all children an equal share in inheritances. It abolished slavery and gave full civic rights to Protestants and Jews. . . . Despite some heady phrasing about the appropriation of counter-revolutionaries' property, the legislators never envisaged anything like socialism. . . . Nevertheless, the main thrust of revolutionary legislation is clear: it substituted the state for the church as the ultimate authority in the conduct of private life, and it grounded the legitimacy of the state in the sovereignty of the people.

Popular sovereignty, civil liberty, equality before the law—the words fall so easily off the tongue today that we cannot begin to imagine their explosiveness in 1789. We cannot think ourselves back into a mental world like that of the Old Regime, where most people assumed that men were unequal, that inequality was a good thing, and that it conformed to the hierarchical order built into nature by God himself. To the French of the Old Regime, liberty meant privilege—a special prerogative to do something denied to other persons. The king, . . . source of all law, rightly dispensed privileges . . . for he had been anointed as the agent of God on earth. . . .

Throughout the eighteenth century, the philosophers of the Enlightenment challenged those assumptions, and pamphleteers in Grub Street succeeded in tarnishing the sacred aura of the crown. But it took violence to smash the mental framework of the Old Regime, and iconoclastic, world-destroying, revolutionary violence is also hard for us to conceive. . . . True, we treat traffic accidents and muggings as everyday occurrences. But compared with our ancestors, we live in a world where violence has been drained out of our daily experience. In the eighteenth century, Parisians commonly . . . witnessed dismemberments of criminals at public executions. And they could not walk through the center of the city without covering their shoes in blood. . . . [R]iots . . . known as "popular emotions"—eruptions of visceral passion—[were] touched off by some spark that burned within the collective imagination.

It would be nice if we could associate the Revolution exclusively with the *Declaration of the Rights of Man and of the Citizen,* but it was born in violence and it stamped its principles on a violent world. The conquerors of the Bastille did not merely destroy a symbol of royal despotism. One hundred fifty of them were killed or injured in the assault on the prison. . . . [The] survivors got hold of its governor, . . . cut off his head, and paraded it through Paris on the end of a pike. . . . A week later, in a paroxysm of fury over high bread prices and rumors about plots to starve the poor . . . , [a] band of rioters then seized . . . , the intendant of Paris, Bertier de Sauvigny, . . . marched him through the streets . . . murdered [him] in front of the Hôtel de Ville, tore the heart out of his body, and threw it in the direction of the municipal government. . . .

It also would be nice if we could stop the story of the Revolution at the end of 1789. . . . But the whole story extends through the rest of the century—and of the following century, according to some historians. Whenever its stopping point, . . . we must come to terms with the Terror.

We can find plenty of explanations for the official Terror . . . directed by the Committee of Public Safety. . . . It was not very devastating . . . by twentieth-century standards. . . . It took about 17,000 lives. Seventy-one percent of the executions took place in areas where civil war was raging; three-quarters of the guillotined were rebels captured with arms in their hands; and 85 percent were commoners—a statistic that is hard to digest for those who interpret the Revolution as a class war directed by bourgeois against aristocrats. Under the Terror the word "aristocrat" could be applied to almost anyone deemed to be an enemy of the people.

But all such statistics stick in the throat. Any attempt to condemn an individual by suppressing his individuality and by slotting him into abstract, ideological categories is inherently inhuman. The Terror *was* terrible. It pointed the way toward totalitarianism. It was the trauma that scarred modern history at its birth.

Historians have succeeded in explaining much of it (not the hideous . . . "Great Terror" when the killing increased while the threat of invasion receded) as a response to the extraordinary circumstances of 1793–1794: the invading armies about to overwhelm Paris; the counter-revolutionaries . . . plotting to overthrow the government from within; the price of bread soaring out of control and driving the Parisian populace wild with hunger and despair. . . .

It would be the height of presumption for an American historian sitting in the comfort of his study to condemn the French for violence and to congratulate his countrymen for the relative bloodlessness of their own revolution, which took place in totally different conditions. Yet what is he to make of the September Massacres of 1792, . . . that took the lives of more than 1000 persons, many of them prostitutes and common criminals? . . . [These] massacres took on the character of a ritualistic, apocalyptic mass murder. Crowds of sans-culottes, including men from the butcheries, . . . stormed the prisons in order to extinguish what they believed to be a counter-revolutionary plot. They improvised a popular court. . . . One by one the prisoners were led out, accused, and summarily judged according to their demeanor. Fortitude was taken to be a sign of innocence, faltering as guilt. . . . If declared innocent, the prisoner would be hugged, wept over, and carried triumphantly through the city. If guilty, he would be hacked to death in a gauntlet of pikes, clubs, and sabres, . . . his body . . . stripped and thrown on a heap of corpses or dismembered and paraded about on the end of a pike.

Throughout their bloody business, the massacrers talked about purging the earth of counter-revolution. They seemed to play parts in a secular version of the Last Judgment, as if the Revolution had released an undercurrent of popular millenarianism. But . . . [this] bloodshed passes the historian's understanding.

It is there, nonetheless. It will not go away, and it must be incorporated in any attempt to make sense of the Revolution. One could argue that violence was a necessary evil, because the Old Regime would not die peacefully and the new order could not survive without destroying the counter-revolution. Nearly all the violent "days" were defensive — desperate attempts to stave off counter-revolutionary coups, which threatened to annihilate the Revolution. . . . [Any] opposition could be made to look like treason, and no consensus could be reached on the principles of politics.

. . . [C]ircumstances account for most of the violent swings from extreme to extreme during the revolutionary decade . . . but not all — certainly not the slaughter . . . in September 1792. The violence itself remains a mystery . . . that may force one back into metahistorical explanations: original sin . . . or the cunning of a dialectic. . . . I confess myself incapable of explaining the ultimate cause of revolutionary violence, but I think I can make out some of its consequences. It cleared the way for the redesigning and rebuilding that I mentioned above. It struck down institutions from the Old Regime so suddenly and with such force that it made anything seem possible. It released Utopian energy.

The sense of boundless . . . "possibilism" . . . was the bright side of popular emotion. [N]ot restricted to millenarian outbursts in the streets, it could seize lawyers and men of letters sitting in the Legislative Assembly. . . .

What children . . . were those men of 1792, with . . . their simple-minded sloganeering about liberty, equality, and fraternity! . . . But we may miss something if we condescend to people in the past. The popular emotion of fraternity, the strangest in the trinity of revolutionary values, swept through Paris with the force of a hurricane in 1792. We can barely imagine its power, because we inhabit a world organized according to other principles. . . . We define ourselves as employers or employees, as teachers or students, as someone located somewhere in a web of intersecting roles. The Revolution at its most revolutionary tried to wipe out such distinctions. It really meant to legislate the brotherhood of man. It may not have succeeded any better than Christianity Christianized, but it remodeled enough of the social landscape to alter the course of history.

How can we grasp those moments of madness, . . . when anything looked possible and the world appeared wiped clean by a surge of popular emotion and ready to be redesigned? Such moments pass quickly. People cannot live for long in a state of epistemological exhilaration. Anxiety sets in. . . . Boundaries soon harden, and the landscape assumes once more the aspect of immutability.

. . . The French Revolution has faded into the past, . . . so far away that we may barely believe in it. For the revolution defies belief. It seems incredible that a whole people could rise up and transform the conditions of everyday existence. To do so is to contradict the common working assumption that life must be fixed in the patterns of the common workaday world.

Have we never experienced anything that could shake that conviction? Consider the assassinations of John F. Kennedy, Robert Kennedy, and Martin Luther King, Jr. All of us who lived through those moments remember precisely where we were and what we were doing. We suddenly stopped in our tracks, and in the face of the enormity of the event we felt bound to everyone around us. For a few instants we ceased to see one another through our roles and perceived ourselves as equals, stripped down to the core of our common humanity. . . .

I think the French Revolution was a succession of . . . events so terrible that they shook mankind to its core. Out of the destruction, they created a new sense of . . . living by the most difficult of revolutionary values, the brotherhood of man.

Of course, the notion of fraternity comes from the Revolution itself rather than from any higher wisdom among historians, and few historians, however wise, would assert that great events expose some bedrock reality underlying history. I would argue the opposite: great events make possible the social reconstruction of reality, the reordering of things-as-they-are so they are no longer experienced as given but rather as willed, in accordance with convictions about how things ought to be.

Possibilism against the givenness of things—those were the forces pitted against one another in [revolutionary] France. . . . Not that other forces were absent, including something that might be called a "bourgeoisie" battling something known as "feudalism," while a good deal of property changed hands and the poor extracted some bread from the rich. But all those conflicts were predicated on something greater than the sum of their parts—a conviction that the human condition is malleable, not fixed, and that ordinary people can make history instead of suffering it.

Two hundred years of experimentation with brave new worlds have made us skeptical about social engineering. In retrospect, the Wordsworthian moment can be made to look like a prelude to totalitarianism. . . . But . . . [the] French revolutionaries were not Stalinists. They were an assortment of unexceptional persons in exceptional circumstances. When things fell apart, they responded to an overwhelming need to make sense of things by ordering society according to new principles. Those principles still stand as an indictment of tyranny and injustice. What was the French Revolution all about? Liberty, equality, fraternity. . . .

The Literary Revolution of 1789

. . . [What] follows . . . [is] one part sociology, one part heresy. . . . [T]he sociology . . . concerns a set of related questions about the facts of literary life under the Old Regime . . . : How many writers were there in eighteenth-century France? Where did they come from? And how did they fit into the social order? . . .

I would estimate the number of writers in France at the outbreak of the Revolution as at least 3000 and probably much more. . . . Three thousand writers in a country of twenty-six million: were they a burden on the economy? a sector of social unrest? a source of ideological discontent? The numbers don't mean much by themselves, and they raise all kinds of definitional difficulties. La Porte defined a "writer" as anyone who has published a book. . . . [This] avoids the anachronism built into the modern notion that a writer is someone who somehow makes his living from writing. . . . Conditions in eighteenth-century France made . . . it virtually impossible to live from the pen. . . . The Republic of Letters was suffering from a population explosion on the eve of the Revolution, and it offered nothing but misery for anyone who tried to rise through its ranks without an independent income.

What were the characteristics of this population? . . . The average age of the writers was 53, and there were more . . . in their sixties and seventies than in their twenties and thirties. This pattern may be something of an optical illusion. . . . [M]any aspiring writers . . . failed to gain any recognition or income [and] gave up writing . . . to pursue another career. The number of these inactive authors cannot be determined. . . . But I doubt that France could have supported . . . even 1000 active writers. . . . [I]t seems likely that the inactive ones identified themselves with "literary France." . . .

The geographical origins of the writers . . . fall into a pattern like that on other maps of cultural life under the Old Regime. . . . Paris soaked up talent from the provinces, and it may well have corrupted some of the country boys who arrived with the dream of scoring hits in the Comédie française and *bons mots* in the salons.

. . . [T]he socio-occupational positions of the authors . . . raise problems about defining categories and sorting out data; but I think it . . . illustrates the relative importance of the three estates. . . . The privileged orders occupied a disproportionately important place in the Republic of Letters . . . one third of all the authors on the eve of the Revolution. . . . [To] characterize literary France by some formula, it would be more accurate to invoke the "mixed elite" favored by revisionist social historians than the "conquering bourgeoisie" of the Marxists.

. . . [T]he writers of the third estate include a high proportion of professional men. . . . By contrast, the commercial and industrial bourgeoisie is almost nonexistent. . . . The largest group of them belonged to what I would call the "intellectual trades": teachers, secretaries, scriveners, librarians, journalists, and actors . . . [who] congregated in cafés and garrets at the heart of the Republic of Letters. . . . [They] provided most of its energy as well as its prose and poetry. . . . It would be misleading, however, to consider these Parisians as "professionals," even if writing itself can be construed as a profession. They supported themselves by intellectual odd jobs, not by selling their wares in the literary marketplace. . . . [M]ost of them lived in misery. A tiny minority penetrated into the world of the salons, where they picked up pensions, sinecures, and seats in the academies. But most writers without an independent income sank into Grub Street, where they lived on whatever scraps they could find. It is impossible to calculate the population of Grub Street, because hack writers had no clearly defined estate or occupation, which could provide them with a social identity. . . . I would estimate that France contained 1000 hungry hacks when the Revolution exploded in 1789.

Did the literary population include many writers from the lower classes? . . . I could find none living among the common people in the country and only nineteen living as shopkeepers or artisans in the 1780s.

Were there many women? The question has some urgency, now that feminist scholars are reworking literary history and rediscovering women writers. . . . The police tracked down every "author" they could find [and] came up with 501, but only sixteen were women. Of course women had great influence on literary life as readers, leaders of salons, and arbiters of taste. . . . But I think the conclusion is clear: only a tiny proportion of "literary France" was female.

. . . [I]t should now be possible to venture a few more conclusions of a sociological sort. Most writers under the Old Regime belonged to a mixed elite, which consisted of a great many members of the privileged orders, an equal number from the professional bourgeoisie, and a large contingent from the intellectual trades. . . . [T]hey lacked writers of the modern . . . kind who live from their pen as independent intellectuals. To be sure, an intelligentsia of sorts had begun to . . . [grow] up around . . . the . . . *philosophes*. But it did not yet have a clear social identity and a firm economic base. . . . [I]t shaded off into Grub Street, . . . which lay outside the categories of civil society. . . .

We are back to my heresy. . . . [T]o make it more heretical still, let me . . . try to formulate it in a more extreme manner: the French Revolution was a literary revolution. . . . Now, . . . I hasten to add that I think the Revolution involved a great deal more than literature. It was an attempt to destroy a whole way of life and to create a new one. It was opposed by its very nature to the cultural system of the Old Regime. And insofar as it transformed French culture, it revolutionized French literature as a social system and the very notion of literature itself. The revolutionaries freed the press, destroyed the academies, scattered the salons, and smashed the system of court patronage. . . . And while they dismantled the institutions of the literary old regime, they made their new variety of literature into an ingredient of a new, revolutionary culture. They repossessed their past and remade literary history. To carry "literarification" so far was not to play a game at all; it was to contribute to the social reconstruction of reality.

. . . [L]et me try to explain. Unlike some revisionists today, I do not understand the Revolution as a political phenomenon derived from the "discourse" of theorists like Rousseau and Sieyés. I think it was a total revolution, in its programs and often in its practice—a revolution in time, space, and personal relations as well as in politics and society; a revolution so big that it could not be comprehended by the people who made it. The twentieth century has accustomed us to mass upheavals, and our history books have laid out revolutions with such clarity that we find it difficult to appreciate the scale and the confusion of the events that took place in France two hundred years ago. To the people in the midst of it, the French Revolution numbed the senses . . . staggered the mind . . . [and] tore their world apart. And when things fell apart, they felt an overwhelming need to make sense of things to find some order in the new regime that was confusedly coming into being. That job fell to the intellectuals among the ranks of the 3000 writers under the Old Regime. . . .

But one cannot remake reality ex nihilo. The intellectuals naturally fell back on their experience and worked with themes that they had inherited from the Old Regime. They opposed Rousseauistic moralizing to Voltairean satire, and they framed their remarks in familiar genres. The form was as important as the content, because the radical journalists and orators did not distinguish style from substance. They hated satire the way they hated high society and they distrusted wit as a sign of an aristocratic disposition.

Their attitudes varied, of course. Some made use of popular strains of humor. But even these seemed treasonous to Robespierre. When he looked back at the literature of the Old Regime, he saw an alien world of refinement and corruption. Although he acknowledged the importance of the Enlightenment as a "preface to our Revolution," he vilified the Encyclopedists. . . . "Men of letters in general" seemed suspicious to Robespierre. Having guillotined a heavy proportion of writers, he deplored their role in the Revolution and singled out only one writer from the Old Regime for praise: Jean-Jacques Rousseau. . . .

I do not mean to imply that the Revolutionaries spoke with one voice or that the literary revolution was simple and unanimous. I am arguing, rather, that it belonged to a common task, which arises in all great revolutions and which was so enormous after 1789 that historians have rarely recognized it—the task of remaking reality from the rubble of an old regime. As products of the literary system peculiar to the Old Regime in France, the writers of the Revolution revolutionized through literature. They began in 1789 by capturing the sacred center of the old literary system . . . and they ended in 1794 by working it into the core of a new political culture.

The Market Woman (Woman of the Revolution). David, Jacques Louis. Giraudon/Art Resource, NY. Musée de Beaux-Arts, Lyon, France.

Postmodern Perspectives

François Crouzet

Industrial Anticlimax and Economic Watershed

François Crouzet's original field of research was the English industrial revolution. His interests subsequently shifted to the history of French economic development in the nineteenth and twentieth centuries. Before embarking on his career as an economic historian, Crouzet studied the French Revolution under Georges Lefebvre. In this selection from an essay he wrote on the French Revolution's economic consequences, Crouzet draws on his expertise in all these fields to evaluate the work of critics of the Marxist interpretation.

The Economic Consequences of the French Revolution: Reflections on a Debate

. . . Discussion of the long term consequences of the Revolution for the French economy is relatively recent. Nineteenth-century historiography concentrated on events and politics. The Revolution was praised for establishing liberty or condemned for its "horrors"; but there was little concern for its repercussions on the growth rate; and historians did not become much involved in debates about the economic consequences of revolutionary legislation. . . . Admittedly, at the end of the nineteenth century interest in the economic history of the Revolution was aroused largely thanks to the influence of Jean Jaurès. . . . But the bulk of this work had to do with the economic origins and aspects of the Revolution. . . . The focus was on the short term, on cyclical fluctuations, and also on the Year II, often seen as an "anticipation" or even as a model . . . [of] present and future state intervention. In any case, revolutionary historiography was self-contained and seldom looked beyond the 18th Brumaire.

To grapple with the problems which concern us here historians had to look beyond traditional chronological barriers and to consider questions about the economic development of France over the last three or four centuries, taken as a whole. In regard to Old Regime France, questions arose as to whether the economy suffered from social and institutional blockages which had greatly hampered development; and as to whether the Revolution had been necessary for breaking these chains, [whether it had] liberated the economy (notably the agricultural sector) from a vicious and paralyzing cycle, and creat[ed] conditions for full-scale modern economic growth. . . .

American and British economic historians on the other hand brought to the attention of their French colleagues (who had long been insensitive to the issue) the fact that the French economy's performance

François Crouzet, Industrial Anti-Climax and Economic Watershed, selections from "Les Conséquences Économiques de la Révolution Française: Réflexions sur un débat" in *La Revue Economique*, numero special: Revolution de 1789 Guerres, et Croissance Economique (XL, Nov, 1989) editor's translation, pp. 1189–1200.

in the nineteenth century and the first half of the twentieth had been less than brilliant . . . markedly inferior [in fact] to that of the other advanced countries. Historians once more discovered that France had made a social and political revolution but that the Industrial Revolution, English in origin, had been a long time in coming (if indeed it had ever occurred in France). Questions then arose about whether the Revolution had played a role in France's "lag," if it had not indeed had pernicious effects which extended far beyond the years 1789–1799. Was the Revolution, in the long term, a liberating force or a factor for backwardness of the French economy? In oversimplified terms this is the question which a number of writers have asked and which will be briefly reconsidered here. . . .

Research into the economic consequences of a cluster of exogenous events—such as a war or a revolution—is usually based on the counterfactual hypothesis that the economy under study would have evolved on the same line as before the accident in question, if this latter accident had not occurred. Deviations from the original trend are considered "consequences" of such events. It should be noted at once that a postulate of this kind is fragile and cannot be demonstrated; moreover, the necessary statistical material for the revolutionary and imperial period exists for Great Britain, but is largely lacking for France. . . . Finally, and most important . . . there is uncertainty about the situation of the French economy on the eve of the Revolution and thus about the trend it might have followed.

Undoubtedly a crisis ravaged the economy in 1789, but we do not know whether it was cyclical, intercyclical, or structural. Was the Old Regime economy caught up in a vicious cycle of stagnation . . . despite the "skin-deep" prosperity of certain sectors? Or was it, despite an acute short-term crisis, healthy and advancing on the right road, i.e., towards English technological progress . . . ?

Perceptions of the pre-Revolutionary economy obviously influence judgments about the Revolution's effects. Depending upon one's point of view, it put an end to prosperity and interfered with development, or it did no more than momentarily aggravate circumstances which were bad enough already and above all it laid the foundation for a new economy.

The war creates a second major difficulty. . . . It clearly had direct consequences, . . . which would not have occurred if peace had been maintained: as was the case with the interruption of French overseas trade following the British blockade, or the "mobilization" of hundreds of thousands of men [for combat]. But revolution and war are not unconnected. Whatever the responsibilities of foreign powers in the outbreak of hostilities, it was the Legislative Assembly and the Convention which declared war on their neighbors and on Europe as a whole. War is an integral part of the Revolution and it is wise not to dissociate the two.

. . . The Wars of the Revolution came to their end under the Consulate and soon recurred as the Napoleonic Wars, [whence] another problem: should research on the economic consequences of the Revolution stop in 1799? Or extend to 1815? Indeed, dissociating the Revolution and the Empire threatens to falsify attempts at analysis. The so-called Napoleonic "episode" created the Civil and Commercial Codes and the durable institutional structures through which France lived for a century and more, and under which nineteenth-century entrepreneurs did business.

As regards the question which concerns us here, as regards everything in fact which relates to the French Revolution, no historian can avoid ideology and political bias. Even if he makes a supreme effort to be objective (I am deliberately using this now old-fashioned word), he is inevitably subject to the influence of his personal choices and preferences in relation to the Revolution. This should be recognized quite frankly . . . ; yet broad areas of agreement remain possible and have even been reached. . . .

It remains to be seen what the Revolution consisted of—in terms of its possible long-term consequences. This doubtless has to do first with the legislation passed by the revolutionary assemblies and the "reforms" which resulted therefrom (e.g., the suppression of the seigniorial regime, the sale of *biens nationaux*, etc.). [It] has to do more generally with institutional and social transformations which . . . had a potential impact on the economy. But the course of events must also be taken into account—phenomena which belong to the short, even the very short, term. (The General Maximum [of prices] was only in force for a few months, but may have had lasting consequences.) It is widely recognized that events can affect . . .the endowment in factors of production, and the nature of demand; . . . that an economy's long-term growth is simply the result of rates of growth, either positive or negative, which it experiences over successive short-term periods.

We will therefore focus on questions having to do with the long-term economic consequences which may have resulted from revolutionary "events," and on related short-term economic fluctuations:

unstable governments, popular uprisings, coups d'etat, civil and foreign wars, insecurity and banditry. There is no need to insist on the multifarious political circumstances of the 1790s, which could hardly have failed to have a negative effect on the economy, by greatly increasing uncertainty and risk. . . . Special mention must be made of the Montagnard repression against the business world—particularly against the Federalists in Lyon, Marseille, Nantes, Bordeaux, that is to say, against the most dynamic economic centers in the France of Louis XVI. The execution of rich merchants surely weakened provincial capitalism . . . [and] was one factor in the emergence of Paris as the nation's economic capital after the Revolution. . . . The Terror's antipathy to business revived and perhaps reinforced Ancien Regime prejudices against "trade."

It is tempting to consider inflation, which lasted about six years, as nothing more than a single short-term episode in France's economic history. . . . The Jacobin [school of historiography] has minimized its perverse effects, as well as the effects of the command economy which resulted from it. But inflation and the General Maximum disorganized economic relations . . . and devoured the working capital of many firms. Many credit networks were disrupted as well. The inevitable after-effect of this hyperinflation was a harsh deflation at the end of the decade, with usurious rates of interest, which paralyzed many businesses. In real terms inflation also depreciated the value of the *biens nationaux*. High yields and possibilities of high appreciation attracted investment capital to [this confiscated land]. . . . On the other hand, inflation reduced the national debt considerably (a lasting effect, since Napoleon did not borrow). Both in the aggregate and per capita France's public debt in 1815 was much less than it had been in 1789 (and less than that of victorious England as well). On the debit side, however, paper money, banks, and credit in general were to be objects of distrust for a long time to come. One consequence was that in the nineteenth century the Bank of France kept a large reserve of precious metals, which by the end of the century may have cost the French economy half a percentage point of growth a year. . . . The state's financial distress brought public works in the transport sector to a complete halt during the 1790s, while in England canals, docks and roads were built on a grand scale in the middle of the war.

. . . France's foreign trade, and its overseas trade in particular, underwent heavy damage during the Revolution and the Empire. . . . As of 1815, the kind of large-scale maritime trade that France had known in the eighteenth century was dead and buried and would never rise again. . . . The figures for French foreign trade would not reach the level of 1789 again until 1825; yet while in the former year it had been equal in value to that of Great Britain, under the Restoration, it was far behind (and would remain so for a long time to come, since it did not catch up with British trade until 1980). This is one of the most serious and lasting consequences of the revolutionary period.

The main cause of the disaster was obviously the "destruction" of San Domingo, . . . which was directly . . . linked to the revolution in France and to the war with England; but on the deepest level it was caused by . . . slavery, which had created an explosive situation in the "Pearl of the Antilles." Pre-revolutionary French commerce depended heavily on the importation and reexportation of sugar and coffee from San Domingo. The rebellious colony having become independent, and very poor, French colonial trade after 1815 was only a shadow of what it had been in the 1780s.

Though ports and maritime regions suffered lasting damage, the consequences of the disasters which befell large-scale foreign trade were less dramatic for the overall economy. A standard complaint, however, is that nineteenth-century France had closed in on herself, shut off from the outside and specially from the open seas. Do not the events of 1789–1815 provide at least *one* explanation of this withdrawal? . . . French industry, in recession at the time the Revolution broke out, experienced an upswing in 1790 and 1791, but some very bad years followed. War sealed off foreign markets and caused lasting damage to the branches of the economy which were most dependent on foreign trade. The domestic market also contracted—particularly for luxury products. There were shortages of raw material and labor. Conversely . . . the military effort of the Terror created new demand . . . ; but this effort lasted only a limited time and had hardly any economic or technical fallout. . . . Even in the Year II, the war effort took no more than 15 percent of the iron industry's output. Overall industrial production fell markedly and had not yet returned to its pre-revolutionary level by the end of the Directory. The situation varied of course from one sector to another; the traditional textile industries—wool, silk, and linen—suffered greatly. With some difficulty, the iron industry held its own. . . . Cotton is a brilliant exception. . . . This industry's production grew during the 1790s, and new machines were introduced. . . . Cotton's ancillary activities, in machine construction and the chemical industry, also made progress (but they were very small).

This performance should not be unduly emphasized . . . nor should it be suggested that the Revolution was its cause. . . . It can be argued that the war with England provided protection for French manufacturers . . . and that, in conjunction with the neoclassical revival, a fall in the standard of living favored cheap cotton cloth at the expense of traditional fabrics. But *indiennes, mousselines,* and Nanking fabrics had been in fashion before the Revolution, and the case can be made that cotton manufacturing would have developed very rapidly whatever happened. All this deserves special attention, of course, because cotton represents the vanguard of the Industrial Revolution, but we should not forget that for the whole of the period 1789–1815 . . . the growth of the cotton industry was markedly less rapid in France than in Great Britain. By the end of this period France had one million mechanized spindles, Great Britain five.

Economic historians . . . have the habit of writing the history of industrialization in terms of competition, . . . above all in terms of differentials in rates of growth. They may be wrong, but this approach is nonetheless enlightening. In this perspective it cannot be denied that the growth of French industrial production was negative during the Revolution, while for the same period England's industrial growth was positive and rapid. . . . The technological aspect must be taken into account as well. In this respect the picture is not as black as it sometimes seems. Necessity—the lack of raw materials and labor—proved once again to be a force for invention or innovation. . . . During the Year III in Elbeuf . . . the departure of adult men for the army stimulated the adoption of machinery to be operated by women and children. Because of the scarcity of men and horses caused by the war, the Committee of Public Safety decided in July 1794 to recommend the installation of Watt steam engines in the mines. . . . Even in the iron industry it is wrong to say that nothing changed, as technical "tinkering" became widespread.

Much is said about the nefarious effects on technological progress of the rupture with Britain, which was the homeland of invention and innovation. Admittedly, this rupture was never complete. English technicians, for example, continued to work in France during the Revolution and under the Empire. Nevertheless, it is difficult not to conclude that transfers of technology would have taken place on a larger scale if Franco-English relations had not been dislocated for twenty-two years. David Landes was thus able to argue that a whole generation was effectively lost; this counts for a lot in the history of industrialization, which has been with us after all for only 200 years. France, already well behind England in 1789 in terms of both technology and economic structure, fell ten or twenty years further behind, and it cannot be doubted that in 1815 English technology was well ahead, in the cotton industry as well. This gap might of course have been closed by rapid technological progress and economic growth after either 1799 or 1815; but such development as occurred . . . was neither sufficiently rapid or long lasting.

In some sense therefore the [crises] of the 1790s held back France's long-term industrial development. This was particularly true because there was no compensatory period of rapid development after the dislocations of the revolutionary period had come to an end. This is all the more surprising since the Revolution brought forth all sorts of institutional changes which would seem a priori to have favored development.

It did away with the "feudal" regime, with the guild system, with state regulation of the economy, with networks of monopoly and privilege, with internal tariffs; it broke fetters, swept away obstacles, promulgated free enterprise, unified markets. Moreover, on the ground thus swept clear the revolutionary assemblies and Napoleon built new institutions of every sort—from the civil code to the *Ecole polytechnique*—which were certainly more in conformity with the needs of an industrialized society than the old regime's had been. The Napoleonic administration, though hardly the self-governing English style night watchman state the Constituent Assembly had wanted, was neither as heavy handed nor as stultifying as is said. The regime . . . which emerged from the dislocations of 1789-1815 held sway over France for more than a century, made allowance for some state intervention, but was in essence a laissez-faire regime, "a juridical structure tailored to the needs of capitalist enterprise" (T. Kemp).

But historians have an unfortunate tendency to bracket political and economic change, to think that since bourgeoisie and growth are linked, and the Revolution of 1789 was a bourgeois revolution, it must necessarily have been a factor in economic growth. It is in fact an error to believe that a complex of judicial, administrative, and financial reforms possesses in and of itself sufficient power to induce technical progress. Institutional change is neutral or ambiguous. At best, it creates possibilities which economic agents exploit or neglect; other factors cause the transition from the virtual to the actual. This is the view of many writers—including Marxists like T. Kemp and Albert Soboul; the latter, for example, recognized that the "bourgeois revolution" in agriculture was a compromise and incomplete: . . . the resistance of the aristocracy obliged the bourgeoisie to seek support among the peasants, particularly small-scale farmers. [The bourgeoisie] was obliged to make concessions to them, which put a brake on the capitalist development of agriculture. Because of the after-effects of the troubles and wars of the Revolution and the Empire, nineteenth-century France had, according to Kemp, "advanced" institutions and a weak and backward industry. Kemp adds that one factor in this paradox is that the revolutionary bourgeoisie was not recruited from the world of business, nor in particular among industrialists. He thus puts himself in the company of the Burkean Alfred Cobban; yet Cobban went much further, of course, seeing the Revolution as the triumph of a class of landed proprietors, who were intensely conservative in economic matters. The Revolution would thus have been fundamentally anti-capitalist . . . a step backward on the road to economic development, . . . a factor in the economic backwardness of nineteenth-century France. Other Anglo-Saxon writers maintain that the Revolution created a "static" structure, wherein innovative changes were discouraged, a "slow growth" economy. . . . Recently, an American scholar, W. M. Reddy, maintained that in the textile industry the Revolution made no changes in social relations, in which the domestic system was perpetuated. . . . He talks of a "world without entrepreneurs" and of a "caricature of market culture" in the nineteenth-century French textile business.

No attempt will be made to discuss these views here, though some of them are highly debatable. England was also ruled by great landed proprietors, but this did not prevent her becoming "the first industrial nation." They do indicate, however, that the idea that revolutionary legislation was wholly favorable to economic progress must be taken with a pinch of salt. . . . The revolutionary concept of property was not frankly favorable to capitalism, the 1790s saw many often successful efforts, not only by the Parisian Sans-Culottes, but by communities everywhere, to put obstacles in the way of capitalist enterprise and technical change—a marginal but genuine factor in economic "lag."

Nor should it be forgotten that "the opening of Careers to Talent" diverted hosts of gifted young men into civil, and above all military, service. In an entrepreneurial culture such as existed in northern England,

Julien Sorel, the son of a sawmill owner in Franche-Comté, would have pushed aside his rustic older brothers, acquired more sawmills, forests, and eventually several ironworks; he would have been elected to the *Corps législatif* of the Second Empire, instead of getting himself prematurely guillotined. . . . In terms of Reddy's formula, we can speak of the state bourgeoisie, which took shape and prospered during the Revolution and under the Empire, as a cartoon bourgeoisie. . . . Within it were to be found many of the "rascals," whom Robespierre had denounced [and who overthrew him]: politicians and top civil servants, generals, . . . speculators, army contractors, purchasers of *biens nationaux*, each and all beneficiaries of "republican profiteering. . . ." This was not an entrepreneurial bourgeoisie. It became rich through its privileged relations with the state. Its enduring ascendancy was surely a factor in economic backwardness. Textile manufacturers counted for very little in comparison, despite the expansion of their business.

The rural economic and social conditions strongly reinforce these arguments concerning the fundamentally conservative character of the Revolution. . . . There is broad agreement that . . . the Revolution consolidated the French system of small scale peasant property and farming, a system which would become even more widespread in the nineteenth century. While great estates had not disappeared, they were proportionally less important than in the rest of Europe, and this system made France distinctive. The French were long proud of being a land of small scale property, a nation of peasants. . . . In our own time this self-satisfaction has given way to an inferiority complex, largely as a consequence of criticism by Anglo-Saxon economists and historians (culminating in a British media campaign against the "medieval" character of French agriculture).

From Arthur Young onwards, a whole line of British observers has harshly criticized French agriculture . . . , in particular the impact of the Revolution thereon. Nineteenth-century writers denounced the equal division of inherited property (forgetting that . . . this antedated the Revolution in many provinces). . . . Some . . . wrote veritable jeremiads on the subject . . . making somber predictions . . . about how the peasants were going to be reduced to the same level as the Irish, [and how] an even bloodier peasant rebellion would break out. . . . John Stuart Mill, on the other hand, defended the French system. . . . This debate actually had a political and ideological aspect [relating to] discussions about large-scale landed property in Britain; its apologists emphasized that equal division among heirs ran counter to property rights and freedom. . . . Several Anglo-Saxon historians (who do not subscribe to this polemical agenda) have recently argued that the Revolution not only failed to bring about any notable technical improvement, but perpetuated bad [agricultural] practices and stymied attempts at modernization which were going on at the time . . . [thus delaying] the Agricultural Revolution and by extension the Industrial Revolution as well.

There is much. . . exaggeration . . . in these arguments. The Revolution may be faulted for consolidating an archaic system, not for creating it. There is room for doubt as to whether the suspension of certain agricultural changes [undertaken] during the monarchy's final years had more than marginally negative effects (and they were perhaps off-set by the positive consequences of the "liberation" of the peasants). The "disappearance of the English peasant" took seven centuries, after all; why was it necessary for France to liquidate her peasantry at a stroke? Overall agricultural production may indeed have shown only modest growth during the Revolution and under the Empire, but the standard of living of the peasants (particularly the least well off) improved, thanks to a well-documented rise in real agricultural wages.

In opposition to these traditional views we find those of recent revisionists . . . that the peasantry was not an obstacle to industrialization in nineteenth-century France, and that its consolidation during the Revolution was not a factor in the country's slow rate of growth. . . . [To Colin Heywood], nineteenth-century France is a "moderately successful case of balanced growth, with a respectable performance"—(a position for which this writer has argued several times).

Was Alfred Cobban right then to say that the economic consequences of the Revolution were astonishingly small for so profound an upheaval? . . . Did the Revolution ruin France? It's a question that is often asked; but nations are not ruined, in the sense that an individual or a business may be ruined. So we have to understand ruin in the sense of impoverishment, as Taine did, when he wrote that the "poor French" were ruined from father to son by Louis XIV, by Louis XV, by the Revolution, by the Empire—a list that may easily be lengthened. It is certainly possible to see the Revolution as one link in the chain of "French misfortune," the long saga . . . of a people for whom nothing succeeds and for whom the "millenarian hopes" of 1789 in particular ended in butchery; but this is a problem which goes beyond the limits of this article. The truth is that the impoverishment of France was limited (it could not be otherwise in a preeminently agricultural country, where the sectors affected—industry and commerce—were in a minority). It is certain that Louis XVIII reigned over a more prosperous country than he had known as comte de Provence, a country in which there was more affluence and less extreme poverty. The economic difficulties of the late Ancien Régime had been followed by conditions of impoverishment in the middle (and even the late) 1790s and by the prosperity of the Empire. In this perspective the Revolution is no more than an interlude, an indentation in an upward curve, in the French economy's long-term process of modernization; but it did not cause any profound structural changes. . . . It is probable that under the Restoration France could have been richer if the institutional reforms which the Revolution had imposed had not been followed by long wars; but it is equally probable that the country would have been less prosperous if the Ancien Regime had continued its course.

William Hamilton Sewell, Jr.

Revolutionary Artisans and the Formation of the French Working Class

William Sewell (1940–) was one of the first American labor historians to apply the methods of cultural anthropology to the study of working-class movements. He is also one of the rare social historians of France whose interests span both the Old Regime and the nineteenth century— as this selection indicates. He shares with other historians in this anthology the distinction of having published in *Les Annales: Economies, Sociétés, Civilisations.*

Artisans, Factory Workers, and the Formation of the French Working Class

Viewed from the standpoint of Britain, the history of French working-class formation is paradoxical. Britain was the homeland of the industrial revolution; the French economy remained predominantly rural and artisanal until the twentieth century. Yet the French were the unquestioned leaders in the development of socialism and working-class consciousness. Most of the great early socialist theorists, with the exception of Robert Owen, were French: "Gracchus" Babeuf, Claude-Henri de Saint-Simon, Charles Fourier, Louis Auguste Blanqui, Pierre-Joseph Proudhon, Louis Blanc. It was also in France, in the revolution of 1848, that socialism first became a mass movement. Given the usual understanding of class consciousness as the product of a burgeoning industrial economy, the precociousness of French working-class consciousness is downright embarrassing. The embarrassment, however, is founded on a set of misunderstandings, both of the nature of French industrial capitalism and of the relationship between class consciousness and the development of factory industry. Although France did not experience a British-style "industrial revolution," French society was nevertheless transformed by industrial capitalism in the nineteenth century. And although French industrialization did not spawn a huge mass of factory workers, it did produce an abundance of discontented artisans who were the mainstay of the early working-class movement, not only in France but in all the early industrial countries. . . .

I. French Industrialization

The key characteristics of French industrialization were a very gradual and early start, continued predominance of handicraft production, relatively slow growth of factory industry, and low rates of population growth. This peculiar pattern left its marks on the French working-class movement. . . .

France never experienced a "take off" of the sort hypothesized by W. W. Rostow—a sudden spurt of output that begins sustained industrial growth. French industrial production began its upward movement as early as the 1750s, before the beginning of the British "industrial revolution," and rose gradually but steadily thereafter. This expansion took place both in rural textiles . . . , and urban industry. . . . The increased productivity that resulted from mechanization and the application of steam power was, hence, not at the origin of modern French industrial growth, but was added to an already expanding base of handicraft industrial production. . . .

Much of the industrial growth of the nineteenth century continued to be in handicrafts. Although the British captured the bulk of the world market for iron and inexpensive cotton and woolen textiles, the French continued to dominate the market for certain luxury goods. The silks of Lyon, . . . and the innumerable luxury products of Paris were among the most important and most rapidly growing industries in nineteenth-century France. . . . Rather than competing directly with British factory-made goods, France continued to exploit its comparative advantage in high-quality products that required highly skilled workmanship. In fact, even the French factory industries that were most successful on the international market . . . specialized in the finest grades of cloth. In addition to craft industries producing for the international market, craft industries supplying the wants of the domestic population continued to thrive. As in all other countries during the first half of the nineteenth century, factory industry was quite limited in scope, and housing, clothing, food, and most other consumer goods continued to be produced by hand. . . .

The classic innovations of the British industrial revolution were adopted later and on a much smaller scale in France than in Britain. In the case of textiles, the British advantage in all but the highest quality goods was so pronounced that most French markets were limited to producing mainly for the internal French market. A large number of textile factories were erected in . . . other cities, and cotton manufacturing was one of the most rapidly growing industries in the country. But in comparison with [British cities] French centers were distinctly second-rate. . . . Mining and metallurgy were important nodes of industrial growth for France, but they were hardly comparable to British and (later) German counterparts. It was the relatively slow growth of the French factory sector that caused J. H. Clapham to wonder whether France ever had a real "industrial revolution," and led the following generation of economic historians of France to write endlessly about the "stagnation" or "retardation" of the French economy in the nineteenth century. But more recent quantitative studies have demonstrated that the concern about "retardation" was misplaced. French output per capita grew at essentially the same rate as British output per capita until World War I, and beyond. The shape of economic growth in France was very different from that in Britain, with French agriculture and handicraft industry playing a more important role, but the economy's overall performance was no less impressive.

One reason that French industrialization differed in form was the low rate of French population growth. French birth rates had already begun to fall by the late eighteenth century, and during the entire nineteenth century France's population increased by less than 50 percent. Britain's population, in contrast, grew by 350 percent in the nineteenth century. . . . In France, a much higher proportion of the population was composed of peasants who were only partially engaged in the cash nexus, and the national territory remained divided into only partially integrated regional markets. . . . These circumstances placed limitations on the possibilities for factory production in France and made it economically rational for a large part of the nation's capital to be invested in agriculture and in handicraft industry. To an earlier generation of economic historians, this French pattern of low population growth and the continued predominance of agriculture and handicrafts appeared stagnant. It is now clear that it was simply an alternative form of industrialization, one that led to rising per capita incomes and eventually to "high mass consumption" as ineluctably as an industrial revolution in the British style.

This French pattern of industrialization had two important consequences for the formation of the French working class. The first was a relative continuity in the urban experience of workers. Owing to low overall rates of population increase, French cities grew much less rapidly during the early stages of industrialization than British, German, or American cities. Between 1800 and 1850 only one of the ten largest cities in France had doubled in population; in Britain all of the ten largest cities had doubled or more than doubled in population . . . in the same years. . . . British cities were also strikingly different in kind from

French cities. Only four of the twenty-five largest cities in France in 1851 were significant centers of factory industry. . . . In Britain six of the top ten cities in 1851 were centers of factory industry. . . . A majority of the great cities of nineteenth-century Britain were essentially creations of the industrial revolution and factory industry, and their urban form and culture reflected this fact. In France nearly all the important cities had long and proud urban traditions, and most of them grew gradually enough that they retained much of their traditional spatial and cultural form through the nineteenth century. With some important exceptions, the class segregation and radical separation of home and work that occurred in the new factory towns of Britain was far less pronounced in French cities. . . . [T]he vast majority of French workers continued to live in mixed centers of administration, commerce, and industry. For this reason, issues of urban space are far less important for the history of class formation in France than in Britain.

The second important consequence of the French pattern of industrialization for French class formation was that artisans rather than factory workers long remained the overwhelming majority of French industrial workers. Even as late as 1876, the industrial population employed in small-scale industry was twice that in large-scale industry. Even in Britain, artisans outnumbered factory workers until past the middle of the century and were disproportionately represented in working-class political activity. But in France the imbalance was far more pronounced. Down to the Commune of 1871, the history of working-class protest in France was essentially the history of artisan protest. The conventional assumption that the class-conscious workers' movement was a product of the factory is even less tenable for France than for other early industrial countries. An account of French working-class formation, therefore, must give special attention to the specific experiences of artisans.

II. Artisans, Textile Workers, and the Dynamics of Industrial Capitalism

The fact that artisan industry survived in France well into the twentieth century by no means implies that it was untouched by the development of industrial capitalism. In fact, capitalism began to transform crafts long before the introduction of English technological innovations in the late eighteenth and early nineteenth centuries. The first handicrafts to feel its effects were woolen and linen textiles. Initially these were urban industries, and as such they were governed by the same kinds of guilds that regulated all other urban crafts. As a longtime staple of interregional and international commerce, the textile industries were subjected to the dynamics of capitalist development very early. By the sixteenth and seventeenth centuries, the merchant capitalists who dominated the textile industry began to put out spinning and weaving operations to rural families who worked in their own cottages and who usually combined these industrial activities with cultivation of a tiny plot of ground. . . . The putting-out textile industry—in which manufacture was rural and domestic, but coordination and control was in the hands of urban capitalists who operated an inter-regional or international market—was the most advanced sector of the capitalist economy in the seventeenth and eighteenth centuries. When cotton manufacture was introduced in the eighteenth century, it followed the same putting-out pattern already established by woolens and linens. The introduction of spinning and weaving factories in the first half of the nineteenth century and the consequent re-urbanization of the textile industry marked not the beginning of industrial capitalism in France, but the arrival of a new stage in the exploitation of an industry that had already been capitalist for at least two centuries.

The history of the textile trades was unique. . . . It was not until the abolition of guilds in the French Revolution and the quickened expansion of national and world markets in the first half of the nineteenth century that industrial capitalism began to have pervasive effects on a broad range of artisan trades. Considered abstractly, capitalism had a uniform dynamic, the same in the nineteenth-century urban artisan trades as in the rural putting-out textile industry of the seventeenth and eighteenth centuries or in the new textile factories of the nineteenth. Systems of production were reorganized to turn out a larger quantity of standardized, usually lower quality goods at a lower cost by a less-skilled labor force, in order to take advantage of expanding market opportunities. But in terms of concrete experiences, what happened to nineteenth-century urban artisans was quite distinct from what happened to textile workers, either in the seventeenth and eighteenth centuries or in the nineteenth.

Scholars have commonly considered nineteenth-century urban crafts to be "traditional," mainly because few of them were affected by important technological changes until near the end of the century. Recent research, however, has revealed a profusion of new exploitative practices that transformed many handicraft trades even without the introduction of new machinery. Entrepreneurs in diverse industries . . . responded to rising demand for their products by turning away from the older practice of making items to order for their clients and instead specializing in standardized, ready-to-use items that could be mass produced and sold at a lower price. Such entrepreneurs thoroughly reorganized existing patterns of production, increasing the division of labor, introducing various subcontracting schemes, diluting workers' skills, or putting out some phase of manufacture to women and children. . . . These practices not only lowered the earnings and reduced the autonomy of workers in the reorganized branch of the trade, but reduced wages for workers who remained in the traditional branch. Exploitation, recent studies make clear, could be as intense in handicraft industries as in factories in the first half of the nineteenth century. . . . This finding is of major significance for any attempt to understand the predominance of artisans in the early working-class movement, since it implies that artisans had as much reason to protest as factory workers. But it goes only halfway. It helps to explain why artisans' rates of participation in protest movements were as high as those of factory workers, but not why they were vastly higher. To explain this disparity, we must widen our inquiry beyond the question of exploitation to explore the ways that different types of workers understood and acted on their workplace experiences.

A useful starting point is the classical Marxist account of the development of class consciousness among factory workers. Marx pointed not only to the intensity of exploitation in the factory but to the increasingly socialized process of production. Gathered together under one roof and constrained to cooperate with other workers in a complex process of production, factory workers would be made aware of the commonality of their interests as wage workers and thereby encouraged to act together on those interests. The problem with this explanation is its excessively literal materialism. Marx assumed that a consciousness of commonality depended on the workers' sheer physical proximity, on their visible and palpable interconnections on the factory floor. In fact, development of collective consciousness is less a matter of recognizing palpable facts than of constructing interpretive webs that give certain facts a special salience. The fact that workers are crowded together into factories does not lead automatically to a recognition of common interest and a feeling of solidarity, nor does the fact that workers labor in scattered workshops necessarily inhibit such a recognition; it all depends on how they understand their work and their relations to one another. But if Marx was wrong to think that the physical arrangement of work would be the crucial factor leading workers to understand that their labor was social, he was certainly right to point out that some such understanding was a necessary condition for collective action and consciousness.

The crucial difference between artisans and factory workers was in the way they understood their labor; the artisans' proclivity for class-conscious action was largely a consequence of a social understanding of their labor that derived from the . . . guild system. . . . In contrast, the relative quiescence of factory workers . . . grew out of a less social, more individualized conception of the relations of production. These different understandings of labor arose from the distinct histories of capitalism in the textile industry and the urban crafts. The growth of a rural, domestic, putting-out organization of the textile industry created a new labor force whose self-conception was not significantly influenced by urban corporate institutions. In urban crafts, corporate institutions and traditions constituted the major framework of productive relations until . . . the French Revolution. Class consciousness emerged in France as a transformation of the artisans' corporate understanding of labor under the twin impact of capitalist development and revolutionary politics. The impact of industrial capitalism on the artisan trades has already been outlined. To discover how artisans became conscious of themselves as members of a working class, we must examine their corporate cultural and institutional heritage, and then determine how this heritage was transformed into a class-conscious workers' movement during revolutionary political upheavals. . . .

III. The Corporate Understanding of Labor

Virtually all the urban skilled trades of Old Regime France were organized in corporations of some kind. These corporations were charted by royal or municipal authority and were empowered to regulate the practice of a trade in a given city. Their powers included: a local monopoly. . . ; quality control. . . ; control over training (no one could work as a journeyman or be accepted as a master unless he had passed a proper apprenticeship); limitation on entry. . . . In the prerevolutionary corporation, labor was nothing if not social. The trade was not composed of individual masters who, as [capitalists] organized production as they saw fit. . . . Nor were workers free to work for whoever offered them the most favorable conditions. Rather, both masters and workers were subjected to the collective discipline of the corporation, which regulated everyone and everything in the trade—ostensibly for the good of the trade as a whole and society at large. The production and sale of goods in the urban skilled trades of Old Regime France was organized by the corporation—a collective body—rather than by individuals connected only by market relations.

Relations of production in the artisan trades were social not only in an institutional but in a moral sense. Corporations . . . were units of pervasive solidarity. . . . [F]or example, masters swore a solemn oath of loyalty to the corporation upon their elevation to the mastership. But the moral community of the trade was manifested above all in the corporation's religious life. The corporation was coextensive with a confraternity established under the protection of the traditional patron saint of the trade. All members of the trade were therefore expected to venerate the same saint and to celebrate his or her festival in common. . . . The confraternity also organized distribution of mutual aid. Every member paid monthly dues to a common treasury . . . and benefits were paid to members who were sick or had fallen on hard times, or to their widows and orphans. . . . The corporation was, in short, a moral community whose members were bound to one another "in sickness and in health 'til death do us part." . . . This does not mean that life in the urban trades was characterized by perfect harmony. . . . Like any human community, trades were riven by innumerable jealousies, . . . and enmities. Above all, they were split by struggles between masters and journeymen. Journeymen were generally excluded from the annual assembly at which the masters discussed the trade's problems and elected officers, and they usually were excluded from the benefits of the confraternity as well. Legally, journeymen were considered to be under the paternal authority of masters, much like children, servants, and wives. But journeymen frequently organized illegal corporate brotherhoods of their own, challenging the masters' authority, claiming a right . . . like that of the masters' corporations . . . to regulate the trade for the common good, and attempting to maintain good wages and working conditions by carrying out strikes. The most powerful of these journeymen's brotherhoods were organized into national federations called "compagnonnage." . . . These brotherhoods maintained rooming houses for itinerant journeymen making their "tour de France" and had an astonishingly elaborate ritual life. Trade "communities" sometimes resembled battlegrounds between rival masters' and journeymen's organizations. Yet the notion that the trade was a community was honored even in these struggles. Both masters and workers claimed to be acting on behalf of the trade as a whole, not for the interests of journeymen or of masters. Here it is significant that the journeymen's brotherhoods invariably chose the same patron saint as the masters'. . . .

Relations between masters and journeymen in a given trade were often tense or bitter, but the tensions and bitterness were founded on a sense of permanent membership in a common community. One might make an analogy with family quarrels that set brother against brother or son against father. Such an analogy has much to recommend it, since family metaphors . . . played an important role in corporate language. Sixteenth-century printers' journeymen studied by Natalie Davis stated the ideal explicitly: . . . "The Masters and Journeymen are one body together, like a family and a fraternity." The analogy with family quarrels is appropriate in another sense, for just as sons could expect to succeed their fathers as they grew to adulthood, so journeymen expected eventually to become masters. . . . Disputes between masters and journeymen were often generational quarrels as much as quarrels between lifetime classes.

In summary urban artisans of the Old Regime understood their labor as social, both in the sense that it was and ought to be given shape by collective regulations of the corporation and in the sense that men working in the same trade formed a solidary moral community. This understanding of labor as social was not, however, class conscious. . . . [I]t included both wage workers and employers in a single . . . trade community. It did not extend community feelings or community regulations beyond the boundaries of the trade. Those who worked in different trades were regarded with indifference at best, and all too often with hostility. The masters' corporations were engaged in constant legal battles with corporations in rival trades, and journeymen of different trades commonly engaged in violent brawls with each other. The sense that all wage workers were . . . members of a single solidary class, was utterly absent in the artisan trades of the Old Regime. It was only in the new society created by the French Revolution that class consciousness could emerge.

The French Revolution effected a far-reaching transformation of the social order. In terms of political theory, at least, France was transformed from a society composed of privileged corporate bodies linked by their common subordination to the crown into a collection of individual citizens, joined together by a social contract that was founded on their natural rights and that guaranteed their equality before the law. In carrying out this transformation, the revolutionaries swept away the artisans' privileged corporations, leaving each artisan legally free to carry on his trade according to his own inclinations, capacities, and interests. The regime of corporate regulation was replaced by a regime of "industrial liberty." At the same time, private property was exalted to the status of a "natural, inalienable, and sacred right" by the Declaration of the Rights of Man and Citizen, and in practice the revolutionary and Napoleonic legal reforms freed the property of artisan masters . . . from any collectively imposed constraints.

These changes did not immediately turn the corporately minded master artisans of the Old Regime into petty-capitalist individualists who henceforth engaged in a ruthless and single-minded pursuit of their own interests. . . . But the legal framework in which they operated was now drastically different. Even before the Revolution, many masters were tempted by the steadily expanding economy of the later eighteenth century to experiment . . . with new ways of organizing production, . . . cutting labor costs in order to produce a larger quantity of standardized products that could be sold below the going price. . . . They continually ran afoul of corporate regulations. But after the Revolution, these "abuses" became perfectly legal exercises of the entrepreneur's "industrial liberty" . . . to dispose of his property as he saw fit. Consequently, even though most masters . . . continued to operate in traditional ways, it was now virtually impossible to stop a more aggressive minority from introducing innovations that cut costs and intensified the exploitation of labor. This had two important results. First, it tended to reduce wages and cause deteriorating working conditions even among employees of masters who did not innovate. Second, within the trade, it caused an increasing heterogeneity of working conditions, of wages, of quality and price of product, and of employer/employee relations. The socially controlled trade community of the Old Regime corporation was gradually being transformed, by the combined action of a new legal system and an expanding market economy, into an anarchic collection of individualized entrepreneurs and laborers.

Not surprisingly, these changes in the handicraft trades quickly gave rise to attempts to reunite the trade community and to restore some measure of corporate control over the productive process. But these attempts were undertaken primarily by workers, not masters. The power of the masters' corporations had rested on their legal privileges, and when these were abolished in the French Revolution, masters' corporations were effectively destroyed. But the legal prohibitions had very little effect on the alternative corporations of the journeymen, because these had always been illegal and were accustomed to a clandestine existence. Moreover, although masters were increasingly disunited, . . . the workers were generally united in their opposition to the new exploitative practices. The result, . . . was a flowering of workers' corporations that attempted to impose far-reaching controls over working conditions in their trades. By the late 1820s, virtually all the skilled trades in the major cities of France had some kind of corporate workers' organization that was actively resisting exploitative practices.

Yet as widespread as the corporate workers' movement of the 1820s may have been, it did not signify the formation of a self-conscious working class. Workers in different trades maintained . . . traditional attitudes . . . toward workers in other trades. And although the workers' corporations could be quite militant in their stance toward masters in labor disputes, they posed no articulate alternative to the existing property system that ensured the masters' continued power. The corporate workers' movement of the Restoration did differ in important respects from [that] of the Old Regime. It was dominated by workers rather than by masters, and it was in opposition to . . . the law and the principles enforced by public authority. But it retained the essential Old Regime vision of the trade as an exclusive solidary community, and assumed that the masters would continue to collect their profits and exercise day-to-day authority in the workshops. The workers' movement of the Restoration retained the forms, language, and vision of the Old Regime journeymen's corporations with only minor changes. This idiom provided the workers with a solid organizational foundation from which to press their claims, but it also limited the kinds of claims the workers could make. It was only when the idiom of the workers' movement was expanded to take in the forms, language, and vision of the French Revolution that the corporate workers' movement could begin to become class conscious. . . .

IV. Revolutionary Political Discourse and the Emergence of Class Consciousness

The French Revolution's transformation of the institutional structure of society was accompanied by the development of a new political language . . . that set the terms in which public claims . . . could be couched—a language of individual citizens, natural rights, popular sovereignty, and the social contract. During the course of the revolutionary and Napoleonic era this discourse developed many variations. Revolutionary language could soon be spoken with a distinct Jacobin, moderate, sans-culotte, Thermidorian, or Napoleonic accent, and it could be used to justify either repression and maintenance of order or struggle and insurrection. It became, in short, a complex and fully articulated linguistic world. . . .

The Restoration in 1814 sharply changed public discourse. Respect for tradition and authority, horror of revolution, and religious piety became the order of the day. Yet the return of the Bourbon monarchy could not restore prerevolutionary political conditions . . . [T]he alternative political discourse of the revolutionary era thrived in the opposition, both in the parliamentary opposition of the liberal constitutional monarchists and in the extra parliamentary opposition of radical journalists and republican conspirators. In 1830, . . . when the inflexible Charles X, attempted to suppress the liberties guaranteed in the Charter, the result was a popular insurrection, the overthrow of the Bourbons, and the establishment of a more liberal Orleanist monarchy. The Orleanist regime restored revolutionary language, though of a moderate and liberal sort, to the center of political life. It was in the social and political struggles following the July 1830 revolution . . . that the artisans of Paris, Lyon, and other French cities transformed their corporate understanding of labor into class consciousness. . . . In the days following the [1830] revolution, Parisian workers, . . . the shock troops of the insurrection, quite naturally expected sympathetic treatment from the . . . new regime. But these initial expectations soon evaporated when Orleanist officials dismissed workers' demand for controls on their trades as assaults on the "liberty of industry." The workers . . . responded by developing a new political and organizational language that met the regime on its own chosen terrain: the discourse of liberty. In doing so, the workers embraced, but also modified and elaborated, the liberal language of the French Revolution. Class consciousness, in other words, was a transformed version of liberal revolutionary discourse. The workers' new political language was worked out on many levels simultaneously: in newspapers and pamphlets, in political organizations, in the statues and practices of workers' corporations, and in strikes and direct actions against the masters or political authorities. . . . Because this movement was complex and multifaceted, any summary description of its discursive practice is bound to oversimplify and distort; nevertheless, some crucial features can be identified.

An articulate minority of workers quickly appropriated revolutionary language, modifying it to highlight the moral and political standing of workers. One example was the appropriation of an argument the Abbé Sieyès had introduced in *What Is the Third Estate?* The Third Estate, he claimed, was the entire nation because it performed all the useful work of society, while the nobility "is foreign to the nation because of its idleness." Sieyès, of course, conceived of useful work as including all the tasks and occupations carried out by the Third Estate. The workers in the early 1830s took one more step and declared that manual labor alone supported all of society. It followed that workers, because they did all of society's useful labor, were in fact the sovereign people. The bourgeoisie, which did not labor, was in effect a new aristocracy. Working-class authors fortified this conclusion by changing the usage of a cluster of important revolutionary words: "aristocrat," "privilege," "servitude," and "emancipation," among others. Bourgeois were dubbed "new aristocrats," who used their "privilege" of property ownership to keep workers in "servitude" as industrial "serfs" or "slaves." This turned the bourgeois constitutional government based on a property franchise into an oppressive "feudal" tyranny, and justified the workers' efforts to gain their "emancipation"—by revolution, if necessary.

The great problem posed by the workers' adoption of revolutionary language was that it initially gave the workers no way of justifying their essentially corporate demands. According to revolutionary discourse, society was composed of free individual citizens, not suprapersonal corporate bodies, and attempts to impose collective regulations on a trade therefore appeared as an infringement of the liberty of the individual. The workers solved this problem . . . by elaborating the idea of "association," which became the key slogan of the workers' movement. . . . The right of association had not been stressed much during the French Revolution, since eliminating all intermediary bodies between the individual and the state had been one of the Revolution's primary tasks. Yet the citizens' right to associate freely with one another was an inseparable part of the "liberté" proclaimed in 1789 and revived so conspicuously in 1830. If the state itself was conceived of . . . as an association formed by the free and equal citizens of the nation and united by bonds of fraternity, it is hardly surprising that citizens should wish to construct more limited associations along the same lines. This was precisely what the workers did in the early 1830s. They rechristened their corporate organizations with such names as . . . "Society of Fraternal Amity," and "Association of Brothers of Concord," and turned them into democratic voluntary associations based on secular humanitarianism rather than exclusive corporations . . . based on the religious idiom of the Old Regime. When workers' organizations became associations, the regulations they proposed became not an assault on freedom of industry but an expression of the associated free wills of the producers, much as laws of a nation were an expression of the general will. In this way their claims for collective regulation were made compatible with revolutionary discourse.

The idea of association was also developed in another distinct direction: . . . in the early 1830s . . . workers and socialists developed the idea of producers' associations or . . . cooperatives. The basic concept, . . . was for workers to establish "associative" workshops in which they would be joint owners of the means of production. These workshops were to be capitalized initially by regular weekly contributions from the associates and would eventually expand to include the whole industry, absorbing masters and workers alike into a unified trade community in which private property would be abolished. The notion of producers' associations was predicated on an ambiguity in liberal discourse. If citizens possessed the right to associate freely, they could use this right to create voluntary organizations intended to overcome the egoistic individualism and anarchy of the current liberal system. By purely peaceful and legal means, workers might eventually hope to supplant private property with associative property, thereby transforming the whole of society.

The final innovation of these years was the extension of the idiom of association to encompass not merely the workers of a given trade, but . . . of all trades. It was in the form of an "association of all trades" that a unified . . . working class first made its appearance in France. . . . [W]hen the long economic depression that followed the revolution of 1830 finally gave way to a sustained boom the workers responded to the favorable economic circumstances with a gigantic wave of strikes that crested in 1833. These strikes were organized . . . by the workers' refurbished corporate trade associations. . . . They were an attempt to establish, by direct action, the unity and collective control over the trade implied by the term "association." In the course of these strikes, workers sometimes also established . . . producers' cooperatives. Although the idea of producers' associations was largely borrowed [from] utopian discourse, . . . it was applied in a thoroughly practical fashion. The main function of producers' associations set up in the fall of 1833 was to strengthen the workers' hand in strikes by providing jobs while the masters' shops were shut down—not, for the time being, to supplant the masters permanently. In other words, producers' cooperatives [were] . . . established to impose collective controls over the trade.

One of the most notable features of the strikes of the fall of 1833 was an unprecedented cooperation between trades. Striking workers in one trade would appeal to other trades and receive moral and material support, which would be reciprocated if and when the second trade went on strike. . . . In the enthusiasm of a strike movement animated by associations, it suddenly became clear to many workers that the spirit of association should be expanded to encompass all workers, and that this could be accomplished by associating their single-trade societies in a grand "association of all the trades." . . . The creation of a class-conscious proletariat was a generalization, a projection to a higher level, of the loyalties that workers in a given trade had long felt for each other. But it was not until workers' corporations were themselves seen as free associations of productive laboring citizens, rather than as distinct corporations devoted to the perfection of a particular craft, that the wider fraternity of all workers became thinkable.

One final feature of [this] strike movement . . . should be noted. . . . [T]he strikers were aided by the revolutionary republican Society of the Rights of Man. Initially a small but militant bourgeois republican sect, the society began to recruit working-class members in 1832 and had come to contain a majority of workers by the fall of 1833, including leaders of some . . . "philanthropic societies." At the same time, the society modified its originally purely political republicanism to embrace various vaguely socialist proposals for economic reform. This new interest in economic and social questions was given practical expression in the help the society extended to the workers in their strikes. Thus, the fall of 1833 saw not only the creation of a new and powerful sense of class consciousness among artisans working in different trades, but also the first steps toward a political alliance between radical republicanism and socialism.

On the level of institution building, the workers' movement of the early 1830s can count few lasting achievements. Once the strike wave had run its course, the government countered with overwhelming force. In the spring of 1834 it . . . outlaw[ed] both the Society of the Rights of Man and most of the organizations the workers had constructed. The workers of Lyon responded with a massive insurrection, which was followed by a smaller rising in Paris. These unsuccessful risings broke the élan of the workers' movement and government repression soon drove its remnants underground. Yet the transformations of the early 1830s created the intellectual, linguistic, and organizational space on which the subsequent workers' movement was built. These transformations established for the first time a class-conscious discourse and institutional practice that was further elaborated by workers over the following decades. . . .

In 1839 and 1840 something of the agitation of the early 1830s returned. There was an abortive rising in Paris in 1839 and a huge wave of strikes the following year. The publication of these works [by Cabet, Louis Blam, and Proudhon] led to an explosion of socialist writings. From 1840 on, socialist ideas became a palpable presence in French public discourse. . . .

As the February revolution of 1848 was to demonstrate, socialism had won a large following among the working class by the late 1840s. . . . In Paris [and] some of the major provincial cities, significant numbers of workers became followers of [various socialists], especially of Etienne Cabet, . . . by far the most successful at proselytizing among workers. But as important as the socialist schools were in developing and broadcasting socialist ideas, they could never have made socialism the mass movement it became in 1848. The socialist schools had two crucial weaknesses. First, they were sectarian and dogmatic. . . . Second, they rejected political action as a means of constructing socialism, relying instead on some combination of moral persuasion and working-class self help. This meant that they could never enlist the large number of politically aware French workers who adhered to the revolutionary tradition of popular political action.

The really massive development of socialism among the working class took place outside the distinct socialist schools and was the consequence of an appropriation . . . of the revolutionary political tradition. It was, in a sense, a continuation of the work begun by the Society of the Rights of Man in 1832 and 1833. The creation of an explicitly republican socialism is associated above all with the names of Louis Blanc, or Blanqui. It was, however, very much a collective development, a broad and loosely articulated collaboration between left-wing republicans, workers, and socialist theorists. . . . Republican socialism was based on two essential ideas. First socialism was a necessary completion of the French Revolution. The legal and political freedoms gained in the first

French Revolution must now be completed by social and economic reforms that would free workers from the tyranny of wealth and egoism and establish a real as well as a formal liberty and equality. And second, this could not be achieved without a political revolution and the establishment of a democratic and republican form of government. By the late 1840s this republican socialism had captured the left wing of the republican movement, and in doing so it had also become the creed of politically conscious workers who would never have embraced the apolitical socialism of the schools. By 1848 there was no significant nonsocialist radical alternative competing for workers' political allegiance; any bourgeois republican who wished to cultivate a working-class following had no choice but to endorse at least a vaguely socialist program.

How thoroughly things had changed since 1830 was made clear in 1848. Whereas the July revolution of 1830 had caught the workers unaware and incapable of articulating an independent program until it was too late, the February revolution of 1848 immediately provoked a massive class-conscious workers' movement throughout France. From the beginning, the workers of Paris pushed the revolution to the left, forcing the provisional government . . . to proclaim a republic on February 24, to proclaim the "right to labor" and the establishment of National Workshops on February 25 . . . , an officially sanctioned "association of all the trades," [which] formed the center of the revolutionary workers' movement of 1848. It not only provided workers with a public forum and a recognized place in the affairs of the republic, but also required them to form unified trade organizations. . . . It was above all in these revitalized corporate trade associations that the workers sketched out their alternative socialist version of the new republic in the brief revolutionary spring of 1848. . . .

The workers' corporate associations of 1848 were little republics, formed in virtually all trades of the capital, based on universal suffrage of the trade, led by elected officers and delegates, and regulated by written constitutions, frequently prefaced by miniature declarations of rights. Their ends were at once economic, social, and political. Economically, the workers' associations asserted control over all aspects of production and exchange. The workers negotiated conventions with masters that fixed uniform wages, hours, and conditions of work for the entire trade. . . . The conventions with the masters reestablished practical collective regulation over the trades. . . . [At] the same time workers launched schemes for associated production that were intended eventually to solve problems permanently by turning private property into associated property. Socially, the workers' associations extended the usual provisions for mutual aid. . . . It was in politics that the workers' associations of 1848 moved furthest beyond their predecessors of the 1830s. In 1848 workers' associations became political actors. . . . They envisioned that the Luxembourg Commission, which they dubbed the "Estates General of Labor," would become a second National Assembly, representing the trade associations that organized and performed all the nation's labor and that maintained fraternal republican solidarity through mutual aid. Workers' associations, . . . the constituent units of a new "democratic and social republic" based on the sovereignty of labor.

This vision . . . was doomed to failure. The victory of conservatives in the elections of April, the abortive workers' *Putsch* of May 15, and finally the bloody repression of the June workers' uprising destroyed the commission and many of the workers' associations it represented. But the workers' movement of the spring of 1848, which in turn was based on the organizational and conceptual breakthroughs made in the early 1830s, set the pattern for the French working-class and socialist movement through and beyond the Commune. The French workers' long-lived ideal of . . . a "federalist trade socialism" grew out of the corporate heritage of the urban skilled trades, as transformed by the revolutionary upheavals of the 1830s and 1848.

Darlene G. Levy and Harriet Applewhite

Revolutionary Women and the Radicalization of French Politics

Darlene G. Levy (1939–) is an intellectual historian. Like Robert Darnton, she came to the study of the French Revolution from a background in the history of the Enlightenment. In the essay from which this selection is taken her focus shifts from ideas in the conventional sense to new concepts that arose among women of the popular classes through their participation in revolutionary politics. Harriet Applewhite (1940–) is a political scientist whose primary interest is the history of the French Revolution. As the scope of the book from which this selection is taken suggests, her original field was comparative politics. Since the book's appearance, her research interests have focused on the political alignment of male revolutionaries as well as revolutionary women.

Women, Radicalization, and the Fall of the French Monarchy

During the spring and summer of 1792, women participated in a movement of political radicalization in revolutionary Paris. Radicalization involved transformations in the principles and practices of sovereignty and citizenship, the development of new measures of political legitimacy, a mobilization of insurrectionary forces, and, eventually, the fall of the monarchy and the establishment of the First French Republic. The massive presence of women, their words and acts, made a historically significant difference in the dynamics and outcome of events. Women dramatically increased the numbers of those challenging the political status quo. They engaged in decisive collective demonstrations of force and acts of violence; they were key actors in the co-optation of the armed force available to authorities who supported the constitutional monarchy. These acts, in combination with women's discourse . . . contributed to the delegitimation of constitutional monarchy, a reformation of rights and responsibilities of citizenship, and a redefinition of sovereignty as the will and power of the people. The constant, often programmed presence of women among the civilian and military forces of a popular opposition dramatized the power of the powerless, to the point where revolutionary authorities of all political sympathies and persuasions acknowledged that this combined physical and symbolic democratic force could not be resisted.

   This transitional period between constitutional monarchy and republic is a moment of extraordinary indeterminacy and openness in the

Darlene G. Levy and Harriet Applewhite, *Women and Politics in the Age of the Democratic Revolution*, (Ann Arbor, University of Michigan Press, 1990), pp. 81–104.

political history of the Revolution, the moment of a surge of women's individual and collective political participation. . . . [U]nder the Constitution of 1791, women had been denied the political rights of citizenship. . . . [K]ey terms in a revolutionary political lexicon derived largely from Rousseauan and classical political philosophy, laws and rights of nature, citizenship, virtue and civic virtue, were gendered to define and legitimate public and political roles for male citizens and exclusively domestic, private roles for women. A body of "recent scholarship interprets revolutionary political opportunities and outcomes for women as largely determined by this political language and by the male-dominated hegemonies it supported and reflected." Our documentation suggests a more complex and indeterminate patterning. In the period between 1791 and the fall of 1793 (when the Jacobin leadership outlawed their organized political activity), women's individual and collective political acts (often grounded in solid traditions sanctioning or even prescribing their involvement in public and political affairs), the competing languages in which these acts were narrated and interpreted, and the political claims and counterclaims with which they were associated, all had the effect of multiplying repertoires of political action and political discourse.

Our interpretation of women's participation in ceremonial, institutional, and insurrectionary politics during the spring and summer of 1792 cautions against reading back into the ever-shifting ideological constellations and power struggles in which women of all socioeconomic categories were caught up between 1789 and 1793, a repressive linguistic-political-military hegemony that the Jacobins established only in the fall of 1793, and even then, only incompletely.

From the middle of the eighteenth century, the monarchy in France had been strained and weakened by the explosion of Enlightenment ideas . . . and most especially by reactions to reforms that royal administrators themselves had initiated. Nonetheless Louis XVI still ruled by hereditary right. His actions were not limited by written constitution; his will was enforced by a strong standing army and by regiments of foreign mercenaries.

Between June, 1789, and September, 1791, the National Assembly instated a constitutional monarchy to replace a monarchy absolute by divine right. In the spring and summer of 1792, a predominantly "passive" citizenry in the politicized sections of Paris, aided and abetted by Girondin and Jacobin radicals, undermined this political system.

They challenged the principle of delegated sovereignty divided between an indirectly elected national legislature and a hereditary monarchy. They dissolved the distinctions that excluded "passive citizens" from voting, serving in the National Guard, and standing for election to political assemblies. And they exploited a collapse of trust in the King to challenge the legitimacy of constitutional monarchy and to claim that the determination of legitimacy rested exclusively with the sovereign nation.

Women of the popular classes . . . of Paris and a handful of bourgeois women were directly in the center of forces that brought about this second revolution of 1792. Revolutionary leaders and radicals often encouraged, when they did not actually program, women's integration into the political nation in arms. Women were conspicuously present in ceremonial/insurrectionary dramatizations . . . of "the will and might of the sovereign nation" such as the series of armed processions of the spring and summer of 1792 that are the subject of this essay.

The actual collapse of the constitutional monarchy on August 10, 1792 resulted from a military confrontation . . . between the King's guard, on one side, and the armed force of the Paris sections and the Departments of France, on the other. However, this change of regime was prepared by a progressive buildup of revolutionary forces and a weakening of resistance in the King's camp and in the national legislature. The principal developments were the King's defection from the Constitution of 1791 and the public's growing attraction to republicanism. . . . The King's flight [in June, 1791] and its aftermath furthered a rapid growth of republican sentiment and the escalation of political activity in the . . . clubs and popular societies, and the radical press. . . . The declaration of war in mid-April 1792 generated insecurity in the capital and intensified public concern over the King's suspicious behavior. These developments widened the breach between the King and his opposition . . . and also shaped the confrontation between constituted authorities, who continued to operate within constitutional limits, and fully mobilized insurgents in the sections who claimed an all-legitimating constituent authority. . . .

In order to analyze selected elements in the mobilization of that popular force during the spring and summer of 1792, we investigated six armed processions through the halls of the Legislative Assembly that involved thousands of men, women, and children, principally "passive citizenry" from the sections and environs of Paris. . . . In each case, we found the participants demanding recognition of their legitimacy and power and receiving that recognition from the national legislature. Second, in the accompanying speeches and through signs, exclamations, gestures, images, symbols, and line of march, the participants, both women and men, built a symbolic significance into their behavior that linked it to radical definitions of citizenship, sovereignty, and legitimacy. Finally, they conspicuously paraded weapons, which carried the threat that armed force would be used. This display of military force, in combination with concrete demands and symbolic representations, in fact coalesced the transformative forces of a second revolution.

We are focusing on two armed processions: the April 9th procession through the Legislative Assembly of soldiers from the regiment of Chateauvieux, armed battalions of National guardsmen, and armed men, women, and children from the sections of Paris; and the June 20th armed procession through the Legislative Assembly and the Tuileries Palace of men, women, and children from the Faubourgs Saint-Antoine and Saint-Marcel. . . .

On April 9, 1792, several deputies from the city of Brest submitted a letter to the Legislative Assembly requesting that forty soldiers from the Swiss Regiment of Chateauvieux be granted permission to appear before the bar of the Assembly. This was a politically charged request. In August, 1790, the Chateauvieux regiment had participated in a rebellion pitting civilian patriots in Nancy and regiment soldiers against the forces of the regional commander, the marquis de Bouillé, acting on orders . . . from his cousin, Lafayette, Commander-General of the National Guard. In the bloody repression that followed Bouillé's reconquest of Nancy, thirty-three soldiers of the Swiss regiment were hanged or broken on the wheel and forty more were condemned to the galleys off Brest. In December, 1791, the Legislative Assembly granted amnesty to these forty soldiers. Between their sentencing and their pardon, public confidence in Lafayette had ebbed and mistrust of National Guard battalions overtly loyal to him was running high. . . . In March, 1792, . . . preparations began for a popular festival to honor the insurrectionary soldiers of Chateauvieux. In a petition addressed to the General Council of the Commune of Paris on March 24, 1792, a delegation that included the patriot and militant Théroigne de Mericourt urged municipal officers to join in honoring the people's martyrs who, "even in chains, have preserved their internal liberty and no king on earth has succeeded in taking it from them. The fatherland has engraved on their chains the formal oath: live free or die. . . ."

On April 9th, . . . the forty soldiers with their escort of National Guardsmen and armed civilians, men, women, and children, arrived at the Assembly. Following a heated debate, the Assembly voted unanimously to admit the Chateauvieux soldiers and, notwithstanding further maneuvering by deputies on the right, they were accorded the honors of the session by a narrow vote and granted permission to march through the hall accompanied by the National Guard. The soldiers' spokesman, Collot d'Herbois, setting the tone for what was to follow, recalled the oath they had sworn earlier in the Revolution to die in defense of the nation. . . . Collot concluded his speech: "May the chains which the soldiers of Chateauvieux bore and which you have broken, be the last which despotism uses to enchain defenders of liberty." In his reply the President attempted to limit the impact of Collot's discourse on the Assembly and the galleries. He recalled that the Assembly had voted the soldiers an amnesty and were adding to this "kindness" a permission for them to appear before the bar, so that the Assembly might receive "the testimony of your gratitude." He then cautioned: "Enjoy its kindness; love your duties; obey the laws." Having delivered himself of this admonition, he accorded the soldiers of Chateauvieux the honors of the session.

At this point, the National Guardsmen who had accompanied the Chateauvieux soldiers paraded through the Assembly, about one hundred strong . . . amid shouts from deputies on the left and spectators in the galleries: "Vive la Nation!" "Vive l'Assemblee Nationalé!" "Vive les soldats de Chateauvieux!" "Vive la liberté!" In their midst marched a citizen named Gonchon, a spokesman for the Faubourg Saint-Antoine (the faubourg of the vainqueurs de la Bastille). He carried a pike, surmounted by a red cap of liberty that was decorated with laurel leaves and tricolor ribbons. Mingling a red cap of liberty that was decorated by laurel leaves and tricolor ribbons. . . . As the procession passed before the President, Gonchon entered the bar and stood there, pike in hand, while troops and civilians paraded past, superimposing their figures on a living emblem of militant citizenship. There followed "a large procession of men, women, children, carrying tricolor flags, pikes, and other emblems of liberty. . . ."

As the procession concluded, Gonchon, speaking for the citizens of the Faubourg Saint-Antoine, announced that his faubourg was manufacturing ten thousand pikes, like the one he was carrying. "They always will be forged for the support of liberty [and] the Constitution, and for our defense." Gonchon and his party were accorded the honors of the session. The Assembly decreed the printing of Collot d'Herbois' speech, but not the speech of the President of the Assembly. The session ended with the approval of a motion that called attention to the fact that the flags given to the Chateauvieux soldiers by various departmental authorities had passed through the space of the Assembly.

This armed procession through the Legislative Assembly . . . can be read from several perspectives. First, the Assembly, seconded by the enthusiastic galleries, repeatedly sanctioned this extraordinary demonstration and everything it signified. Initially, the Assembly voted to receive the Chateauvieux soldiers and granted permission to their supporters to march armed through the Assembly. Then, after their spokesman defined their cause as the struggle of "liberty against despotism," the Assembly further underscored its approval of the demonstration and its legitimation of a radical reading of the right and responsibility of the citizen to resist oppression and to die in defense of liberty. It voted to print Collot's speech; it refused to print the speech of its own President, in effect repudiating his discourse. . . . The motion noting that tricolor flags from the departments had passed through the political space of the legislature added still another dimension of legitimacy to the procession and carried the message of a bond of solidarity uniting the rehabilitated soldiers with National Guardsmen armed civilians, and all sections of the political nation . . . , a de facto legitimation of the right of popular insurrectionary resistance.

Second, as the procession . . . took over the space of the Legislative Assembly, the marchers filled that space with politically charged signs of a militant citizenry. The liberty cap on a pike . . . linked the citizen's right to liberty, [to] self-defense, . . . to resist oppression, and his possession of the weapons with which to enforce all three. Furthermore, this processional ritual . . . recast the separate identities of the marchers into a collective identity. They all enacted a drama in which insurrectionary soldiers were reidentified as heroic citizens. . . . The whole was represented as the reunion of a great national family, the other face of which was a united nation in arms. What this procession dramatized most palpably and concretely was the message that the entire passive citizenry of France was being integrated into a national force, men, women, and children . . . forming a *tableau vivant* of militant sans-culottes citizenship.

While accounts mention armed women, they do not focus special attention on them. We propose to stop the moving picture of this procession in order to magnify and analyze female militancy as one element in a larger dramatic depiction of the national family, on the march, pikes in hand.

In an article . . . appearing in the February . . . 1792 the radical journalist Prudhomme called attention to the symbolic and military significance of the pike, a weapon already being produced in large numbers in the Paris sections as an alarmed population began to calculate the consequences of a declaration of war. "[U]niversally accessible, available to the poorest citizen," the pike was an emblem of independence, equality under arms, vigilance, and the recovery of liberty: "A pike in the hand of every citizen is terrifying for malevolent persons that it announces an armed nation's continual surveillance." . . . Prudhomme proposed that every citizen . . . be armed with two pikes, "one for the repose of this household, the other for the safety of the republic." At the same time, he conspicuously eliminated half the nation's potential pike bearers by denying the right of women to bear these arms. Dismissing what he described as a proposal by Théroigne de Mericourt to organize and lead a phalanx of Amazons, Prudhomme cautioned: "Let pikes be prohibited for women; dressed in white and girded with the national sash, let them content themselves with being simple spectators."

On March 6th, less than a month after this article appeared, a delegation of "citoyennes de la ville de Paris," led by Pauline Léon, an outspoken revolutionary activist, presented to the National Assembly a petition with more than 300 signatures concerning the right of women to bear arms. The petitioners grounded their claim in an appeal to the right to defend one's own life and liberty and to resist oppression, rights guaranteed in article two of the Declaration of the Rights of Man and of the Citizen. . . . They also claimed for women the political/moral attributes of revolutionary citizenship, including civic virtue, and they based that claim partly on the evidence of recent revolutionary history. They represented their participation in the journée of the fifth and sixth of October, the women's march to Versailles and their return to Paris with the King in tow, as the act marking their political transformation into militant patriots. . . . They renewed the oaths they had sworn earlier in the Revolution to live free or die. They requested permission to arm themselves with pikes, pistols, sabres, and rifles . . . and to engage in military maneuvers. . . .

The Assembly's response . . . was ambiguous. The President invited the delegation to attend the session. A deputy expressed his fear that if the petition were honored, "the order of nature would be inverted." The delicate hands of women "were not made for manipulating iron or brandishing homicidal pikes." As serious motions crossed with parody, the Assembly decreed a printing of the petition . . . and promptly passed to the order of the day.

A conservative journalist remarked, commenting on the inconclusiveness of the Assembly's action and on the precedent that might be set by it: "Perhaps in interpreting this decree, women will arm themselves nonetheless"; to avoid a dangerous confusion the Assembly ought to have declared that there was no cause to deliberate on the matter in the first place.

While the Assembly hesitated between "liquidating" and tolerating women's demands for the right to bear arms, the General Council of the Paris Commune and the mayor, Jerome Pétion, took action to honor women's militancy publicly, reward it officially, and instate it as a model of female citizenship, all this just four days before the armed procession through the Assembly to honor the Chateauvieux soldiers. . . . Pétion argued that while French mores generally kept women out of combat, it was also true that "in the moment of danger, when the fatherland is in peril," women "do not feel any the less that they are citoyennes." "We are not adequately sensitized to the importance of forming citoyennes." He noted that until now it has seemed as though men have wanted only to subjugate women. . . .

This evidence strongly suggests that in the weeks preceding the April 9th procession, a concept of female citizenship was emerging. This concept dissolved distinctions between active/passive, male/female citizens and the public/domestic spaces where citizenship could be acted upon; combined women's right of self defense with their civil obligation to protect and defend the patrie; and placed these rights and duties directly in the center of a general definition of the rights and responsibilities of citizenship. Thus, the armed women who marched on April 9th . . . representing a united national family in arms, at the same time embodied a driving force of radicalization, the principle and practice of militant citizenship.

This picture of an armed national family is the clean, sharp inverse of the radical journalists' earlier depictions of unarmed families brutally gunned down by Lafayette's troops. . . . The incendiary journalist Jean-Paul Marat filled the pages of his *Ami du peuple* with provocative word pictures of "poor old men, pregnant women, with infants at their breast!, massacred in cold blood." "The blood of old men, women, children, massacred around the altar of the fatherland is still warm, it cries out for vengeance. . . ." The arming of passive citizens, including women, in the spring of 1792, turned upside down Marat's provocative picture of the world of the weak; activated an involuntarily pacific (because legally "passive") citizenry; and placed the mobilization of half the population behind the radical leadership's escalating estimates of the strength of the national family in arms.

The armed marchers of . . . June 20, 1792, started out from the Faubourgs Saint-Antoine and Saint-Marcel. They . . . moved through the streets and avenues of the right bank of Paris, into the halls of the Legislative Assembly, and then through the residence of the King in the Tuileries Palace, symbolically reclaiming these spaces for the people and reconsecrating them to the work of executing the general will of the sovereign people.

On June 16, a delegation from the sections of these two working class faubourgs had informed municipal authorities of their plans. Their purpose was to plant a liberty tree in the Tuileries Gardens . . . and to present petitions to the Legislative Assembly and the King "relative to the circumstances." They asked for authorization to dress in the uniforms and carry the arms they had used in 1789. The key to the circumstances to which the delegation alluded was a collapse of the King's credibility, entraining a new crisis of confidence in the constitutional monarchy. The crisis was prepared in a generalized climate of fear, uncertainty, and mistrust as the nation suffered its first defeats in the war. . . . It was precipitated by the King's dismissal of his liberal Girondin ministry following his veto of legislation that . . . authorized the preparation of a camp beneath the walls of Paris to receive 20,000 troops from the departments.

The Council of the Commune refused to authorize the armed procession announced on June 16. . . . This action had no impact on the organizers and participants who continued with their preparations from bases in the general assemblies, clubs, and popular societies of their sections. A section meeting convoked on the night of June 19th . . . was attended by more than a thousand citizens, men and women, who were repeatedly and strenuously urged to march, armed, on the 20th.

This same night [Pétion] . . . developed a strategy of placing all armed marchers . . . under the authority of [National Guard] commanders, thereby legitimating an extraordinary armed force composed of National Guardsmen and all citizens, passive along with active, women and children along with men. During the night of June 19–20, the royalist Department of Paris vetoed [this] . . . scheme; and the following morning, [Pétion] . . . dispatched municipal authorities to the faubourgs with orders to prevent or disperse the procession.

When these municipal officials arrived in the sections of the two faubourgs, they were met by thousands of fully mobilized citizens, National Guardsmen, men, women, and children, ranged in formation, armed, and preparing to march. An officer dispatched to the Faubourg Saint-Marcel reported a portion of its battalion already in marching formation, fully armed, with the battalion's cannon at the head of its line of march. . . . After attempting to reason with them the officer and his colleagues concluded that there was no way to persuade these "volunteer soldiers, citizens, and the women who are with them" to "lay down their arms and return their cannon to the corps de garde. . . ." They were going to march armed because . . . they feared being repulsed by force, especially at the Tuileries Palace. Officers . . . dispatched to the Faubourg Saint-Marcel reported coming upon a troop of men armed and in uniform, with horse-drawn cannon at their head, and accompanied by "a tremendous number of persons of all ages and both sexes, armed and unarmed." They refused to lay down their arms or abandon their march. . . . They argued that they knew what the law was as well as anyone else; they were armed only to assure that it was respected and observed. They also argued that there were legitimizing precedents for armed processions of this kind. . . . Finally, the marchers made it clear that they were armed to repel force with force, if necessary. . . . In the end the marchers closed all discussion by taking action: "So the whole troop of them, giving way to their impatience, began to cry out: that's quite enough of all this; forward march, Monsieur le commandant, forward march!"

At the very moment when officers in the field were meeting with insuperable resistance to their efforts to stop the march, the Municipality of Paris confronted the necessity of relegitimating it. Notwithstanding explicit instructions to the contrary from the Department, the Municipality decreed that the Commander-General of the National Guard issue all necessary orders "to assemble under the flag citizens in all kinds of uniforms, with all kinds of arms, who will march thus assembled under the command of the officers of the battalions."

Starting out from the two faubourgs, the armed marchers joined forces on the right bank, marched together through the streets and . . .

arrived at the Tuileries Gardens, planted a commemorative liberty tree and regrouped outside the Legislative Assembly. Meanwhile, inside, the deputies engaged in a tense debate over whether and under what conditions these petitioners should be admitted: with arms? without arms? in a delegation? Vergniaud, a deputy on the left, warned that if the law against armed demonstrations was applied, a massacre would result . . . [with] men, women, and children . . . shot down. Finally under mounting pressure from the . . . multitude . . . , the vote was taken: a delegation would be received.

The delegation's address to the Assembly, . . . established the marchers' claims and linked them to a republican ideology rooted in principles of popular sovereignty, militant citizenship, and political legitimacy as an expression . . . of the will of the sovereign people. First, the orator established an identity between the marchers and the French people. The orator later expanded this explosive claim: the marchers are the people and the people is the sovereign. . . . In his conclusion, the speaker returned to the most immediate reality, the real strength of the force actually concentrated behind the doors of the Assembly. "This is the petition not only of the inhabitants of the Faubourg Saint-Antoine but of . . . Paris." "[A]nd of the entire realm," a deputy added, completing the orator's extraordinary representation of this procession as a mobilized sovereign people. . . .

Second, the orator underscored a matter of fact of which this sovereign people, . . . fully mobilized, was an armed force. "We come to assure you that the people are prepared to take extreme measures to avenge the majesty of the outraged people." He justified a recourse to insurrection . . . by an appeal to natural right, the right to resist oppression . . . in Article Two of the Declaration of Rights.

Third, the orator proclaimed that the armed sovereign was the supreme authority, its will was insuperable. No other will . . . could prevail against it. . . . "A single man must not influence the will of a nation of twenty-five million souls." The orator reread the constitutional crisis between the King and the Assembly as a confrontation of . . . the will of the sovereign people . . . [and] the traitorous Catalines in the Assembly, a veto-wielding despot on the throne, and pusillanimous judges in the courts. Implicit in the warnings . . . expressed through this discourse was the doctrine that the will of the sovereign people . . . stood before and behind all constitutions, institutions, and laws as the source, expression, and ultimate measure of their legitimacy. In one such double-faced message, the orator professed respect for the Constitution, then immediately appealed beyond it to the force of the armed sovereign. . . .

The President of the Assembly tried to parry the thrust of these declarations with a lecture on the respect owed to the laws . . . but to no avail. The Assembly voted to allow the armed procession to parade through the hall.

In the hour and a half that followed, thousands of marchers . . . enacted concepts of militant citizenship and popular sovereignty and dramatized the principle that the will of the people is the source and measure of political legitimacy. Their barely ceremonial behavior, veering between processional performance and insurrection, undercut and threatened to dissolve prevailing constitutional arrangements. In this sense the procession of June 20th previewed the new republican order in the making.

The marchers played out a political self-definition that their spokesman had articulated in his speech. They represented themselves as the sovereign people in arms. As they paraded through the hall, indeed took it over, observers identified detachments of National Guardsmen . . . interspersed with children, women . . . and men with swords and guns. A sympathetic enthusiastic eyewitness, Mme. Jullien, described the marchers as "all intermingled in the true spirit of equality and fraternal union, . . . the real sovereign. . . ." [W]eapons were reported: long pikes, guns, axes, . . . knives, pitchforks, sticks, bayonnets, large daggers, clubs, and great saws. Armed women were described separately as wearing liberty caps and carrying sabres. In . . . [an] engraving the women were depicted carrying pikes and swords. Notwithstanding the immense numbers, the staggering variety of costumes and arms, the melange of civilians and trained military, and the combinations of all ages and both sexes, a kind of order, unity, discipline, and hence additional power was created and sustained by the line and rhythm of a march to drumbeat, martial music, and refrains of "Ca ira."

Exclamations, cries, emblems, signs, and speeches linked the marchers as a palpable, forceful physical presence to the principles and powers of popular sovereignty. . . . A banner . . . carried by a woman marcher, proclaimed on one side, "Liberty! Tyrants, tremble. The French are armed!" and on the other, "Equality. Reunion of the Flags, Saint Antoine and Saint-Marceau." A third bore the inscription on one side, "When their country is in danger, all the sans-culottes are alert," and on the other side, "Tremble tyrants, your reign approaches its end." A placard bore the message, "Warning . . . to Louis XVI: The people is tired of suffering, liberty or death." In the middle of the procession a marcher delivered a speech in which he equated the avenging force present on the floor of the Assembly with the power of millions: "It is . . . twenty million men whom we come to offer, it is an entire nation which must arm itself to combat tyrants, [the nation's] enemies, and yours."

. . . [These] symbolic trophies of victory . . . carried the message that an invincible sovereign, a people twenty million strong, was capable of piercing its enemies full of holes, tearing out their hearts . . . physically eliminating them from the political system, constitutional guarantees notwithstanding. When the marchers targeted aristocrats and tyrants as enemies of the sovereign people, they explicitly named Louis XVI, whose . . . veto they read as the chief obstacle to the execution of their sovereign will. At the same time, their placards proclaimed their loyalty to the Constitution of 1791, which explicitly authorized the monarchical executive's exercise of a suspensive veto power. When the marchers paraded through the Assembly, their cries, "Long live the law!" . . . mingled with their shouts of "Long live the sans-culottes!" . . . "Down with the Veto!" one of their banners bore the inscription, "The Constitution! Live free or die! The Constitution or death!" They meant what they said; they were loyal to the Constitution, as they understood the matter. . . . [T]he Constitution, . . . [and] all constituted authorities . . . [were] only the instrument of an armed, sovereign citizenry, . . . the ultimate source of the system's legitimacy.

These new meanings of citizenship, sovereignty, and legitimacy symbolically inverted the constitutional arrangements of 1791. . . . Having traversed the Legislative Assembly, the marchers . . . broke through the gates of the royal palace and charged up the staircase armed with sabres, pikes, sticks, and rifles (and dragging a cannon). They literally cornered the King and the royal family in their private quarters. . . . With greatly increased numbers and more threatening gestures. The marchers' invasion of the King's space turned it into a battleground between the King's will . . . [and] the will of the sovereign people. They concretized the recalcitrant will of the King in his veto power and attempted to bend that will [to] . . . the popular will. The King's consent to withdraw his vetoes would be the only acceptable sign of conversion and anything less only further evidence of tyrannical governance. As they . . . filed past the King . . . , they practiced a politics of persuasion through threats, insults, verbal and physical displays of force, the exhibition of symbolic trophies, offerings of transformative patriotic emblems, self-acclamations, and pledges of allegiance and solidarity to one another: "Long live the Nation!". . . . "Down with the King!" "Down with the Queen!" They paraded two hearts impaled on pikes. One was made of wood or painted carton and bore the inscription, "Heart of M. Veto"; the other was a bloody animal heart with a similar inscription. One marcher filed past the King and held out to him a liberty cap that he had placed on the end of a long stick. The King took it. He put it on his head. Applause and shouts rang out: "Vive la Nation!" "Vive le Roi!" "Vive la liberté!" The liberty cap, alas, did not transform the will of the King. A woman held out her sword, decorated with flowers and a cocarde, a striking emblem of . . . the people's festive harmonization of wills through the application of armed might. The King took it and brandished it and joined the crowd in shouts of "Vive la Nation!" Then he reiterated his refusal to retract his vetoes, proclaiming his fidelity to the principles of the Constitution.

In the end, neither side scored a clear victory in a battle of wills that strained ceremonial ritual to the breaking point. After the siege had lasted more than six hours the mayor and municipal authorities finally moved the demonstrators out of the palace. However, two guards reported overhearing the section chief, Santerre, comment as he left the chateau, ". . . We will . . . make . . . [the King] give in"—an unambiguous expression of this collective determination to break the King's will and incorporate it into the will of the people.

Witnesses on the scene were quick to seize the larger import of the day's events. The American diplomat Gouverneur Morris wrote in his diary: "His Majesty has put on the Bonnet rouge but he persists in refusing to sanction the Decrees. . . . The Constitution has this day I think given its last groan." . . .

On June 21, 1792, the Legislative Assembly decreed that under no circumstances would "any armed gathering of citizens be admitted to its bar for purposes of parading through its meeting hall or presenting itself before any constituted authority without prior legal authorization." The legislation came too late. The armed processions, repeatedly legitimized by the deputies' votes to receive and honor them, had functioned successfully as ceremonial demonstrations of the breadth, scope, and strength of a fully mobilized democratic force in the revolutionary capital. . . .

Women were at the center of a mass-based political and military movement in Paris that gathered force and momentum through the spring and summer of 1792 and culminated on August 10, 1792, in . . . the collapse of the constitutional monarchy. We have analyzed one ceremonial and insurrectionary expression of this movement of revolutionary radicalization and democratization. Months before the constitutional monarchy fell and a republican system was established, these armed processions mediated a collective expression of the principles and practices of popular sovereignty, militant citizenship, and political legitimacy defined as the expression of the popular will. We have called attention to the contribution of women . . . , who reformulated, democratized, and claimed for women fundamental political principles and rights that later were enacted in the armed processions, like the right to bear arms both in self-defense and as a patriotic act. We have emphasized the numbers and visibility of women in ceremonial demonstrations of collective strength, which prepared the events of August 10, 1792.

One might ask nonetheless: What historical difference did the women really make? Did women's active participation change any outcomes? Are the historians missing much when they leave women out of their . . . analyses of revolutionary radicalization? We want to speak to these questions.

Three days after the events of June 20th, the Procurator-General of the Department of Paris, P. L. Roederer, forwarded to the mayor and municipal officers a letter he had received from a Parisian cloth merchant named Mouton. Mouton reported overhearing the conversation of three poorly dressed men as they watched his wife working behind the counter: "There's a young strong woman; this one will make a good marcher. . . . [W]e must put her on our list." Mouton linked these remarks to . . . a well-known strategy "of forcing peaceful citoyennes to march in the middle of tumultuous crowds in order to paralyze the force responsible for disciplining them." . . . [Pétion] reported back to the Department that he had forwarded the two letters to the municipal police and had ordered them to take appropriate precautionary measures.

As he wrote these orders, . . . [Pétion], under attack for having failed to use force . . . to disperse the armed procession of June 20th, rushed into print with a self-defense. His answer to his critics was that neither he nor anyone else could have commanded the force capable of halting the march. All battalions from the two faubourgs were marching with cannon and arms, followed by large numbers of armed citizens and a multitude of unarmed citizens, Pétion argued. Any force mobilized against the marchers could only have been composed of National Guardsmen.

In that case, the Guardsmen would have been opposing fellow Guardsmen, combating citizens armed with pikes, opposing unarmed men, confronting women, battling with children. ". . . [W]ho could have answered for the lives of these persons who are the most precious to the nation. The very idea of this carnage makes one tremble"; ". . . to whom would this bloody battlefield have been left?" Three-quarters of the National Guard would have refused to fire on their fellow citizens, . . . [T]hey all shared the marchers' motives, given that the Legislative Assembly already had set precedents when it tolerated earlier processions. Other observers acknowledged that [Mayor Pétion] . . . was right about June 20, there was no way to oppose this popular force with force.

In short, authorities of all convictions who would have had to give the orders perceived that the participants in the insurrectionary processions of June 20 had shaped themselves into a new symbolic, political, and military force and represented themselves as a national family in arms that could not be vanquished. On August 10, 1792, that turned out to be the case; on June 20, it already was considered by authorities to be the case, in part because of the presence of women.

. . . We suggest that radicalization in revolutionary Paris involved a coalescing of the democratic aspirations, strategies, energies, beliefs, and ideals of individuals and groups into a force that was perceived as invincible by authorities well before it scored the costly military victory at the Tuileries that brought down the monarchy. Women participated in the armed processions that shaped that force; added their numbers to its mass; contributed to formulating and communicating its fighting principles and demonstrating its strength. Women's solidarity with that force, coupled with the symbolic representation of all these armed marchers as a national patriotic family in arms, convinced the authorities that the power of these crowds of predominantly passive citizens who identified themselves as the sovereign people was . . . irrepressible.

We are not able to reconstruct all . . . that motivated these political actors; but we suggest that the experience of involvement in ceremonies, deputations, and insurrections during the spring and summer of 1792 furthered the development of political consciousness. For example, the petition bearing more than three hundred signatures that Pauline Léon and a delegation of women brought to the Legislative Assembly on March 6, 1792, clearly attests to the women's understanding of their entitlement to the rights and responsibilities of citizenship. Léon insisted on women's natural right to self-defense: ". . . society cannot deny the right nature gives us unless you pretend the Declaration of Rights does not apply to women and that they should let their throats be cut like lambs. . . ." She also claimed for women attributes of civic virtue that, in both neoclassical and Rousseauan variants of the "male language of virtue," were reserved exclusively for men. "We are citoyennes and we cannot be indifferent to the fate of the fatherland." In . . . the processions of April 9th and June 20th, the leaders armed women, handed them . . . emblems of liberty, and led them through the national legislature and the Tuileries Palace. They also dissolved prevalent distinctions between the domestic roles and private virtues of women and the political roles and civic virtues of men. They empowered the powerless and hailed their militancy as formidable demonstrations of popular sovereignty. These processional and insurrectionary performances were symbolically charged acts. Notwithstanding efforts to control and direct such acts, they retained a subversive potential to blur or invert gender roles and, beyond that, to dramatize radically new political identities for women as members of a militant, sovereign citizenry.

The breadth, scope, and impact of women's engagement in the events of 1792 are remarkable. Radicalization meant in part a collective application of force that opened up the possibility for an expanded legal and constitutional definition of the rights and status of citizenship. Women's acts of power in the Revolution were very real. Women enlarged the demographic base of the democratic revolution; by the summer of 1792, the presence of women in a crowd in a procession . . . made the use of countervailing force problematic, if not impossible. Their participation in revolutionary dramaturgy strengthened the psychological and political bonds linking the individual and the nation. Their most radical discourse linked their roles as militants to fundamental principles and rights of citizenship, like the right to bear arms. Male radicals remained profoundly ambivalent about the political implications of women's involvement. Nonetheless, they recognized women's weight as political actors; they tolerated and even orchestrated women's participation in the ceremonies and demonstrations of armed force that contributed to democratizing the process of legitimation and practices of sovereignty and citizenship.

Our focus on the crisis of 1792 has brought into relief neglected aspects of women's central involvement in the dynamics of revolutionary radicalization. It also reveals that women's political status, claims, strategies, and opportunities remained relatively open and fluid at this critical historical juncture. Following the events of August, 1792, this indeterminacy favored women's escalating struggles for political identity in the new revolutionary system and their efforts to shape and transform the language of politics to express and legitimate their claims. Eventually a victorious republican leadership encoded legal and constitutional definitions of citizenship that democratized, universalized — for men — rights of political citizenship, access to political office, the suffrage, and the right to bear arms in the National Guard and other armed forces, while underscoring women's continued political passivity and further validating the gendered models of nature, citizenship, and virtue that rationalized it. But in 1792, and for more than another year, until the Jacobin repression of women's organized political activity in October, 1793, these definitions did not have a decisive impact on women's escalating militancy, their progressively more radical and militant counterdefinitions, claims and practices of citizenship through institutional and insurrectionary political interventions. At all levels, a shifting republican leadership persevered in its uneasy toleration and episodic exploitation of women's de facto but not de jure political status without, however, resolving the issues of gender and citizenship that this double-faced politics had exposed.

Tzvetan Todorov

The Birth of Conflicting Nationalist Traditions

After leaving communist Bulgaria, Tzvetan Todorov (1939–) made a name for himself in France as a structural philologist. His interests subsequently shifted to history. Throughout his career he has been an outspoken critic of Marxist totalitarianism. Like Mona Ozouf, he holds a position at the *Centre national de la recherche scientifique* in Paris. In his historical studies, Todorov has been concerned with the relation of the self to the other in an increasingly impersonal world. He comes to grips with this problem by identifying with thinkers who are at odds with him — and often with each other. In this selection from *On Human Diversity*, he considers the nationalism of the French Revolution from the perspectives of two eighteenth-century philosophes who represent what many historians believe to be incompatible strains in Enlightenment thinking, the rational liberal aristocrat Montesquieu and the sentimental democrat Rousseau.

On Human Diversity: Nationalism, Racism, and Exoticism

Nations and Nationalism

. . . All of us belong to communities that speak the same language, inhabit a common territory, have certain shared memories, and follow the same customs. . . . On the other hand, all of us belong to communities that guarantee our rights and impose obligations on us—communities of which we are citizens, communities that may enter into armed conflict with one another. On the one hand there are cultures, on the other there are states.

As for nations, they are both political and cultural. Whereas cultural and political entities have always existed, the nation as such is an innovation introduced in Europe in modern times. Antonin Artaud clearly distinguished between two types of nationalism based on these two aspects of nationhood, while noting his own preference. "There is cultural nationalism, in which the specific and distinguishing quality of a nation and its works is asserted; and there is what we may call civic nationalism, which in its egocentric form ends up as chauvinism and is translated by customs restrictions and economic conflict, if not all-out warfare." . . . Not only do the forms of nationalism based on each of these aspects of nationhood differ from one another, but in certain respects at least they are opposites. Cultural nationalism . . . leads toward universalism—by deepening the specificity of the particular within which one dwells. Civic nationalism . . . is a preferential choice in favor of one's own country over . . . others — an antiuniversalist choice.

Montesquieu . . . sought to interpret the nation as a cultural entity. In the vast project of *The Spirit of the Laws*, what he calls the "'general spirit' of a nation" . . . plays an essential role. . . . This spirit is the outcome of a whole series of factors: forms of government, traditions, mores, geographical conditions. . . . In what sense does the spirit of the nation lead to universality? In his *Pensées* . . . , speaking of religions, Montesquieu suggests a response that could be applied just as well to nations. "God is like the monarch that has several nations in his empire: they all come to pay him tribute, and each speaks in her own language." This aphorism establishes parallels among three series of terms. (1) God is unique and universal, while religions are multiple and diverse; there is no contradiction, however, for each religion constitutes a different path for advancing toward the same point. (2) Languages are multiple, yet for someone who knows more than one language, the same meaning can be revealed through each. (3) Several nations may have the same king, and all may pay him tribute: while they may be materially different, these tributes are equivalent in the monarch's eyes. . . . Now religion, language, and political institutions are all elements of the spirit of a nation['s] culture . . . : we may thus reasonably suppose that the same relationship is found there. Culture is like a language that provides access to universals; one culture is not, *a priori*, better or worse than another. "The various characters of the nations are mixtures of virtues and vices, of good and bad qualities." . . . But it is absolutely essential to have a culture: without language, there is no access to meaning.

The civic or political sense of . . . "nation" is entirely different. As a first approximation, we may say that this sort of nationalism arises from the expressed preference for one's "own" over all "others," a phenomenon that seems to have been recognized from earliest antiquity as a characteristic of all human groups; it is what might be called their patriotism. In his *History*, Herodotus describes the Persians as follows: "They honor most of all those who dwell nearest them, next those who are next farthest removed, and so going ever onwards they assign honor by this rule; those who dwell farthest off they hold least honorable of all; for they deem themselves to be in all regards by far the best of all men, the rest to have but a proportionate claim to merit, till those who dwell farthest away have least merit of all." . . . But at this rate, who among us is not Persian? Patriotism of this sort would merely be the transposition of individual egocentrism to the level of the group. And just as egocentrism seems to be, if not a universal human trait, then at least an inevitable one during . . . childhood . . . , the privileged treatment of one's "own" people at the expense of "others" characterizes at least certain phases of the history of peoples. In short, egocentrism is a spontaneous reaction that arises prior to any education; we shall refer to it here as "the rule of Herodotus." But we have not yet encountered modern nationalism.

How are we to evaluate patriotism, understood in this way? We might say, on the one hand, that there is not much to be proud of in an attitude that is after all rather self-centered. However, we must also note that, in passing from the individual to the group, self-centeredness does not come out unscathed. There is a radical difference between "taking care of oneself" and "taking care of one's own." The valorization of the group has a double aspect: it implies turning one's back on the lesser entity (the self) as well as on the greater entity (other groups, humanity as a whole). Attachment to the group is at once an act of solidarity and an act of exclusion.

True schools for solidarity are found in groups smaller than the nation: the family or clan, then the village or neighborhood. Here is where children learn to overcome their own innate egocentrism. The exclusion of others is entirely relative. A child knows that other families exist, and cannot imagine life without them, but she also learns that a higher loyalty binds her to her own: this loyalty involves both a right to receive help and a duty to give it. The earliest notions of morality are acquired here, and we may wonder whether this mode of acquisition is not also the only one solid enough to be able to endure and spread. Auguste Comte thought . . . that familial affections constituted "the only real transition from egocentric instincts to universal sympathies." . . . Love of humanity is not worth much if it does not begin as love of one's neighbors. This latter sentiment is thus not to be condemned; quite the contrary: it must be present if it is to be extended, through individual development, from people who are close at hand to the whole of the human race, as the principles of morality dictate.

But a nation is not the same sort of spontaneously formed group. First of all, nations are much larger than families or neighborhoods, and this fact entails two consequences. On the one hand, any given nation is too large for anyone to know all its members . . . , or even to have a great deal in common with them. On the other hand, it is large enough to give individuals the illusion of infinite size and . . . bar . . . the way to "universal sympathies." . . . It is neither a genuine school or solidarity (moreover, it requires that family loyalties be abandoned) nor a useful transitional stage in the evolution toward respect for humanity in all its forms. That is why history is full of examples in which family devotion coexists with tolerance for foreigners, whereas nationalism never leads to universalism.

It is important to distinguish between the two meanings of the word "nationalism," for . . . we shall be inclined to judge them differently. But are we really dealing with a simple case of homonymy? Is there no significant relation between the two uses of the term? A relation does of course exist, but it resides in the object itself, not in the concept that encompasses the object. As it happens, the nation as culture, the set of individuals who have a certain number of features in common, partially *coincides* with the nation as state, a country separated from others by political borders. And in reality the two are quite often connected: it is because a national cultural consciousness exists that the idea of political autonomy can evolve; conversely, the state (nation) can allow the culture (nation) to assert itself and flourish. The fact remains that the concepts themselves are independent, and to a certain extent opposed, since the universal is the contrary of the particular. What is more, the common culture is not necessarily national in scope, . . . and the existence of an autonomous state is neither sufficient nor necessary for the survival of a particular culture. But if state and culture are not rigorously interdependent on the level of logic, their interdependence may become imperative under certain historical circumstances.

Here we need to introduce another distinction between two meanings of the word "nation," both . . . political. . . . The first . . . , which we might call "internal," took on considerable importance on the eve of the French Revolution and in its immediate aftermath. The nation is a space of legitimation, and as a source of power it is opposed to kingly or divine right. People act in the name of the nation, instead of referring to God or monarch; they cry "Long live the nation!" instead of "Long live the king!" This space is then perceived as a space of equality: not the equality of all inhabitants, to be sure (women and the poor are excluded), but the equality of all citizens; people turn to the "nation" in order to combat social privilege or regional self-aggrandizement. The second, or "external," sense of the word "nation" is quite different: here one nation is set in opposition to another nation rather than to the king, or the aristocracy, or geographical regions. In this sense the French constitute one nation and the English another.

Once again the two meanings of the word are not unrelated, but once again the relationship is limited to the . . . identity of the object. Under the Old Regime in France, individuals did not identify strongly with their country. As Renan put it, "the handing over of a province was only a transfer of property from one prince to another; the inhabitants remained largely indifferent." . . . How can anyone identify with one country in preference to another, if a royal marriage is all it takes to bring about a change in citizenship? How can anyone believe that a war is of personal concern when it results from the whim of a prince? On the other hand, as soon as the nation, in the sense of its citizenry as a whole, has become the locus of power, each of its members may consider the state as his own; this is how modern "external" nationalism is introduced. Voltaire had already noted this: "A republican is always more strongly attached to his own country than a subject is to his; and for this good reason, too, that men have a greater regard for their own property than for that of their master." . . . The fact remains that the intention underlying the two concepts is once again different and even opposed since the "internal" nation proceeds from the idea of equality, while the "external" nation implies on the contrary a preferential choice in favor of one's own country over all the others, thus implying inequality.

It is precisely the encounter between these two meanings, internal and external, cultural and political, that has given rise to the specifically *modern* entities of nation and nationalism. They are characterized by the fusion of what I am trying to keep separate here. Legitimation via the nation instead of God has been viewed as inseparable from preference for one's own country at the expense of universal principles, membership in a culture—which is undeniable and unavoidable—has come to justify the requirement that cultural and political entities should coincide. Still, what concerns us here is less modern nationalism in its full extent than patriotic feeling (which has existed from time immemorial) in its recent manifestations.

. . . In its relation to values is patriotism a form of absolutism or of relativism? The patriot has an undeniable preference for certain values—but not in the name of an absolute system. A consistent patriot ought to recognize that everyone is entitled to prefer the values chosen by her own country. Patriotism is thus a form of relativism, but a tempered relativism. The radical relativist refuses to pronounce any value judgments at all; the patriot agrees that any reference to absolute and universal criteria must be rejected, but he introduces an alternative basis for judgments: to paraphrase Pascal, one might say that a person born on one side of the Pyrenees owes an absolute allegiance to French values, while the same person born on the other side of the Pyrenees would owe just as strong an allegiance to Spanish values. As Charles Maurras, one of the best-known theoreticians of French nationalism, pointed out, from this perspective it is necessary to look for the good; yet "this good will be not absolute Good but the good of the French people." . . . In this respect patriotism is the perfect mirror image of *exoticism*, which also forswears an absolute frame of reference but does not give up value judgments; exoticism is the opposite of patriotism in that it valorizes what does *not* belong to one's own country. In the abstract, like any relativist, the patriot may proclaim equality among peoples . . . ; still, in practice, the patriot is almost always also an ethnocentrist. No sooner has my relativist judgment been pronounced than I render it absolute: being a Frenchman, I declare that France is superior to all countries, not just for me but for everyone.

A national value may coincide with a value that claims universality; in many instances patriotism is not opposed to universalism. It is nevertheless always possible to conceive of a situation in which the two conflict and in which it is necessary to choose between universal values and national values, between love of humanity and love of country. The state of war, in particular, multiplies the opportunities for this sort of conflict. Two questions then arise. Is it possible to reconcile patriotism with cosmopolitanism, attachment to national values with love of humanity? And if not, which of the two should we prefer?

In the eighteenth century, Helvétius, Voltaire, and Rousseau offered negative answers to the first question in their writings. Helvétius denies the existence of natural law, since justice is only what best suits a given community. . . . "In all ages and nations, probity can be only a habit of performing actions that are of use to our country." Universal probity is thus a contradiction in terms: one cannot imagine an action that is useful in exactly the same degree to all nations; humanitarian virtue, like all other universals, "is nothing but a Platonic chimera." . . . Patriotism and universal love are thus incompatible: "It is evident that a spirit of patriotism, a passion so desirable, so virtuous, and so worthy of esteem in any citizen, is, as is proved by the example of the Greeks and Romans, absolutely exclusive of the love for all mankind. . . . It is necessary that the private interest of nations should submit to a more general interest, and that the love of our country, becoming extinguished in the heart, should give place to the more extended flame of universal love: a supposition that will not be realized" for a very long time. . . .

Which of the two . . . is preferable? Given that one . . . is impossible, there can be no doubt about . . . Helvétius' respon[se]: humanitarian sentiment, . . . a personal illusion, must be sacrificed to civic virtue. . . .

Voltaire takes the opposite tack. He, too, believes that love of country and love of humanity are incompatible, and this troubles him. "It is sad that men often become the enemies of the rest of mankind in order to be good patriots. . . . This . . . is the human condition: to wish for the greatness of one's country is to wish evil to one's neighbors. The man who would wish his country never to be either larger or smaller, richer or poor than it is, would be the citizen of the world." But of the two terms . . . , Voltaire places a higher value on the universal, even though he knows that, especially as they age, people become sentimental about their fatherland and prefer bread at home to biscuits abroad.

As for Rousseau, who read and pondered Helvétius' text, he warrants a more extensive look. In his writings, the opposition centers on the terms "citizen" and "man," the latter term designating, sometimes ambiguously, both the human being viewed as inhabitant of the universe and the private individual. The citizen's path and the man's do not coincide, for obvious reasons. Their endeavors have different goals: the happiness of the group in the one case, that of the individual in the other. . . .

Rousseau comes back to this distinction in the chapter of . . . *[The] Social Contract* [on] "civic religion." This time . . . the citizen . . . is not named; as for the man, he is no longer Socrates but Christ, and the difference lies between "the religion of man and that of the citizen." . . . But the substance of the terms remains the same: the universalism of one of these religions is opposed to the patriotism of the other. Owing to its universalism, the Christian religion is incompatible with the objectives of nationhood. "Far from attaching the citizens' hearts to the State, it detaches them from it as from all worldly things." . . . "Since the Gospel does not establish a national religion, a holy war is impossible among Christians." . . .

We cannot say that one of these terms is valorized here at the expense of the other; rather, there are two independent value systems at work, and we cannot simply eliminate one of them. If we were to give up citizenship, we could no longer guarantee the application of the law . . . ; if we were to forget about humanity, Rousseau suggests, we would be denying our own most intimate feeling that tells us, when we see another human being . . . that we belong to the same species. The universality of the Christian religion has already contributed to marking the difference between the two systems, by "separating the theological system from the political . . ." ; it must be said that this theology turned universal is nothing other than ethics. Politics and ethics thus cannot be confused. . . .

Rousseau does not stop at indicating the difference between these two paths; he declares that they are radically incompatible. At least, this is his outlook [in] *Emile:* "Forced to combat nature or the social institutions, one must choose between making a man or a citizen, for one cannot make both at the same time." . . . The success of civism is in inverse proportion to that of "humanism." "Good social institutions are those that best know how to denature man" . . . : here the word "denature" concerns "natural man" (or "man") insofar as he is opposed to the citizen. "The legislator who seeks both [these virtues] will not get either one: this harmony has never been seen; it never will be seen, because it is contrary to nature, and because one cannot give a single passion two objects." . . . Rousseau's vision is dramatic: where others [see no] divergence, he sees an irreducible opposition.

In a further complication, Rousseau is convinced that this contradiction . . . is a source of irreparable unhappiness . . . the main source of unhappiness in human beings. "What causes human misery is the contradiction . . . between nature and social institutions, between man and citizen. . . . Give him over entirely to the state or leave him entirely to himself, but if you divide his heart you destroy him." . . . As composite beings, we cannot achieve either ideal; by dint of serving two masters, we are no good either to ourselves or to others. "Make man whole, you make him as happy as he can be." . . . "To be something, to be oneself and always one, a man must act as he speaks. . . . I am waiting to be shown this marvel so as to know whether he is a man or a citizen, or how he goes about being both at the same time." . . .

Just what features are derived from the position of citizen? The latter is wholly defined on the basis of the notion of fatherland; "man," on the other hand, is the one who does not wish to privilege his own people at the expense of the rest of humanity. Civic education has as its primary function the inculcation of patriotism. "The newly-born infant, upon first opening his eyes, must gaze upon the fatherland, and until his dying day should behold nothing else"; a citizen is a patriot or he is nothing at all. "That love makes up his entire existence: he has eyes only for the fatherland, lives only for his fatherland; the moment he is alone, he is a mere cipher; the moment he has no fatherland, he is no more; if not dead, he is worse off than if he were dead." . . . To make education more effective, each state must add education via cultural nationalism to its civic nationalism. It must protect and encourage national institutions, traditional customs, costumes, ceremonies, games, festivals, spectacles: all these are forms of social life that help attach the citizen to his country (so long as they are forms specific to that country and to no other), by making the cultural and the political coincide. Rather than feeling like a "man," the citizen formed in this way will feel like a Pole, or a Frenchman, or a Russian; and since patriotism will have become his "governing passion" . . . , all his values will be derived from the national values: "This is to say: you must turn a certain execrable proverb upside down, and bring each Pole to say from the bottom of his heart: *Ubi patria, ibi bene.*" . . .

The obverse of this love for everything that belongs to one's country is a certain contempt for whatever does not belong to it, and especially for foreigners. The ideal classical city-states provide examples: the Spartan ensures that equality reigns at home, but he becomes inequitable as soon as he crosses the borders of his homeland; similarly, "the humanity of the Romans extended no further than their domination." . . . The reign of equality at home does not prevent people from practicing slavery or colonialism abroad: such is the logic of patriotism. "Every patriot is harsh to foreigners. They are only men. They are nothing in his eyes. This is a drawback, inevitable but not compelling. The essential thing is to be good to the people with whom one lives." . . . Thus, if today's Poles want to follow the classical example, they need to manifest their "instinctive distaste for mingling with the peoples of other countries" . . . Once again, this reasoning is not at all paradoxical; it might even be considered trivial: to defend and exalt one's fatherland means preferring it to other countries (and to humanity). Such is the logic (and the ethics) of the citizen: Cato is a better citizen than Socrates. But is that really what Rousseau believes? In other words, is he on the side of patriotism or of "cosmopolitanism"?

A number of references to cosmopolitanism can be found in Rousseau's writings, and they have sometimes been used to argue that Rousseau's position was subject to change. This is not in fact the case. His earliest declarations on the subject appear in the "Discourse on the Origin of Inequality," where he sings the praises of "a few great

Cosmopolitan Souls" who rise above national frontiers and who "embrace the whole of Mankind in their benevolence." . . . Thereafter, although he no longer uses the word "cosmopolitan" in the same sense, Rousseau maintains the same principle: virtue and justice are on the side of humanity (but it would be more accurate to speak of humanitarian virtues, or equity).

What are we to make, then, of the texts in which Rousseau appears to denigrate cosmopolitanism? Let us take a closer look. Rousseau in fact attacks "those supposed cosmopolites who, justifying their love of the homeland by means of their love of the human race, boast of loving everyone in order to have the right to love no one." . . . But it is clear that his criticism is directed toward self-professed cosmopolites rather than real ones: what he is actually condemning is the dissociation between words and deeds that characterizes the "philosophers" (we would call them intellectuals) who hide their self-centeredness behind general pronouncements (the conservative Burke, in England, the utopian Comte, in France, are in this respect Rousseau's faithful disciples, even though they see themselves as his opponents). Rousseau makes the same accusation later on, but this time the word "cosmopolitan" designates only the latter form of love of one's fellow man: "Distrust those cosmopolitans who go to great length in their books to discover duties they do not deign to fulfill around them. A philosopher loves the Tartars so as to be spared having to love his neighbors." . . . How much easier it is to defend remote worthy causes than to put into personal practice the virtues one is professing: the love of distant peoples is less costly to the individual than the love of his nearest neighbor. This does not mean that one must love only one's neighbors, but that one must love foreigners as well as—and not instead of—one's own people.

In reality, Rousseau never retreats from his attachment to universalist principles. However, he does shift back and forth between the citizen's perspective and the individual's (again, both roles are worthy of respect), and he explores the logic of both positions in order to describe their various characteristics. When he says, referring to contempt for foreigners, that "this drawback is inevitable but it is slight," Rousseau is speaking not for himself but for the citizen (Helvétius); when in the first version of *On the Social Contract* he speaks of universalism as "healthy ideas". . . , it is the man, not the citizen, who is speaking. There is no contradiction here.

But Rousseau goes still further. Not satisfied to present two equally coherent systems of values between which one might make an arbitrary choice, he explores the relation between them and concludes that man must be placed above citizen. "Let us first find the cult and the morality that will belong to all men, and then when we need national formulas, we shall examine their foundations, their relationships, their conventions, and after having said what belongs to the man, we shall then say what belongs to the citizen." . . . The man takes precedence over the citizen: such is the order dictated by reason—which does not prevent circumstances from dictating the reverse order. "We do not really begin to become men until after we have been citizens." . . . We are born in a particular country; it is only through an effort of will, by rising above ourselves, that we become "men" in the full sense—that is, inhabitants of the world. Rousseau is even more categorical in one of his autobiographical texts: "In general, any party man, by that alone an enemy of the truth, will always hate J. J. . . . Now there is never any disinterested love of justice in these collective bodies. Nature engraved it only in the hearts of individuals." . . .

Patriotism, then, has an inherent flaw. By preferring one segment of humanity over the rest, the citizen transgresses the fundamental principle of morality, that of universality; without saying so openly, he acknowledges that men are not equal. Moreover, a Spartan or a Roman has a limited sense of equality even within the community, since women and slaves are excluded; in Poland—a modern Sparta—as well, everything that is feminine is avoided. Now true morality, true justice, true virtue presuppose universality, and thus equal rights. And yet in order to be able to exercise one's rights one must belong to a state, and thus be a citizen: there are no rights except within a juridical space underwritten by the establishment of a frontier separating inside from outside. The expressions "rights of man" and "world citizen" thus both entail internal contradictions. In order to have rights, one must be not a man but a citizen; yet—with apologies to Voltaire—only states have citizens, not the world. To be in favor of rights thus implies being on the side of the citizen, and yet the best principle of justice is that of universality.

If Rousseau is to be believed, the opposition is radical, irreducible. And yet we are all both men and citizens, or ought to be. What are we to do? The response Rousseau seems to suggest involves several phases. We must first take advantage of all the situations in which the two "passions" tend in the same direction; we must then be lucid as to their incompatibility in all other instances, rather than being misled by good intentions; finally we must aspire to modify the laws of the nation in the name of the laws of humanity, while continuing to remember that we always remain citizens of a particular state whose laws we must obey. The path he recommends in *Emile* is that of an obedient but potentially critical citizen. Correspondingly, in order to be acceptable, a society need not resemble the one described in *On the Social Contract*; all that is required is that individuals be able to exercise their judgment freely in that society and be able to act according to that judgment. Rousseau is not at all an "idealist," either: he knows perfectly well that only a compromise can meet these contradictory requirements, and he prefers lucidity to the euphoria of illusions.

. . . Those very voices that claimed affinity with Rousseau in 1789 turn out to be impervious to his teaching: the Revolution aims to satisfy both man and citizen. No conflict between the two is thinkable, even if their noncoincidence is noted. Thus, in *Qu'est-ce que le tiers état?* . . . Sieyès identifies readily with natural reason, or natural law, whereas his discourse in fact starts with the idea of the nation. When he distinguishes between the two, it is in order to link to everything. It is the source of everything. Its will is always legal; indeed it is the law itself. Prior to and above the nation, there is only "*natural* law" . . . : And if the two were not in agreement?

That question does not trouble Sieyès. It is true that he is thinking first and foremost about the "internal" meaning of the word "nation," but his formulas also allow for an interpretation in the "external" sense. All the more so in that the reference to natural law is not always maintained: "The national will . . . never needs anything but its own existence to be legal. It is the source of all legality. . . ." What Sieyès wants to dispense with here is divine right, or the rights of kings, or any legitimation based on privilege, but at the same time he affirms the nationalist credo: the nation is always right; being "the source and the supreme master of positive law" it cannot itself be judged. . . . Failing to differentiate between the two "nations" thus also amounts to opting for the nation over humanity, for patriotism over cosmopolitanism.

The fact that the first Declaration of Rights, written in August 1789, is the one known as "of Man and of the Citizen" is already paradoxical for anyone aware of the distinctions Rousseau established and the incompatibilities he disclosed. The seventeen articles of the Declaration never envisage a potential conflict between the rights of each party. Taking up Sieyès idea, Article 3 says: "The principle of all sovereignty resides essentially in the Nation"; but it is the "internal" sense of the word that is invoked here, as the remainder of Article 3 suggests: "Nobody, no individual can exercise authority that does not emanate directly from it." . . . In the constitution itself, which dates from September 1791, Title VI is devoted to "Relations of the French Nation with Foreign Nations"; the question of conflict is at least evoked here, and it is settled in the sense of a preference for humanitarian principles. "The French nation renounces the undertaking of any war in view of making conquests, and will never use its forces against the freedom of any people." . . . In other words, in deciding whether or not a war should be fought, the question is not whether the war is useful to France but whether it is right in itself—that is, whether it is right from the standpoint of humanity.

Under the impetus of the revolutionary developments, a certain reflection on the relations between France and the world was elaborated. Clubs of foreigners favorable to the Revolution were founded, and even a club of foreign patriots (!); a confederation of "Friends of Truth throughout the World" was established in France. On June 19, 1790, a delegation of foreigners appeared before the National Assembly. The delegation was led by Anacharsis Cloots, a German baron who had lived in France for many years and who transmitted to those present the fervent congratulations of the universe. "The trumpet that sounds the resurrection of a great people has reverberated in the four corners of the earth, and the songs of joy of a chorus of twenty-five million free men have woken people long buried in slavery. The wisdom of your decrees, Gentlemen, the union of the children of France, this ravishing picture gives despots cause for concern, and it gives legitimate hopes to the enslaved nations." The next day, during an outdoor meeting, "M. Danton . . . said that patriotism should have no limits but the Universe; he proposed to drink to the health, freedom, and happiness of the entire Universe." Cloots gave himself the title of ambassador . . . of the human race and he dated his letters from "Paris, headquarters of the world." And Durand-Maillane wrote in 1791, in his *Histoire apologétique du Comité ecclésiastique* . . . , that the new constitution "has to make the people of France happy, and, by imitation, all people. . . ."

Similar formulations, however empty or naive they may seem to us, in fact prepared the way for a certain interpretation of the relations between man and citizen, cosmopolitan and patriot, that we shall encounter again in Michelet. France and more specifically the French Revolution became exemplary incarnations of the route of the universe. . . . The liberation of the French showed the way to the rest of humanity, and

French decrees or the French constitution came to serve as models for all other countries. Patriotism and cosmopolitanism thus could conflict only for people who came from countries other than France, since as patriots they owed allegiance to their own country and as men they owed allegiance to France, the incarnation of humanity! The French, on the other hand, could be patriots with a clear conscience, for in working for France they were defending the interests not of a particular country but of the entire universe.

We find the same ideas even in the draft of a declaration that Robespierre presented on April 21, 1793, though he himself was hardly tender-hearted toward foreigners as a general rule: "Men of all countries are brothers and the various peoples must help each other according to their abilities, like the citizens of a single State [here we see the return of the fallacious analogy familiar to the Encyclopedists]. He who oppresses a single nation declares himself the enemy of all." . . . The constitution of June 1793 postulates, in Article 118, that "the people of France are the friend and ally of free peoples," which leaves us with the corollary supposition that, as Robespierre says, oppressor peoples are France's enemies. Is France thus to be charged with the universal mission of making liberty reign throughout the world? It is true that Article 119 also says that the people of France do not "involve themselves with the government of other nations," which amounts to requiring them simultaneously to take part and to remain neutral; but it is perhaps characteristic of constitutions to authorize a variety of behaviors. . . .

In fact, at the time of the Revolution itself, the behaviors at issue were not exempt from ambiguity. Certain revolutionary declarations gave an interventionist cast to universalist principles. One decree, adopted by the Convention of November 19, 1792, granted "fraternity and aid to all peoples seeking to recover their freedom," thus opening the way to future "exportations" of the Revolution. Cloots himself also chose the policy evoked in Article 118: in the name of the rights of man, he wanted to make war on all other countries, until Revolutionary ideas finally triumph. "Our situation requires the scalpel of Mars; the abscess that troubles us must be lanced with bayonet blows." The result was supposed to be the installation of a single State, and the submission of all to the same perfect laws (Condorcet's dream). "I propose an absolute leveling, a total reversal of all the barriers that interfere with the interests of the human family," Cloots wrote in *La République universelle* . . . "I defy anyone to show me a single article of our Declaration of Rights that is not applicable to all men, in all climates": Cloots, himself a foreigner by origin, often sounded more chauvinistic than the French, and his universalism was only another name for his Francophilia; as for the Revolution, it became dictatorship when it was exported.

The rights of man can thus serve, in certain instances, as pretexts and weapons of war, somewhat as the Christian religion served the Crusaders. In other circumstances, the revolutionaries appealed to abstract equality among nations, and thus preferred Article 119 to Article 118; such was the position of Danton and Robespierre in particular. But what is perhaps more telling is that, in order to defend their own country, the incarnation of the revolutionary victory, the French had to turn against outsiders. Robespierre's violent diatribes against the English are familiar: "I do not like the English, for my part, because that word makes me think of an insolent people who dare to make war on the generous people that has reconquered its liberty. . . . I have hope only in our soldiers and in the profound hatred the French have for that people." By the same token, all foreigners living in France found themselves under accusation: they were to be arrested and imprisoned. In a logical—and absurd—conclusion, their supporters were also to be accused: Cloots himself was attacked by Robespierre, who reproached him for belonging to the "foreign party" and for wanting to be called a "world citizen" rather than a "French citizen." . . . And Cloots ended up on the scaffold.

Thus, despite their common attachment to universalist ideas, and despite their disagreement as to which concrete policies to follow (export the Revolution or come to terms with neighboring governments), Cloots and Robespierre in fact converged in their preference for the French over other peoples; the difference is that Robespierre practiced this preference at home, whereas Cloots wanted to impose it abroad. For both, then, patriotism won out over universalism. From this point on, the price of ignoring Rousseau's wisdom would be hypocrisy or inconsistency.

Let us now leap more than one hundred years forward to the end of the nineteenth century, a period whose way was paved by the French Revolution. The final years of the century, marked by the Dreyfus affair, witnessed the constitution of two "leagues": the League for the Rights of Man, in February 1898, and the League for the French Fatherland, in January 1899. It is hardly necessary to add that the goal of the second league was to combat the first. Man and citizen, humanitarian and patriot found themselves on opposite sides of the barricade, as Rousseau had predicted, and contrary to the hopes of the nineteenth century republicans. It was not these republicans who turned out to have understood Rousseau but rather Charles Maurras, who hated him and who declared: "A fatherland is a union of families constituted by history and geography; its principle excludes the principle of the liberty of individuals, of individual equality," in other words, it excludes humanitarian principles. . . .

In these conflicts between patriots and humanitarians, some chose the camp of "man" and may have paid dearly for it, like Jaurès (whose thinking was not exempt from ambiguity on this point, however). Others preferred the "citizen": Maurras was one of the more eloquent among the second group. Criticizing the revolutionary amalgam of man and citizen, he wrote: "It is a doctrinal truth, in a philosophy very remote from daily life, that the fatherland is in our day the most complete and the most coherent manifestation of humanity . . . ; one French nationality moreover having a special claim to represent it [here the narrow ground of agreement between Robespierre and Maurras is evident]. However, these are the theses of a scholar sitting at his desk. If one is seeking an active value in this order of things, one must proceed differently and declare that patriotic feelings exist; humanitarian feelings do not exist, or have so little existence that they are scarcely conceivable except in opposition to the national ideal: instead of motivating it, they get in its way." Maurras is perhaps wrong to argue for the superiority of patriotism on the basis of its greater extension in the world (it is right because it is a fact); but he still remains faithful to Rousseau ("we become men whereas we are born nationals"), and he is right to denounce the illusion of continuity between man and citizen.

At least since the Second World War, nationalist discourse has become the specialty of antirepublican and antidemocratic movements. These two tendencies were already reconciled during the war of 1940, but only because German fascism was the enemy (thus an enemy on two counts); the recent colonial wars, on the contrary, bring the conflict clearly to light. When Maurras says that patriotism, "conceived in its historical marrow, in its hereditary essence, . . . resembles all the ideas against which democracy has risen up in all times"; he forces the issue without betraying it; his heirs, today's nationalist movements, oppose the entire array of democratic parties. This obviously does not imply any sort of withering away of nation-states. These exist as an effect of modern social structures; the nation easily outlives nationalism. But the existence of a nation-state does not require the adoption of a patriotic ideology. . . .

Suggestions for Further Reading

Differences among historians about the French Revolution's place in history are one aspect of an enduring debate about whether its effects were good or evil. This debate inspired much of the research on which the selections in this book are based. In the twentieth century the debate itself has become an object of historical inquiry. Stanley Mellon covers the beginning of the debate during the Bourbon Restoration in *The Political Uses of History* (Stanford, 1958). Paul Farmer traces its later stages under the Third Republic in *France Reviews Its Revolutionary Origins* (New York, 1944). Other books deal with particular points of disagreement among the revolution's apologists and critics. One of the most influential of these specialized studies is Augustin Cochin's *La crise de l'histoire révolutionnaire, Taine et Monsieur Aulard* (Paris, 1909) which deals with conflicting interpretations of the revolution's causes. Cochin focuses on two interpretations, *la thèse du complot*, favored by conservatives, which attributes the radicalization of the revolution to the conspiracies of an ideologically motivated minority, and *la thèse des circonstances*, favored by historians of various leftist colorations, which explains, and excuses, revolutionary excesses by invoking the force of circumstance. A later anthology edited by William F. Church, *The Influence of the Enlightenment on the French Revolution* (Lexington, Mass., 1964), traces one major facet of the controversy Cochin studied from the revolutionary period to recent times.

Church's anthology is one of a series published by D. C. Heath under the title *Problems in European History*. The selections in another book in this series, Ralph W. Greenlaw's *The Economic Origins of the French Revolution: Poverty or Prosperity?* (Boston, 1958), documents an historiographical dispute that cuts across the ideological line drawn by Cochin. In this perspective Mathiez comes down on the same side as Alexis de Tocqueville and on opposite sides from Lefebvre.

Greenlaw edited another Heath pamphlet that deals with the debate between opponents and proponents of the Marxist version of the Bourgeois Revolution, *The Social Origins of the French Revolution: The Debate on the Role of the Middle Classes* (Lexington, Mass., 1975). Subsequent studies chart this argument's later phases—notably G. Comninel, *The French Revolution: Marxism and the Revisionist Challenge* (London, 1987), who surveys most of its course, and Steven L. Kaplan, *Farewell, Revolution: 1789–1989*, 2 vols. (Ithaca, N.Y., 1995), who takes it down to the bi-centennial year. (The second volume of Kaplan's book, *The Historians' Feud*, contains an absorbing picture of the acrimonious relations between Furet and Michel Vovelle, Soboul's successor as "official" historian of the revolution, as the bi-centennial commemoration took shape.) The great English Marxist historian Eric Hobsbawm published another book on the debate soon after the bi-centennial, *Echoes of the Marseillaise* (New Brunswick, N.J., 1990), in which he predictably sides with the "orthodox" historians but provides a valuable account of the context within which the quarrel between Marxists and revisionists arose. Just before the bi-centennial another English historian, Geoffrey Best, edited *The Permanent Revolution* (Chicago, 1988), a book of essays dealing with various historiographical controversies, one of which, Norman Hampson's "The French Revolution and Its Historians," is especially balanced and thorough.

Understanding the revision of the "orthodoxy" and the "paradigm shift" that followed from it ultimately requires scrutiny of Alfred Cobban's work [particularly *The Social Interpretation of the French Revolution* (Cambridge, U.K., 1964) and his earlier essay, "The Myth of the French Revolution" (London, 1955)] and familiarity with some of the research on which he based his conclusions. Robert Forster's *The Nobility of Toulouse in the Eighteenth Century* (Baltimore, 1960) provided ammunition for Cobban's attack on the Marxist premise that "feudalism" obstructed capitalism under the Old Regime. André-Jean Tudesq's, *Les Grands Notables en France (1840–1849)*, 2 vols. (Paris, 1964), synthesizes much of the evidence that Cobban uses to undermine the more basic "orthodox" postulate that the Revolution brought capitalists to power.

The man who revised the Restoration version of the Bourgeois Revolution, Alexis de Tocqueville, has been the subject of many studies. Some of these deal with *Democracy in America*, most others with his place in the development of liberal thought or with his life [the now standard biography is André Jardin, *Alexis de Tocqueville: 1805–1859* (Paris, 1984)]. Very few have to do with the "paradigm shift" which his writings on the Revolution initiated. Richard Herr's *Tocqueville and the Old Regime* (Princeton, N.J., 1962) tells the story of how this book came to be written. The best account of the book's impact at the time and on the future is an essay by J.-P. Mayer, "L'histoire de l'influence de l'Ancien Régime," which concludes the first of the two volumes devoted to *L'Ancien Regime* itself in Alexis de Tocqueville, *Oeuvres complètes*, 18 vols. (Paris, 1951–1986), II, 335–353, of which Mayer was general editor. This volume begins with a laudatory introduction by Georges Lefebvre (pp. 9–30). Both essays raise serious questions about Furet's claim to have rescued Tocqueville's historical work from neglect. Furet's reassessment of Tocqueville's historiographical significance is a major talking point in *Interpreting the Revolution*, as the selection from that work in this book indicates, and in a subsequent article, "Quinet et l'Ancien Régime," *Commentaire*, VII (1984), 341–350. For a contrast ing view of Tocqueville's place in historiography see Marvin R. Cox, "Tocqueville's Bourgeois Revolution," *Historical Reflections/Réflexions historiques* XIX (Fall 1991), 279–300, and "Tocqueville's Revision of the 'Orthodoxy,'" *Selected Papers of the Consortium on Revolutionary Europe* (1995), 196–198.

It is Tocqueville's own writings, rather than those of commentators, which best explain his historiographical stature. *The Old Regime and the Revolution* provides an outstanding example of how a first-rate mind compresses complex research material into a compelling thesis. His perspective on his own times is well presented in John Stone and Stephen Mennell (eds.), *Alexis de Tocqueville on Democracy, Revolution and Society* (Chicago and London, 1980) and in Roger Boesch (ed.), *Selected Letters on Politics and Society* (Berkeley, 1985).

A number of monographs testify to the impressive stature that Hippolyte Taine attained during the Age of Positivism. Two of these, one from the first decade of the twentieth century, Paul Lacombe, *Taine: historien et sociologue* (Paris, 1909), and the other from the 1930s, Karl de Schaepdryver, *Hippolyte Taine: Essai sur l'unité de sa pensée* (Paris, 1938), deal with his work as an historian. Furet wrote an appreciative ar ticle on Taine for *The Critical Dictionary of the French Revolution* [trans lated by Arthur Goldhammer (Cambridge, Mass., 1989)] which he edited with Mona Ozouf. This points to a possible revival of interest in Taine. There are no signs of a serious revival of interest in Aulard. A spe cial posthumous issue of his journal *La Révolution française* (October– December 1928) commemorated his work. He was also the subject of a full-dress study shortly after World War II, by Georges Belloni, *Aulard: Historien de la Révolution française* (Paris, 1949). But his standing today is summarized in the title of a recent article by James Friguglietti,

"François Alphonse Aulard: Forgotten Historian of the French Revolution," in Boris Blick and Louis Patsouras (eds.), *Rebels against the Old Order: Essays in Honor of Morris Slavin* (Youngstown, Ohio, 1994). Taine and Aulard are the primary focus of Augustin Cochin's *La crise de l'histoire révolutionnaire,* cited above.

There has been fairly sustained interest in Jean Jaurès since his death in 1914. A major biography was published in 1962 [Harvey Goldberg, *The Life of Jean Jaurès* (Madison, Wis., 1962)]. As in Tocqueville's case, however, this interest has had more to do with Jaurès political ideas and public life than with his interpretation of the Revolution. Significant among the few studies of *L'Histoire socialiste* are two articles in Maurice Dommanget, *La pensée socialiste devant la Révolution française* (Paris, 1966), one by Dommanget, "Sur Jaurès historien de la Révolution française," and the other by Madeleine Rebérioux, "Jaurès historien de la Révolution française." Rebérioux and Gilles Candar recently edited a book on *Jaurès et les intellectuels* (Paris, 1994). For a recent appreciation of Jaurès' contribution to revolutionary historiography, see Lawrence H. Davis, "Jean Jaurès, Karl Marx, and the French Revolution." *Selected Papers of the Consortium on Revolutionary Europe* (1995), 196–198.

The standard work on Albert Mathiez is James Frigulietti, *Albert Mathiez, historien révolutionnaire* (Paris, 1974). To understand the high esteem in which this Marxist historian once was held students should consult his works of social history, particularly *La vie chère et le mouvement social* (Paris, 1927). To compare his approach to political culture with that of post-Marxist historians like Mona Ozouf it is useful to look at his early work entitled *Les origines des cultes révolutionnaires* (Paris, 1904).

Those interested in understanding Georges Lefebvre's commanding stature at the time of his death should look at the issue of the "orthodox" journal *Les Annales historiques de la Révolution française* that was dedicated to his memory in 1960. The basis for his enduring reputation as a social historian is well articulated in P. M. Jones, "Georges Lefebvre's Peasant Revolution 50 Years on," *French Historical Studies* (1989). Richard Cobb's essay on Lefebvre in *A Second Identity: Essays on France and French History* (Oxford, 1969), pp. 84–100, shows how deeply personal his commitment to Marxism had become in his declining years. Lefebvre's own works from earlier periods of his life explain why, despite his acceptance of the Marxist "paradigm," he cannot plausibly be seen as a rigidly Marxist historian. Two highly readable cases in point are *The Great Fear of 1789: Rural Panic in Revolutionary France* (New York, 1973), originally published in 1932; and his classic narrative account of the events of 1789, *The Coming of the French Revolution*, translated by R. R. Palmer (Princeton, N.J., 1947), originally published in 1939 as part of the official commemoration of the revolution's sesquicentennial.

Soboul's reputation has suffered more lasting damage. As a social historian, he continues to have his defenders. For a relatively recent account of his ideas and his contemporary standing, see Geoffrey Ellis, "The Marxist Interpretation of the French Revolution," *English Historical Review*, 93 (1978). David Caute's *The Fellow Travelers* (New Haven, 1988) shows that Soboul's relationship with the communists was more troubled than his advocacy of a "disciplined worker's party" would suggest.

François Furet established his reputation as a post-Marxist historian, and laid the foundation for subsequent post-Marxist interpretations with the first work excerpted in Section IV, *Interpreting the Revolution*. To follow his evolution from his beginnings as a Marxist to his present position as chief critic of the "orthodoxy" it is useful to look at *La Révolution* (Paris, 1965–66), a text he wrote jointly with Denis Richet, that appeared at about the same time as Cobban's *Social Interpretation*. The narrative is a sustained critique of the "orthodoxy's" major propositions, but its underlying assumptions illustrate the hold which Marxist categories continue to have on post-Marxist historians. This text went through several editions until it was succeeded by *Revolutionary France*, the second of Furet's works excerpted in Section IV. For a full appreciation of the post-Marxist vision of the revolution, the book to consult is the *Critical Dictionary of the French Revolution* cited above. This contains articles by a number of scholars on all the standard subjects with which revolutionary historiography has been concerned [e.g., "The Estates General," "The Terror," "The Sans-Culottes"] and others that have to do with aspects of revolutionary political culture to which the post-Marxists themselves have given prominence [e.g., "The Festival of the Federation," "Public Spirit," "Regeneration," "Vandalism"]. "Anglo-Saxon" historians Keith Baker and Colin Lucas have edited another major anthology on this subject that contains entries by authorities in both Europe and the United States, *The French Revolution and the Creation of Modern Political Culture*, 2 vols. (Oxford, 1987–1988). Mona Ozouf elaborates on some of her own views of revolutionary political culture in both these works and in *L'homme régénéré: essai sur la Révo-lution française* (Paris, 1989).

For an introduction to the *Annales* school to which both Furet and Ozouf belong, see Peter Burke, *The French Historical Revolution: the Annales School, 1929–89* (Stanford, 1990). The pertinence of historicist literary criticism for the writing of history is explained in a book of essays that Lynn Hunt edited and introduces, *The New Cultural History* (Berkeley, 1989). Her attempts to apply this method to the history of the revolution are carried forward in a recent monograph, *The Family Romance of the French Revolution* (Berkeley, 1992), and an anthology, *The French Revolution and Human Rights* (Boston, 1996). Two works are essential to an understanding of Robert Darnton's background: *The Business of Enlightenment: A Publishing History of the Enlightenment* (Cambridge, Mass., 1979), in which he explains the importance and complexity of eighteenth-century print culture, and *The Great Cat Massacre and Other Episodes in French Cultural History* (New York, 1989), in which he explains and illustrates the usefulness of cultural anthropology for social history.

For an appreciation of François Crouzet's complex perspective on the Revolution's socio-economic significance the essential work is *Britain Ascendant: Comparative Studies in Franco-British Economic History* (Martin Thomas, trans., New York, 1990) in which he documents France's economic inferiority to England during the early stages of industrialization and concomitantly charts the distinctive path which the French took to economic modernization. For a fuller picture of the uses to which William Hamilton Sewell, Jr. puts cultural anthropology in his study of the French working classes see his *Work and Revolution in France: the Language of Labor from the Old Regime to 1848* (Cambridge, U.K., 1980).

Essays by other historians in the Levy-Applewhite book excerpted in Section V deal with the impact of the revolution on women in other countries. The book as a whole extends to gender studies the thesis set forth by R. R. Palmer in his *The Age of the Democratic Revolution*, 2 vols. (Princeton, 1964), that the upheaval in France formed part of a general offensive against the old aristocratic order that was as significant for its effects within a broadly defined "Atlantic world" as in France itself. An earlier study of women in the revolution is Joan B. Landes', *Women and the Public Sphere in the Age of the French Revolution* (Ithaca, N.Y., 1988).

Readers interested in revolutionary nationalism, the subject of the selection from Tzvetan Todorov's *On Human Diversity*, may consult Jacques Godechot's book, *La Grande Nation: l'expansion révolutionnaire de la France dans le monde de 1789 à 1799* (Paris, 1956) and his article, "Nation, patrie, nationalisme, patriotism en France au XVIIIe siècle" in *Annales historiques de la Révolution française*, 206 (1971). It is Tzvetan Todorov who best illustrates the self-conscious commitment of postmodern thinkers to breaking down barriers between traditional disciplines. Another historical work that he undertook in this spirit is *The Conquest of America* (New York, 1984) — an influential book among American students of multi-culturalism. History students interested in post-modernism itself will profit from Marshall Berman's *All That is Solid Melts into Air* (New York, 1988), in which a Marxist thinker redefines Karl Marx's legacy for a world in intellectual flux.